ADVANCE PRAISE FOR DWARFSPLOITATION

"Dwarfish reviews about dwarf films seems an odd basis for a book, but it's surprisingly entertaining and enlightening and respectful about the little folk. A snappy, unique guide to all films Dwarf."

– Joe R. Lansdale, author of *Bubba Ho-Tep*

"This book is truly a one-of-a-kind. An inspired idea, and an equally-inspired book. Chris Watson and Brad Paulson have created something special with "Dwarfsploitation." In an age when there seems to be books about every aspect of cinema, these authors have discovered a niche that had yet to be explored. Kudos."

– Andrew J. Rausch, author of *Turning Points in Film History*

"The first time I went to the Library of Congress to do research on midgets in film, I was directed to a single tattered volume produced by the MGM publicist on "The Wizard of Oz." I was astounded. The literature was virtually non-existent. Later I had a special assignment involving dwarf-tossing, and I sought out any dwarf-tossing trade association that could possibly be of any assistance. Again, my exertions were frustrated. That's why, when I first heard that "Dwarfsploitation" was in the works, I was cautiously hopeful but still ready for a Billy Barty headbutt to the nuts. I'm happy to say that the resulting book is a resource that we've needed for 60 years, and should take up permanent residence on the Ikea children's-room book shelves of anyone shorter than 4-foot-4."

– Joe Bob Briggs, author of *Joe Bob Goes to the Drive-In*

"Brad and Chris's book stands head and shoulders above the run of the mill cinema book types. It makes little people everywhere stand a little."

– James Bryan, director of *Don't Go in the Woods*

"Paulson and Watson's book is a unique perspective to say the least. We seem to have books on everything these days, so, why not something that is entertaining, informative and celebrates our little friends in cinema."
– Robert Davi, actor from *License to Kill*

"It was a short read and I loved it. Don't overlook it!"
– Joe Estevez, actor from *Soultaker*

"Wow, I'm impressed! This has to be the most comprehensive guide to cinematic dwarves that you'll ever read. Meticulously researched, with hysterically funny yet genuinely fond comments by the authors, running the gamut from dwarfsploitation to 'normal' life. A must-have for any film-fan's library."
– scream queen Brinke Stevens

"A salute to Little People everywhere that belongs on every film aficionado's desk. Horror film makers: A demented dwarf is icing on the cake. I am working one into my next film. I'm the man that discovered both Luis Dejesus and Herve and can say without fear of contradiction what they lacked in height they made up in talent and *length*."
– Joel M. Reed, director of *Bloodsucking Freaks*

DWARFSPLOITATION

by

Brad Paulson

&

Chris Watson

BearManor Media

2012

Dwarfsploitation

© 2011 Brad Paulson and Chris Watson

All rights reserved.

For information, address:

BearManor Media
P. O. Box 71426
Albany, GA 31708

bearmanormedia.com

Typesetting and layout by John Teehan

Published in the USA by BearManor Media

ISBN—1-59393-276-6
978-1-59393-276-3

Table of Contents

Foreword by Lloyd Kaufman 1

Introduction by Chris Watson 5

Dwarftionary 9

Dwarf Reviews 11

Afterword by Brad Paulson 307

Special Thanks 311

About the Authors 313

The authors of this book fanboy a photo op with *Wizard of Oz*'s Jerry and Elizabeth Maren.

Foreword
by Lloyd Kaufman

This Foreword is Dedicated to the Late Zelda Rubinstein
May Her Memory "Come Into the Light."

Greetings from Tromaville! Lloyd Kaufman here, President of Troma Entertainment and Creator of the Toxic Avenger. I am honored that Chris Watson has asked me to write the foreword to his book on The Dwarves. The Dwarves are a great band and I had the privilege of using tracks by this stellar musical combo on the soundtrack of *Citizen Toxie—* Hey! Look who's here! It's Chris Watson, author of this very tome! What up, dude?

> Chris Watson: Lloyd! Lloyd! This book is about dwarves, as in those little people, not the band, you dummy! Didn't you read this book!?

D'oh! Little people!... Hmmm... little people... Well, I really don't have any idea how to proceed except to draw from my personal experience with dwarves in my movies and in my life. I hope, dear reader, that you are okay with this. We all have certain preconceived notions and prejudices about dwarves. For example, I recently was surprised to see a dwarf coming out of New York's trendy Bloomingdale's department store. I was surprised to see that she was loaded with purchases stacked up so high she could not see. Then I was surprised with myself for being surprised. I wondered, "Why can't dwarves be trendy and shop at trendy stores?" Maybe my Bloomingdale's dwarf had just bought a designer gown to wear in a movie starring Super Dwarf Peter Dinklage (*The Station Agent, Death at a Funeral*) or perhaps she had a hot date. In which department did she shop? Children's clothing? Hell, for all I know, she was buying dishes! See what I mean?

The point is there were hundreds of shoppers streaming in and out of Bloomingdale's, but I chose to focus on this dwarf and give her a lot of thought. Normally, I would hold the door open for a female; would the dwarf be offended by this? Would she think me condescending? Would she think that I opened the door for her because I thought she was disabled? For some reason, I did not hold the large, heavy front door for her and she had to flop around like a cartoon cricket, struggling against the over-sized and heavy portal. I do not believe I am alone in my instinctive reaction to spotting a dwarf. Otherwise, why would this book exist?

Overall, my relationship with dwarves is sort of love/hate! When I was five years-old, I was first exposed to dwarves when my father took me to Ringling Brothers' Circus. As I sat in the stands I watched these dwarves run about the tent. At first, I thought that they were children. I wanted to play with them!

With the closing of many circuses and the out-lawing of side show freaks, one could only then see dwarves in movies. One film that made an early impression on me was Tod Browning's 1932 horror masterpiece, *Freaks*. Later, I also enjoyed the artwork of Toulouse Lautrec not just because he made great poster art, but in *large* part because he was a *small* part! By the way, I was very, very disappointed that the original Hollywood movie about Lautrec, *Moulin Rouge*, did not feature a genuine dwarf, but a crappy actor walking on his knees. Thank heavens Baz Luhrmann's 2001 remake at least had some real dwarves in the can-can dance line!

Unfortunately, I started to hate dwarves when I saw those munchkins in *The Wizard of Oz*. They are shit-eating dwarves, and little shits – all of them! It wasn't until we founded Troma Entertainment and we released *Blood Sucking Freaks* that I saw a performance by a dwarf that, to this day, is the most compelling performance by a dwarf until the gregarious Robert Reich became Secretary of Labor under President Clinton. "Ralphus," played by the late Luis De Jesus, immortalized himself on screen in *Blood Sucking Freaks* by kidnapping, violating, and sadistically torturing, beautiful gyno-Americans! So began my first love affair with dwarves.

The first little person I actually worked with was Norma Pratt – Well, strike that. Actually, the first dwarf I "worked" with was in the bush[1] of Chad Africa, during my "year off from Yale." I had sexual intercourse with her. She was named Dieudonnée (her name translated means "God Given") and she wore a wrap-around piece of cloth with President John F. Kennedy's image on it. I still get a big piece of wood whenever I see that Zapruder film—Now back to Norma Pratt, who appeared in my 1982 film *Stuck On You!* Even though

Norma's scene called for her to have five gallons of milk dumped on her head, she was ecstatic because she was playing "a real" person and that her part had nothing to do with her being a dwarf! So why don't dwarves want to play dwarves in movies? I have heard that Super Dwarf Peter Dinklage also says he does not want to be typecast as a dwarf. What is wrong with playing a dwarf? I am a drunk and am happy to play a drunk in movies (*Rocky*, *The Janitor*, *Zombiegeddon*)! I am happy to get the work! Dwarves probably find it easier to get on film than normal people, no? They should be happy to be typecast! Norma Pratt's *Stuck on You!* shoot went very, very well! As for Norma's appearance in 1983's *The Toxic Avenger*, however, things got a bit sticky – literally. You see, Norma was not at all thrilled by having to perform in a scene in which she played a "real" mom and handed a pair of her movie son's cum-stained pants over to a clerk at a dry cleaning establishment. She was further aggravated when I made the artistic decision to have Toxie throw her into a clothing dryer. After that shoot, Ms. Pratt failed to return my phone calls. What attitude! I guess when it came down to it; she would have preferred a G-rated dwarf role rather than playing an R-rated "real person."

While working on *Citizen Toxie: The Toxic Avenger Part IV*, we faced serious problems as dwarves were in high demand due to the popularity of "Mini-Me" from the *Austin Powers* series. I had originally intended to use little people for the in-womb battle between the fetus Toxic Avenger and fetus Noxious Offender. However, with the very *tall* prices demanded by these very *short* individuals, coupled with their demands for limousines to pick them up, just to be auditioned, I ended up having to use children for that scene, and was forced to break numerous child labor laws! So I again began to despise little people. Almost everyone else was working on Troma movies for free. Why did these little ego-maniacs not "get it?" Why were they not satisfied with just the joy of being involved with something they could believe in?! How 'bout my Troma slogan: "Let's make some art!"—eh?

Now, some may be saying, "Wait a minute, Lloyd! Didn't Hank the Angry Drunken Dwarf play the part of God in *Citizen Toxie*, and you loved Hank, no?" Yes, dear readers, the late Hank the Angry Dwarf did, in fact, play the part of God in that movie. He was such a sweet guy that I agreed to the hefty payment he requested. However, I forbade him to drink and also gave him the opportunity to act and not just behave like a drunken freak as he had to do on the *Howard Stern Show*. Hank made it clear to the cast and crew that he did not buy my act. But that's not unusual. Tall people also do not buy my act! He could have used his hilarious scene in *Citizen Toxie* for his "acting" reel! I think that Hank could have made it as a sober movie actor but instead he went back to being a falling-down drunken freak for Howard Stern—and died! So I am angry at this dead, angry, drunken dwarf.[2]

In recent years, I feel that dwarves and I have reached a more comfortable, less tumultuous place in our relationship. I currently am the elected Chairman of the Independent Film and Television Alliance (IFTA) and I had the pleasure of working with super-dwarf Ed Gale on a didactic video for IFTA about getting bank loans for independent movies. We hit it off so well that Ed refused to accept money for his appearance in this video. This was a far cry from the dwarves I had dealt with ten years earlier who wanted me to have limousines pick them up for auditions! So now I love dwarves!

As you can tell by reading this introduction, I am confused as to my own relationship with and prejudices about little people.[3] One thing that makes me feel better, however, is that thanks to dwarves I believe that I am not the only one with a small penis![4] Love 'em or hate 'em, dwarves have indeed been an important influence on my movies/love life and an essential part of the world-wide cinematic industry. So, enjoy Brad and Chris's book and may it help us all to realize and overcome our dwarf-related prejudices. Above all, dear reader, remember Hans Christian Andersen's immortal words:

Thumbelina,
What's the difference if you're very small?
When your heart is full of love,
You're nine feet tall.

– Lloyd Kaufman
President of Troma Entertainment
and Creator of the Toxic Avenger
New York City
February 24, 2010

Notes

1. This was in 1965, before George W. made "bush" a bad word.
2. I am also angry at Howard Stern and hold him responsible for Hank's demise.
3. There was nothing confusing about my relationship with Dieudonnée in Africa, however—I just want to make that clear.
4. Actually Dieudonnée's vagina was quite ample, so disregard my prejudicial statement about penises – except for the part about my having a small one.

Introduction
by Chris Watson

Dwarf. Midget. Little person. Little guy. Shorty. Wee man. Little creature. The list of what they've been called could go on forever, but they prefer "little person." Sure, it's confusing if you use movies as a reference. For instance, if you were to watch *Little Cigars* (1973) you would be confused from such quotes as, "Don't ever call a midget a dwarf!" However, times have changed and as Martin Klebba says in *Feast 2: Sloppy Seconds* (2008), "It's little people motherfucker!" While both of these films tried to remind the viewer of what was politically correct at the time, both of these films are considered Dwarfsploitation.

Resources for information on little people in film are scarce. As author Joe Bob Briggs said, "The literature is virtually non-existent." There are currently no websites devoted to little people or books about them available. So, then, what is "Dwarfsploitation?" The simple explanation is to say "to exploit a dwarf in film." However, it's not that simple.

A grand example of "Dwarfsploitation" falls in multiple categories. A common category would be using a dwarf actor to play a character, such as when Ed Gale played "Chucky" in the *Child's Play* series or Warwick Davis played "Wicket" in *Return of the Jedi* (1983). While both actors gave terrific performances, enhancing their characters far above what those characters would have been had they just been robotic, they are never given the chance to be seen or heard on screen. Unfortunately, they become the unsung heroes of classic cinema.

In a similar fashion, there are several films where a little person will show up out of costume but with no lines—they are there for no reason other than they are a dwarf. For instance, in the bad comedy *Freshman Orientation* (2004), the lead of the movie is on stage performing. In a truly cliché moment, the crowd gets into his performance. The director, perhaps feeling the scene wasn't working, cuts to a little person's hands clapping and then pulls back to feature a dwarf actress who neither speaks nor shows up again in the film.

Another common category would be "size differential." Take how dwarf actor Weng Weng is introduced in the classic film *For Your Height Only* (1981); two normal height policemen walk towards the screen and then split off to reveal a little person. Another example can be found in *Dahmer Vs. Gacy* (2010) in a scene where Jerry Maren, "the lollipop kid" from *Wizard of Oz* (1939), is seen doing a mime routine next to an over-sized "Gacy." The "size differential" in both is used to get a cheap laugh at the expense of the actor's height.

Falling in a sub-category of "size differential" would be "a little person with a large object." What makes Weng Weng films so great is that we get to see this little person with lots of large guns. In the recently unearthed *D' Wild Wild Weng* (1982), Weng Weng mows down a bevy of bad guys using a large machine gun that's attached to his jeep. If it were an average height person on the back of that jeep, it would not be nearly as memorable.

There's also the obvious "ways to insult a dwarf" category. It is rare for a little person to appear in a film and not be referred as something other than their character name. They can be referred to as movie references such as "Oompa Loompa," "Willow," "Munchkin," "Mini Me," "Ewok" or references to size such as "shorty," "little guy," "little one," "wee man"… the list goes on. Even in the more prestigious little people films like *The Station Agent* (2003) and *Frankie Starlight* (1995), they get referred to as "midget" and "wee kid."

These are common traits of many films that commonly exploit a dwarf actor. While Native and African Americans have had their depictions discussed and altered, very little is ever said about the depiction of dwarves in cinema. Why do they laugh maniacally? Or why are they commonly angry?

It is notable that this is not a new trend. Dwarf actor John George was working during the silent era, his first screen credit being *Bobbie of the Ballet* (1916). Several of his films would be nothing more than extra roles where he was exploited without even getting a line.

While several talented dwarf actors would come around, the most notable and recognized was Michael Dunn. He received an Academy Award nomination for his work as an intellectual story-telling dwarf in

Ship of Fools (1965) and was nominated for a Tony award in 1964 for *The Ballad of the Sad Cafe*. Unfortunately, as his career progressed he would work mostly in bit roles in more prestigious films such as *Madigan* (1968) and would be forced to play parts in films like *Dr. Frankenstein's Castle of Freaks* (1974) where he was a horny, necrophiliac dwarf. In the end, even the most talented dwarf actor is relegated to pure exploitation films.

If you are the type that needs proof, this book is for you. While trying to celebrate the dwarf actor and their work, we also made it our duty to point out exploitation moments that are in each film. After a description of each film and the actors in them is a list of "dwarfsploitation" moments. I hope that after you read this book you will have a larger appreciation for all the wonderful and talented dwarf actors there are and have been like we do.

Dwarftionary

As dwarves inspired us to write this book, so did they also inspire us to speak and write in our own vernacular. Since we realize not everyone speaks Dwarfish, we've provided the meanings to some of the terms the new reader may be confused by here:

Dwarfsploitation
   A film genre that derives its entertainment from the exploitation of people 4'10" and under.

Dwarficidal
   1 - A dwarf with suicidal tendencies, or in the case of this book
   2 - A filmmaker who derives unhealthy pleasure from capturing the deaths of dwarves on screen.

Dwargasm
   An ecstasy-like bodily response resulting from the extreme joy of exposure to dwarves.

Sizeist
   A person who harbors a negative bias toward dwarves.

Tallie
   Normal sized person.

Fabio
   Good looking normal-sized person.

Dwarf-curious

A person who enjoys watching dwarfs. This can branch out as far as sexually.

Honorary dwarf

Not officially a dwarf, but uncannily small for a tallie. Celebrity examples are Danny Devito, Tom Cruise, Sylvester Stallone, etc.

Dwarf Reviews

The Adventures of Baron Munchausen (1988)

Written by Charles McKeown and Terry Gilliam
Directed by Terry Gilliam
Starring John Neville, Sarah Polley, Oliver Reed, Eric Idle, Uma Thurman
Featured dwarf: Jack Purvis

When a performance about Baron Munchausen is being put on, it is interrupted by the Baron himself. He tells the tale of he and a group of misfits saving a city under siege. Of course, a group of misfits doesn't seem to be complete in cinema without the use of a dwarf (played by Jack Purvis). In this case the dwarf has a special talent of blowing (no, really). When in battle, the dwarf stands off to the side and just blows, knocking over the enemy's shelter and sending soldiers flying—definitely the highlight of the film. The film is as wild as Terry Gilliam's other tales but the use of a dwarf certainly adds to the film.

Dwarf stagehand.
Dwarf with sword.
Dwarf with big ears.
Dwarf tattooist.
Dwarf playing cards.
Sweeping dwarf.
Dwarf leads tallie.
Dwarf with cane.
Dwarf can "blow over a forest with just one breath."
Dwarf floundering.

Dwarf blows over baddies.
Dwarf falls over.
Dwarf excited and cheering.
Dwarf hugged.

The Adventures of Rocky and Bullwinkle (2000)

Written by Kenneth Lonergan
Directed by Des McAnuff
Starring Robert De Niro, Rene Russo, Jason Alexander and Piper Perabo
Featured dwarf: Ed Gale

Based upon the popular cartoon series, there is a scene where the President of the United States is meeting with his staff. When discussing how three agents were sent to infiltrate RBTV but disappeared, Randy Quaid's Cappy von Trapment character says, "It's almost as if there was a mole in the White House." Cut to the President with a mole standing next to him taking notes. The mole is played by dwarf legend Ed Gale, who is wasted here in costume without any lines. He's not even in all the shots. This one is a waste of time both as a film and as a dwarf watcher.

Dwarf in costume.
Dwarf revealed behind larger objects.
Dwarf with small glasses.
Dwarf takes notes.
Dwarf there and then not.

Alice in Wonderland (1933)

Written by Joseph L. Mankiewicz and William Cameron Menzies
Directed by Norman McLeod
Starring Charlotte Henry, Lillian Harmer, Alison Skipworth
Featured dwarf: Billy Barty

In the best scene of the movie, and a very odd one at that, the legendary little person Billy Barty pops up as a baby that is aggressively being thrown around while being sung a lullaby by someone that looks closer to a character from a McDonald's commercial. Tossed around madly, we get some close ups of Barty bawling his eyes out before he's thrown to Alice. Alice ends up taking off with him but when he turns into a pig she quickly sets him loose. This one is just weird enough that it's worth a look.

> Dwarf as baby.
> Dwarf tossed around.
> Awkward dwarf face close ups crying.
> Dwarf tossed.
> Turns into a pig.

Alien From L.A. (1988)

> Written by Regina Davis, Albert Pyun, and Debra Ricci
> Directed by Albert Pyun
> Starring Kathy Ireland
> Featured dwarf: Deep Roy

When a "big boned" beauty passes into an alien world, she becomes a hot property. To profit from her, a witch-like woman takes her to "Mambino," played by Deep Roy, who is very much like an alien version of the Godfather. Deep Roy only has a few scenes but plays the weirdo character just fine. The movie is considered a horrible movie and I agree with anyone who says this. I would only suggest this film to someone I don't like.

> Dwarf with magnifying glass.
> Angry dwarf.
> Dwarf in make up.
> Dwarf with long eyelashes.
> Dwarf laughs maniacally.
> Dwarf caresses tallie's face.

American Drive-In (1985)

Written by David Allen Ball and Krishna Shah
Directed by Krishna Shah
Starring Emily Longstreth, Pat Kirton, Joel Bennett
Featured dwarf: Phil Fondacaro (as H.G. Golas)
"Even with her naked, I steal the scene!"

American Drive-In (1985) is the story of a handful of misfits who come together at a drive-in. Just as you get bored watching the film, dwarf legend Phil Fondacaro shows up sitting in a vehicle, writing a letter to his agent. He's apparently half playing himself, as he mentions in the letter that he still gets fan mail from *Hard Rock Zombies* (1985)—the film they are also playing at the Drive-in— but then goes on to complain that George hired every stinking midget on the West Coast but his agent couldn't get him in—Fondacaro actually played an Ewok in *Return of the Jedi* (1983). We then discover his name is Rocky Magellan (and Phil uses the pseudonym H.G. Golas for the REAL movie credit instead of Phil Fondacaro). Why they didn't just let him play himself, or at least his pseudonym, baffles me.

When Phil's character comes on screen, the movie cuts back to him going, "This is a good movie. This is a really good movie." This is repetitive for a while until a youngster pulls a prank by moving the speaker system to the vehicle of two tallies having sex. As Rocky's "best scene" comes on screen, Phil as a Nazi zombie on top of a cow, the moaning of the two tallies having sex is heard.

As if that wasn't enough insult to our dwarf friend, later on he tries to buy some popcorn. Being a true actor, he finds himself unable to come up with fifty cents. Luckily, an adoring tallie "drops" him some money.

Rocky disappears again and doesn't show up much but is in it enough to almost make the movie worth watching. It's an okay movie made better by the appearance of Phil Fondacaro almost playing himself. While watching himself on screen, Phil says, "Thank God every day for my extraordinary talent." So do I.

Dwarf has hard time getting in car.
Dwarf zombie.
Dwarf Nazi.
Dwarf on cow.
Angry dwarf.

American Pie Presents: Beta House (2007)

Written by Erik Lindsay
Directed by Andrew Waller
Starring: Shannon Beckner, Steve Talley, Eugene Levy
Featured dwarf: Jordan Prentice

The *American Pie* sequel before this, *American Pie: The Naked Mile* (2006) brilliantly introduced a rival fraternity comprised entirely of dwarves, with the exception of the one tallie they allowed to join due to the fact he was a legacy. One of the film's main subplots revolved around the feud between Jordan Prentice's dwarf fraternity and Stifler's tallie fraternity. The movie blatantly appears to end with the promise of a continuation between the dwarf and tallie rivalry. This was perhaps one of the greatest endings I had ever seen put on film since I was all but promised a sequel with the same returning dwarf fraternity. When it reached that moment in the film I had to fight back a powerful dwarfgasm. And I was expecting an even more explosive dwarfgasm with "Beta House" as my natural expectation was that the filmmakers would either double the number of dwarves and/or amount of dwarf screen time. Sadly, this never happened.

Instead, we have a completely different plot thrown in which involves the rivalry between a nerd fraternity and a dwarf fraternity and the *American Pie* series goes back to its generic, straight-to-video, cookie-cutter-plot origins. This sequel would have been great if it would have been a dwarf fraternity, but all they did instead was the reverse of *Revenge of the Nerds* (1984) with tallies. Without dwarves, there's just not much to see here. There are a few funny scenes however, and the brilliant Jordan Prentice does appear, doing his best "Deep Throat" from *All the President's Men* (1976) impression as he gives vital information to his former arch nemesis Stifler about how to take down the nerd fraternity. His cameo is a good one and does involve the best visual gag of the film but it's not nearly enough to recommend for viewing. It is with great sorrow that I say I don't know if I'll ever be able to watch another installment of this series. Once they abandoned dwarves, so did my loyalty to the franchise.

Stifler meets tallie and dwarf in trench coat and glasses.
Dwarf positioned in front of tallie.

Dwarf and former arch tallie rival abandon differences to work together and take down a nerd fraternity.
Dwarf seals nerd tallie's fate with his top secret information.
Tallie bangs dwarf.
Dwarf with flashback hair.

American Pie: The Naked Mile (2006)

Written by Erik Lindsay
Directed by Joe Nussbaum
Starring Steve Talley, Candace Kroslak, Eugene Levy, Jessy Schram, Angel Lewis
Featured dwarf: Jordan Prentice
"It's little person, fucknut!"

If you're familiar with the *American Pie* series, you know they're basically sex comedies that use the clichéd device of the main character falling in love as a pass so they can put as many boobs, sex jokes and flying semen gags as possible in the movie. They push the R-rated smut button as far as they can, rivaling the late night Cinemax movies (which were often coined 'Skinemax') due to their massive amounts of filth and smut. This installment pushes the sleaze button so far it's the closest *American Pie* installment to porn yet. However, there is one other thing that sets it apart from the other sequels... the introduction of a rival dwarf fraternity!

After seeing this movie for the first time I couldn't believe my eyes. I was ready to watch something completely generic, my finger ready to push the fast forward button. But as I watched, I felt like I had witnessed the most brilliant idea I had ever seen in a movie in quite some time. My hat goes off to both Nussbaum and Lindsay for the introduction of a dwarf fraternity as well as the fact they were smart enough to give them extensive screen time, which is not hard to do since the leader of the dwarf fraternity is played by the extremely talented Jordan Prentice.

The film starts off in traditional *American Pie* fashion as the lead character gets caught whacking off (a flying semen joke is of course included here). Shamed, he's given the opportunity to redeem himself when his girlfriend (hot for a tallie) agrees to have sex with him. There is of course a mix up and his deflowering is delayed while he goes to college to visit his greasy cousin. Here, he's faced with the incredibly tough decision of whether he's going to bang a hot sorority girl there or wait until he gets back home to bang his girlfriend. Or, perhaps find some way to bang both? Boy, the characters in these *American Pie* movies have a rough life, don't they? Fortunately behind this generic, paper thin plot exists the dwarf subplot.

The minute they appear, the magic of dwarves breathes an indescribable new life into the film. After we're treated to the wonderful visual of an entire football team of dwarves, Stifler explains to his team of tallies that the dwarves are their rivals, their arch nemesis. They compete with the tallie fraternity in everything: girls, sports, you name it. Not only that, but the dwarves have defeated the tallies for the last five years in a row in football. A brutal game ensues where the dwarves give the tallies a run for their money, building up to a wonderful shot where Prentice bursts out of the mud and attacks like some kind of micro version of John Rambo (even though Stallone is fairly dwarfish himself). But the rivalry doesn't stop there. The dwarves cockblock the tallie fraternity in a bar. One of them even jumps up on a chair to stare a tallie down. Then we're treated to tallie/dwarf sexual tension, a close up of a sexy female dwarf shaking her booty and the coup de grace: dwarves running naked! This is pure dwarfsploitation but there is a counterbalance since the dwarf fraternities are such collective bad-asses in sports, taking the tallie's women and trading insults. Once again, dwarfsploitation is under the thin veil of dwarf empowerment. This is a must see for the dwarf appreciator and wisely uses dwarves to distinguish itself from the usual straight-to-video fare. Kudos to the filmmakers!

> "They're midgets!"
> "Did I do too much nitrous? A midget fraternity?!"
> "This is where every midget in America wants to be."
> "I can't believe we lost to midgets!"
> "That midget quarterback stole my girlfriend last year!"
> "We got cock blocked by some midgets at the bar."
> "What is this, 'Enter the Midget?'"
> "We got to get those fucking midgets!"
> "You and the lollipop guild punch like a bunch of five year olds."
> Dwarf makes out with hot female dwarf.
> Dwarves let tallie in as a legacy.
> Dwarf fraternity undefeated for five years.

Dwarf flies through air and tackles tallie.
Dwarf bites tallie's leg.
Dwarves do a victory line dance.
Dancing dwarf.
Dwarf hangs off tallie's back as he makes a touch down.
Dwarf comes out of mud like Rambo.
Dwarves cockblock tallies.
Girl calls dwarves cool and sexy.
Dwarf jumps on chair to stare down tallie.
Dwarf disrespects his own girl friend.
Dwarves jump out of van wearing masks and attack Stifler.
Naked dwarves.
Dwarf runs naked mile with bunny ears on head.
Stifler hits on hot dwarf dancing and holding bottle.
Tallie slaps dwarf's ass.
Dwarf/tallie flirting.
Tallie sex tape of himself and hot female dwarf.

The Angry Red Planet (1960)

Written by Sid Pink, Ib Melchior
Directed by Ib Melchior
Starring Gerald Mohr, Nora Hayden, Les Tremayne, Jack Kruschen
Featured dwarf: Billy Curtis

Once again, cheated with the prospect of seeing dwarves and barely given anything in return. This film, about an expedition to Mars where several stiff-moving, cheesy-looking, puppet-like creatures are shown, makes us wait and wait and wait and then only gives us a glimpse of Curtis in the Martian outfit. And, in classic dwarfsploitation form, we never see his face. If you blink or fast forward, you're likely to miss it. Watch if you're a sci-fi enthusiast but don't even think twice about viewing it if you're looking for dwarves.

Martian dwarf.

Anguish (1987)

> Written by Bigas Luna
> Dialogue by Michael Berlin
> Directed by Bigas Luna
> Starring Michael Lerner, Talia Paul, Angel Jove, Clara Pastor
> Featured dwarf: Zelda Rubinstein
> "See what happens when you disobey mother?"

This is an incredibly bizarre movie where the dwarf psychic from *Poltergeist* (1982), Zelda Rubinstein, has a tallie son (Michael Lerner) whom she's incredibly maternal with, not to mention controlling. To give you somewhat of an idea of just how incredibly weird this movie is, at the beginning of the film, a pigeon is stuck behind a cupboard. Rubinstein tells her tallie son to get the pigeon out without hurting it. The pigeon stuck in the wall and the tallie trying to get it out and not upset mother makes for an incredibly bizarre and tense scene. When the tallie does manage to get the pigeon out of the wall, the dwarf takes it in her hands and talks to it as if it were her own, much smaller child. She creepily looks at the pigeon and tells it, "See what happens when you disobey mother?"

Then her tallie son goes to work as an orderly in an optometrist's office and gets fired for screwing up an uppity rich tallie bitch's contact lens order. His dwarf mother does not take too kindly to the fact that her tallie son has just been fired. So, for revenge, she hypnotizes her boy into killing people and ripping out their eyeballs to add to her collection. (Yes, it's an eyeball collecting dwarf!) This is a truly excellent moment for the dwarf-curious since we have basically a spinning dwarf's head with a spiral ring behind it hypnotizing her tallie son into killing for her. Now, if you've never seen a spinning dwarf's head before, you're in for a treat with this film. I certainly can't think of any other movies that have utilized this concept. Plus, beside all of this, the dwarf never really leaves us, even when she's not onscreen! Her disembodied voice follows her tallie son wherever he goes when he's killing people, constantly guiding and giving him proper homicidal instructions. Now what a great, unique way to get more dwarfsploitation in a movie! Add a disembodied dwarf voice! And here's the clincher: all of what I've described is actually a movie within a movie!

The overly maternal dwarf mother to tallie plot is actually part of a movie called *The Mommy* that people inside of a seedy Los Angeles movie theatre are watching. When it gets to the parts of the dwarf hypnotizing her tallie son into killing, a man who looks like the lizard from the *Spider-Man* movies (Angel Jove) is hypnotized into killing people in the theatre in ways that mimic the tallie son's killings in *The Mommy*. So to recap, we have some very unusual forms of dwarfsploitation being displayed in *Anguish* (1987). There's a creepy dwarf, combined with a psycho-esque mother dwarf, combined with dwarf hypnosis, combined with psychotic Manson-style dwarf getting other people to kill for her, combined with dwarf telepathy, combined with dwarf-movie-within-movie telepathy.

Damn, when you think about it, that's one powerful dwarf! Certainly one I wouldn't want to mess with! "Go towards the light!" Whatever you say, creepy-voiced dwarf. The last thing I'd want to do after watching this movie is disappoint mother. Kudos to Spanish director Bigas Luna for giving us forms of dwarfsploitation we never knew existed, combined with one of the most bizarre psychological dwarf horror movies ever made. If you've never seen it before, this is certainly one worth checking out.

> Knitting dwarf.
> Dwarf talks to snail.
> High angle shots of dwarf.
> Dwarf listens to voices through a seashell.
> Dwarf hypnotizes son.
> Dwarf gives creepy reactions on phone.
> Delusional dwarf.
> Psychotically maternal dwarf.
> Hypnotist dwarf.
> Extreme close-up of dwarf mouth.
> Spinning dwarf vision.
> ECU - dwarf eyes.
> Dwarf communicates telepathically for her tallie son to kill.
> Movie within a movie victims hear dwarf voice.
> Disembodied, hypnotizing dwarf voice.
> Dwarf has powers over people in theatre.
> Dwarf has tantrum and knocks over crystal ball.
> Dwarf steps on nail and wails.
> Dwarf attacked by pigeons.

Ankle Biters (2002)

Written and directed by Adam Minarovich
Starring Adam Minarovich
Featured dwarf: Michael Moore
"3 feet tall, two inch fangs"

Within the opening four minutes of *Ankle Biters* (2002), you know you're in for a classic film. Every camera movement/style that is possible in the world of Micro Cinema is instated during a chase scene between a tallie and a couple of dwarf vampires. There's nothing more impressive than dwarves scaring the crap out of a tallie wearing a Tool t-shirt. I'm not sure if it's the fangs that scares him or the horrible gang wear they have on but nonetheless it's a very entertaining introduction that only gets better as Adam Minarovich shows up with his dwarf sidekick "T-Bone," both of which are packing heat. You get everything in these four minutes that you could dream of; dwarves fighting each other, dwarf firing a gun, dwarf jumping off a VERY small ledge…it's just insanely brilliant. Just brilliant.

As if the opening five minutes, ending with T-Bone in the side car of Minarovich's motorcycle, wasn't enough, we get the rest of the movie. Right after the opening credits we get a real treat—the reason behind the title. It seems a couple of wannabe badasses have crossed the country to sell the dwarf vampires a sword in the middle of nowhere on a railroad track. When one of the tallies shoots the black vampire and threatens to do the same to the others, they are both attacked at the ankles. Several gratuitous shots of ankle biting later, we get a tallie jumping off a bridge to escape these dwarf vampires (he ran well too, despite having his ankles gnawed on, so I'm a little confused). All of this in the first ten minutes and this film did not make AFI's top 100 films list. I'm flabbergasted. Appalled. Outraged. And I'm not done. After all, this is a classic.

Within the next few minutes we are treated to a good ol' bar fight as Minarovich and his dwarf buddy T-Bone try to figure out what exactly is going on. As soon as the shit hits the fan, T-Bone jumps onto the bar to land a kick in the face of a tallie and moments later he's sending a bottle crashing on the head of another tallie that was trying to get Minarovich from behind. As if that wasn't enough, the dwarf punches another tallie and then jumps on the back of yet another tallie while punching him. When finished, the dwarf and Minarovich do some weird high five variation to celebrate. Did I mention this is all within the first fifteen minutes? Brilliant.

As the movie continues, it does get old. Honestly, though, they made it hard to top the first fifteen minutes that are like a dwarfsploitation lover's wet dream. The rest has some random kills by the vampire dwarves, killing everything from fat guys to mechanics to teens smoking dope. Minarovich and T-Bone become a bickering couple, making one wonder why this dwarf would stick around with such an asshole.

One can complain that the movie is this or that because of its micro budget. The effects are laughable. While a lot of effort was put into the shots and making it bad-ass, they forgot to read the manual on how to use their lenses, giving the shots a circular shape through a large portion of the film. The acting is horrendous. The story is lame at times, with plenty of plot holes, and yet the movie is brilliant. It would not be brilliant if it did not feature so many wonderful dwarves. The movie would not have been made with dwarves had it had a budget. So, we are forced to appreciate what we are given and that is a micro-budget dwarf vampire movie that is like a bastard love poem to dwarves everywhere. Thank you Mr. Minarovich.

Weird dwarf noises.
Dwarf POV.
Dwarf with doo rag and shades taunts tallie.
Camera scales up dwarf's body.
Dwarf vampires chew on tallie.
Referred to as "shorty."
Dwarf with gun.
Eddie Murphy-looking dwarf fights tallie.
Close up of dwarf hand firing gun.
Dwarf leaps off foot tall ledge.
Two dwarves fight.
Slow motion close-up of feet walking.
Dwarf in side car.
Redneck dwarves buy sword on train tracks.
Dwarf shot by greedy tallie.
Dwarves bite ankles.
Close-up of dwarf head.
Dwarf leaps onto barstool.
Dwarf stands on bar to kick tallie.
Dwarf hits tallie on head with bottle.
Dwarf celebrates beating up tallies.

Referred to as "shorty."
Vampire dwarves gnaw on fatty asking for money.
Slow motion shot of dwarf vampires walking down street.
Dwarf wants tacos.
Dwarf vampires attack mechanic.
Dwarves come out of lockers.
"Yeah, I need some help. I need some help right now. There's some little dwarves attacking my brother with a sword."
Dwarf flips off tallie.
Dwarf punches tallie in crotch.
Dwarves attack police.
Dwarf with bow.
Dwarves stalk teens.
Dwarf slapped and knocked over by hot blonde.
Dwarf drinking.
Dwarf on tallie's shoulders while spinning a basketball.
Dubbed-over midget laughing.
Dwarf picks up tallie and twirls him around.
Dwarf crotch violence.
Dwarf jumps higher to fight tallie.
Dwarf shot with shotgun.
Dwarf gives large growl.
Dwarf jumps on tallie to bite neck.
Close up of dwarf feet.
Slow motion shot of dwarf running towards camera.

At the Circus (1939)

Written by Irving Brecher
Directed by Edward Buzzell
Starring The Marx brothers
Featured dwarf: Jerry Maren (as Jerry Marenghi)

Jeff Wilson (played by the singer/actor and not the dwarf actor Kenny Baker) is happy. He finally has the money to pay off the evil Carter the money he owes him so that nothing stands in the way of him marrying the girl of his dreams. It all goes downhill when Carter has Goliath (Nat Pendleton) and Little Professor Atom (played by dwarf legend Jerry

Maren really wants to sock this tallie in the kisser.

Maren) steals the money from him. It's up to the Marx brothers to solve the mystery and save the day. The movie is overfilled with music numbers that fall flat and only offers a few laughs but is good for a lazy Saturday afternoon. Maren is very childlike at this point despite chomping on a cigar and having a 'stache. Had he been given more lines this movie might not have been so mediocre. There is one good scene where Maren is being interrogated by the Marx Brothers. Groucho is trying to get Jerry to give a cigar when one brother continuously has a cigar every time Groucho asks Jerry for one and the other sneezes so hard it knocks Jerry's house apart. The scene is cheesy but funny, and by far the best moment of the whole film.

> Cigar-smoking dwarf.
> Dwarf shadow.
> Thieving dwarf.
> Room is labeled "tiny house."
> Tallies can't fit into room.
> Groucho only shakes with two fingers.
> Dwarf picked up and passed around.
> Referred to as "midget."

Attitude For Destruction (2008)

> Written by Jeremiah Campbell
> Directed by Ford Austin
> Starring Monte Hunter, Simon Burzynski, Jed Rowen, Annmarie Lynn Gracey
> Featured dwarf: Mighty Mike Murga

Attitude For Destruction (2008) is about a rock band named Hollywood Roses who get offered a deal under one condition… they get rid of their lead singer, Drake. Naturally, the band kills and buries the

Bloody dwarf mayhem. Courtesy of Ford Austin.

poor bastard. Things go most excellent for them until Drake's girlfriend makes a deal with the Devil for revenge. Director Ford Austin utilizes dwarf actor Mighty Mike Murga very early on by having him show up during a virgin sacrifice. The sacrificial victim is fully nude as the dwarf enters shirtless, covered in blood and carrying a goblet. He approaches the victim's killer and begs for blood and gore. She obliges and fills the dwarf's cup. The dwarf goes to town and gets his fill, chowing down on the blood and gore and having a great time with it.

The dwarf's role in the film certainly didn't have anything to do with the plot and it seemed to be in there for nothing more than just the weirdness factor of having a dwarf in the film… and I find nothing wrong with that! It's sheer dwarfsploitation for the sake of dwarfsploitation and at least the dwarf wasn't wasted in a sci-fi scene where his face is covered up. You're at least able to see the little guy in all his buff, blood-drenched dwarf glory. It's simply a more honest approach at dwarfsploitation than other movies who don't want to admit that's what they're actually doing. This film knows dwarves sell and how to market them. On a further note, *Attitude for Destruction* also contains a unique dwarfsploitation plot device: during the villain's exposition scene toward the end of the movie, the footage from the earlier dwarf scene is shown to complement the voiceover. This is what I'd like to call maximizing both dwarf screen time and dwarfsploitation. After all, no rock/horror film is complete without dwarves. Kudos to the filmmakers!

Warning! This movie contains a very angry dwarf. Courtesy of Ford Austin.

Shirtless dwarf.
Blood-drenched dwarf.
Goblet-holding dwarf.

Growling dwarf.
Begging dwarf.
Blood-and-gore-eating dwarf.

Austin Powers in Goldmember (2002)

Written by Mike Myers and Michael McCullers
Directed by Jay Roach
Starring Mike Myers, Beyoncé Knowles, Seth Green, Michael York, Robert Wagner
Featured dwarf: Verne Troyer
"Just because you're one eighth their size doesn't mean you deserve one eighth of their respect, does it?"

Mike Myers further cements his reputation as a dwarf appreciator with this one. After watching it, one can clearly see that dwarf appreciation wasn't just a passing hobby with Myers. It's something he's clearly fascinated with and that's what I admire about Myers the most: his dedication to maximizing screen time for dwarves. Roach wastes no time in getting the dwarf into the movie, a smart choice from a proven director. Clearly, he realized how important the dwarf was to the success of the *Austin Powers: The Spy Who Shagged Me* (1999) and knew he'd better not waste any valuable dwarf potential, and I'm proud to say he doesn't. *Goldmember* (2002) is filled with dwarfsploitation. Yet it strangely doesn't come off as offensive because the whole thing, after all, is very tongue in cheek and Myers and the dwarf have such good chemistry together.

What really separates the movie from *The Spy Who Shagged Me* (1999) is the fact that the dwarf actually has an arc in this movie. This film may be a comedy filled with sophomoric, scatological humor but there is certainly something to be said for the emphasis on making the dwarf's character much more important and relative this time around. In this installment of the series, Dr. Evil's real son is so pissed off that his father has essentially abandoned him for his dwarf clone, Mini-Me, that he actually stops questioning and protesting Dr. Evil's methods and instead becomes more like the father that he despises. When Dr. Evil sees the diabolical progress his son has made, and the fact that he's made his dream come true by buying him sharks with lasers attached to their foreheads, he suddenly becomes a proud father for the very first time in his life. Unfortunately, this moment comes at a high cost to Mini-

Me, because Dr. Evil chooses his son over his own clone.

A tear came to my eye as the poor dwarf realizes his moment of rejection, accepts it, tilts his head to the side in one of the most sorrowful, human as a puppy dog moments I've ever seen and wheels himself out of the room. Fortunately, for the audience and dwarf appreciators everywhere, the dwarf realizes that Dr. Evil didn't really love him. He knows that he deserves to be with someone who truly respects him, so the dwarf defects and goes to Austin Powers' side. What happens next is indeed one of the funniest moments in the movie as Michael Caine, playing Powers' natural-born pervert father, asks the dwarf if everything is okay with him and if he has a wang proportionate to his dwarf body. The dwarf agrees to drop his trousers, and after doing so, Caine describes the dwarf's unit as something that looks like a baby's arm holding an apple. The two become fast friends as do Powers and the dwarf, but not before a misunderstanding leads to a tallie/dwarf battle that tops their previous throw down in *The Spy Who Shagged Me* (1999).

The most notable difference between the brawl in this movie and the one from the previous installment is the fact that the dwarf bites Power's crotch during the fight and gets lockjaw. Powers also puts a pillowcase over the dwarf's head, covering his entire body and slinging it around, destroying various objects around the place. From this point on, we're treated to a number of dwarfsploitative outfits such as a mini Austin Powers outfit and a wetsuit which was my personal favorite because it was like seeing a dwarf version of Jacques Cousteau.

> Honorary dwarf Danny Devito chomps on cigar and blasts away with machine gun.
> Dr. Evil carries Mini-Me in front of him in a baby carrier.
> Sleeping dwarf.
> Chocolate-eating dwarf.
> Dwarf attacks Seth Green like a mad dog after trying to take his chocolate. Dr. Evil restrains him by pulling him back on a leash.
> Dwarf moons the court after being sentenced and slaps his own ass.
> Dwarf dressed like a gangbanger in do-rag and jail clothes walks with swagger in prison.
> Dwarf stands on bench to address prisoners with Dr. Evil.
> Dwarf dances in front of prisoner while singing.

Dwarf rides on top of Austin Powers' motorcycle.
Dwarf dressed in rap gear.
Dwarf wears giant clock around neck.
Dwarf spotlighted against wall trying to escape from prison.
Dwarf repulsed as Goldmember eats his own peeling skin.
Dwarf hits Dr. Evil in crotch with fake meteor.
Gun-pointing dwarf.
Pants-dropping dwarf.
Rejected dwarf.
Bird-flipping dwarf.
Dwarf disturbed by Fred Savage's mole.
Dwarf uses mini katana to open letter.
Dwarf punted into mini fridge.
Dwarf breaks mini bottle to fight Austin Powers.
Dwarf hind kicks Powers in crotch.
Dwarf's body covered with pillowcase.
Dwarf runs into wall while wearing pillowcase.
Dwarf dressed up as Austin Powers in backseat of mini car.
Dwarf writes in mini notebook.
Dwarf sexually harasses Beyonce.
Dwarf in mini scuba outfit.
Dwarf humps Beyonce's leg.
Dwarf hides in bottom of Austin Power's henchman outfit.
Dwarf in shadow's hand looks like Mike Myer's wang.
Dwarf strapped upside down to Austin Powers.
Dwarf flies out of shaft and hits wall.
Shin-kicking dwarf.

Austin Powers: The Spy Who Shagged Me (1999)

Written by Mike Myers and Michael McCullers
Directed by Jay Roach
Starring Mike Myers, Heather Graham, Michael York, Robert Wagner, Rob Lowe
Featured dwarf: Verne Troyer
"Breathtaking. I shall call him Mini-Me."

Jay Roach changes what was most likely to be a one hit wonder into a bona fide blockbuster trilogy by adding a dwarf. The addition of Verne Troyer as Mini-Me, the clone of Dr. Evil, is one that can only be described as divine intervention and should serve as a sequel guidebook for future generations of filmmakers to study. Essentially, what Mini-Me does best is counterbalance the large amount of screen time Mike Myers has as multiple characters. A little Mike Myers, after all, goes a long way. But a whole lot of dwarf, on the other hand, never seems to last long enough. Watching Verne Troyer in the movie makes you want to have your own dwarf sidekick. The movie allows the viewer to live out their own fantasy of what it would be like to have their very own dwarf clone.

I believe one of the main reasons this film was so financially successful was because it connected on a primal level with many people, and it did so for this very reason: everyone wishes their friends were more like them, right? Well, imagine how awesome it would be if your best friend were a clone of you. Dr. Evil realizes this, so much so that he pretty much gives his real son (Seth Green) the brush-off so he can spend more time around the dwarf version of himself and pamper the little guy to boot. He gives the dwarf twice as much love as he ever thought about giving to his son. As I was watching, it made me wonder, if I had two sons, one a tallie and one a dwarf, who I'd love more. Well, off the top of my head I'd have to say the dwarf, so I guess I'm going to have to side with Dr. Evil on this issue. I mean, after all, you can't really blame him. Mini-Me is absolutely adorable, even when he's at his most evil. It would be impossible to get mad at a kid like that. He does exactly what Dr. Evil does, including speaking in finger quotes, stroking a hairless cat, riding on the front of his bike, playing a mini piano on top of his big piano, the list goes on.

The filmmakers also do a good job here in giving us a few new and unusual forms of dwarfsploitation such as the dwarf dry humping a giant laser, dressing up as a baby with a blowgun and getting lockjaw on Austin Power's crotch after biting it. Like I said before, *Austin Powers: The Spy Who Shagged Me* (1999) should be required viewing for film schools across the world for its unique device of adding a dwarf to ensure Blockbuster gold.

    Dr. Evil dwarf clone.
    Dr. Evil mimicking dwarf.
    Hairless cat-stroking dwarf.
    Dwarf flips off Seth Green.
    Dwarf attempts to eat cat ear.

Dwarf in levitating chair.
Dwarf jumps through time portal.
Bonnet-wearing dwarf with a blowgun, in baby carriage.
Dwarf rides in front of Dr. Evil's bike.
Dwarf drags large briefcase.
Dwarf in rotating chair.
Dwarf makes finger quotes.
Dwarf scurries across table.
Dwarf dry humps giant laser.
Dwarf plays mini piano on top of Dr. Evil's large piano.
Close up of dwarf hands playing piano.
Dancing dwarf.
Dwarf in "Moonraker" style outfit.
Horn-honking dwarf.
Dwarf hangs from ceiling pole.
Dwarf fights Austin Powers.
Spitting dwarf.
Dwarf is stuck on Austin Power's crotch after biting it.
Dwarf scat into space through Austin Power's spacesuit.
Dwarf flies through space.
Dwarf docks inside large penis ship.
Dwarf takes a needle shot in the ass.

Bad News Bears (2005)

Written by Bill Lancaster, Glenn Ficarra and John Requa
Directed by Richard Linklater
Starring Billy Bob Thornton
Featured dwarf: Pancho Moler
"Get out of here, you're creeping the kids out!"

When a drunken ass of an ex baseball player (Billy Bob Thornton) takes over a rag tag little league team that everyone is trying to get out of the league, he tries every trick in the book to get them going. When one trick fails, he goes over to the bench to reveal a dwarf in uniform. When he tells the dwarf, "Kevin," that it's not going to work out, Kevin asks for his payment, which appears to be a 1.75L bottle of vodka. He then tells Kevin to get out because he's creeping the kids out. As Kevin leaves he fakes out the kids, continuing his torment. The movie itself is bland and mediocre. The dwarf joke is one of the few that is rather funny so don't let the set up fool you as the screen time of Pancho is very, very limited.

Dwarf as kid.
Dwarf taking vodka as payment.
Dwarf scaring kids.
Dwarf being treated poorly.

Bad Santa (2003)

Written by Glenn Ficarra & John Requa
Directed by Terry Zwigoff
Starring: Billy Bob Thornton, Tony Cox, Brett Kelly, Lauren Graham, Bernie Mac, John Ritter
Featured dwarf: Tony Cox
"You can't drink worth a shit, you know that?" - Billy Bob Thornton
"I weigh 92 pounds, mother fucker!" - Tony Cox

Billy Bob Thornton and Tony Cox are perfectly cast in this movie about a thieving tallie/dwarf duo, but it's dwarf actor Cox who is the real star of *Bad Santa* (2003). This is a film that near flawlessly utilizes many elements of dwarfsploitation without giving Cox a shitty role. Yes, it exploits him. It places him in a little elf outfit with funny ears and yes, it puts him in a mini snowman outfit and makes him crawl through air vents like a micro version of Bruce Willis from *Die Hard* (1988).

All these elements aside though, Cox has one of the greatest, meatiest dwarf roles in cinema history. He is technically Billy Bob's sidekick, but often the line is obscured because Cox has such a strong character in the film. Instead of being the goof-off, fuck-up, or manic sidekick, Cox is the one that holds things together when Billy Bob goes crazy and falls off the wagon almost every single time we see him on screen. The dwarf constantly struggles to keep the team together and apologizes for Billy Bob pissing people off in the movie and almost getting them fired. It's hilarious to think about because as far as characters are concerned, the dwarf is actually the father figure to the spoiled, childlike Billy Bob.

The only difference is that the sizes between father and son are completely reversed here, and even though Cox is cast as the straight man and constantly lectures Billy Bob for almost ruining everything for the both of them, he's still childlike in his own way. He throws tantrums, is incredibly foul-mouthed, and fulfills the angry dwarf stereotype perfectly. He also allows himself to be bossed around by his Asian tallie girlfriend who is not very time conscious when it comes to the robberies they commit. She wants what she wants and wants her dwarf boyfriend to get it for her. So, in summary, Tony Cox's character is angry, foul-mouthed, fatherly and pussy-whipped. Now, that's what I call a multi-layered dwarf exploitation role. In fact, it's one of the best ever. *Bad Santa* (2003) is a must see for the dwarf completist and dwarf-curious alike.

Dwarf elf.
Thieving dwarf/tallie duo.
Dwarf in snowman suit.
Dwarf thief.
Dwarf dates ball busting tallie.
Dwarves dance with Billy Bob.
Drinking dwarf.
Lecturing dwarf.
Dwarf walks next to smoking and drinking Santa in elf outfit.
Dwarf wears funny elf ears.
Dwarf hypes up kids to see Santa.
Dwarf/tallie argument.
Dwarf crawls through vent.
Dwarf negotiates with Bernie Mac and fails.
Extreme-cursing dwarf.
Dwarf tries to beat up Billy Bob Thornton.
Dwarf spars fat kid.
Fat kid punches dwarf in crotch.
Dwarf punches fat kid in crotch.
Dwarf kisses mannequin's breasts.
Dwarf jumps and can't reach mannequin's fur.
Dwarf clubs mannequin's leg to get to fur.
Dwarf pulls gun on Billy Bob.
Dwarf in gunfight with cops.

Basket Case 3: The Progeny (1992)

> Written by Robert Martin, Frank Henenlotter
> Directed by Frank Henenlotter
> Starring Kevin Van Hentenryck, Annie Ross
> Featured dwarf: Benny Phipps

This acid trip of a movie is part three in the *Basket Case* series and offers a ton of weirdo monsters that are part of a freak family that's about to get bigger—one of the freaks is pregnant. Grandma Ruth (Annie Ross) takes her group of freaks on a field trip to the freak doctor's house. Chaos ensues as the police discover there's a reward out for the twins from the first two "Basket Case" movies. The freak puppets are great and weird and it is hilarious to watch them do everything from singing on the school bus to ordering burgers at a fast food joint. The freaks would not be complete without the stereotypical dwarf freak with a mutated face, credited to a Benny Phipps (her only film credit as of this writing). She's given nothing to do and isn't even there in several of the group shots. For fans of extreme weirdo cinema only.

> Dwarf involved in group singing.
> Dwarf running.
> Dwarf gazing up.
> Dwarf reading the Holy Bible.
> Sobbing dwarf.
> Dwarf extra.

Bedtime Stories (2008)

> Written by: Matt Lopez and Tim Herlihy
> Directed by: Adam Shankman
> Starring: Adam Sandler
> Featured dwarves: Mikey Post, Sebastian Saraceno, Debbie Lee Carrington
> "Big people stink!"

Adam Sandler and Disney teamed up for this *Cinderella* reworking where he's a maintenance man at a Hilton-esque hotel who is trying to get a shot at running the place. He finds out that when he tells his niece and nephew bedtime stories, they come true. Luckily, during a cowboy and Indian bedtime story where Sandler and the leading lady are about to kiss, the nephew throws in the suggestion of an angry dwarf kicking him. The dwarf, played by Mikey Post, then runs off angrily to a mini wagon train of other dwarves. As Sandler asks, "Why'd you do that?," Mikey turns to him and replies with, "Because I'm angry." When the situation happens in reality, Mikey surprisingly kicks him and joins a Gremlin full of dwarves, driven by Sebastian Saraceno.

The moment easily delivers the best, if not the only, laugh out loud moment of the movie. It also keeps with the stereotype of so many other movies that depict dwarves as angry.

There's also a goblin that appears during one of the sequences that is apparently played by the beautiful Debbie Lee Carrington. Why keep such a lovely woman under mask? And why kick her?

> Angry-kicking dwarf.
> Dwarf having trouble getting into car.
> Flying goblin dwarf.
> Dwarf extra.
> Dwarves in cowboy outfits.

Big Top Pee-wee (1988)

> Written by Paul Reubens, George McGrath
> Directed by Randal Kleiser
> Starring Paul Reubens, Kris Kristofferson
> Featured dwarf: Mihaly "Michu" Meszaros

A big storm sends a traveling circus to Pee-wee's farm. He lets them stay so they can do their show and even agrees to be a part of it. Unlike the current residents of Pee-wee's town, who all appear to be complete bastards to him, the freaks in the traveling circus are much better human beings. They could care less that Pee-Wee is the town eccentric who talks to his pig, creates mutant vegetables, owns a hot dog tree and has his animals sleep in beds inside their stables as if they were all part of some strange, animal prostitute farm. They accept Pee-wee for the kind, sensitive farmer he is, and to sweeten the pot, they have a dwarf as part of their crew who wears a funny hat that makes him look like Toad from the "Super Mario Bros" video games.

The director constantly chooses angles to draw attention to the dwarf's height, having him stand on boxes, be manhandled by the circus strongmen, etc. However, he also gives the dwarf a heart of gold, having him stand up for Pee-Wee and demanding that everyone listen when he speaks. If only everyone could have a kind-hearted dwarf friend like this! There is nothing extraordinary the dwarf does but he is present throughout the entire movie and is a consistently funny and entertaining character. This, combined with the incredibly bizarre elements of the movie, make it an easily recommendable view.

To top everything off, Kris Kristofferson's character (Mace Montana) has a wife that's the size of Tom Thumb. This is not technically a dwarf role but I would consider her character to be part of the honorary dwarf department. Among many other things, the fact that Kristofferson has a wife that fits in his hand and no one in the movie acknowledges it to be anywhere out of the ordinary is hilarious. I don't know in what universe this film exists, but it's certainly not this one.

> Funny-hat-wearing dwarf.
> Dwarf attempts to pull a morbidly obese woman out of a trailer.
> Bird's eye view of dwarf in circus.
> Circus strongman lifts up dwarf in celebration.
> Dwarf stands on a chair next to Benicio Del Toro.
> Dwarf sits next to a morbidly obese woman.
> Film keeps cutting back to enthusiastic, celebrating dwarf.
> Dwarf in suspenders and Freddy Krueger-esque shirt.
> Dancing clown/cowboy dwarf.
> Top-hat-wearing dwarf.

Bill and Ted's Bogus Journey (1991)

> Written by Chris Matheson, Ed Solomon
> Directed by Peter Hewitt (as Pete Hewitt)
> Starring Keanu Reeves, Alex Winter, William Sadler, and Joss Ackland
> Featured dwarves: Ed Gale, Arturo Gil

In *Bill and Ted's Bogus Journey* (1991), dwarves appear in Martian suits as the most brilliant scientists in the universe, otherwise known as

"Stations." When Bill and Ted are killed by evil robot versions of themselves, there's a section of the movie where they enter Heaven and plead with God to get another chance at life on earth. God grants their requests and points them in the direction of the Stations, who look like freakish versions of *Fraggle Rock* creatures with their puppety features and elongated snouts. Their cracked-out design appears to be made by someone high as a kite. They speak in gibberish with cartoon voices, yet several of the brilliant minds in Heaven, including the likes of Albert Einstein, seem to understand what they're saying without any confusion.

Bill and Ted convince the Stations to help build good robot versions of themselves to take down the evil robot versions of themselves. From there on out, we're treated to the dwarf Stations helping Bill and Ted buy supplies at the store and morphing into one tallie Station to actually build the robots. This is a part I didn't understand; why would they have to morph into a tallie to build the robots? Couldn't they just do it as two separate dwarves? What are the filmmakers trying to say: that the dwarves are more powerful as one tallie than two dwarves? Sounds like blatant sizeism to me.

Regardless of this point, the dwarves are fun to watch in their cracked-out outfits, even if they do cover up the face and body of two of our favorite dwarf actors, Ed Gale and Arturo Gil. The end of the movie gives us an added bonus of the dwarf Stations joining Bill and Ted's band and playing the drums to a sold-out concert. Rock on, Wyld Stallions!

> *Fraggle Rock*-looking dwarf aliens.
> Scientist dwarf aliens.
> Cartoon voice dwarf aliens.
> Hardware-shopping dwarf aliens.
> Robot-building dwarf aliens.
> Drum-playing dwarf aliens.

Bird (1988)

> Written by Joel Oliansky
> Directed by Clint Eastwood
> Starring Forest Whitaker
> Featured dwarf: Tony Cox

We know Eastwood is a dwarf appreciator from his masterpiece *High Plains Drifter* (1973). Unfortunately, the same instincts were not followed through in the film *Bird* (1988). After waiting a hundred and forty two minutes and six seconds, a dwarf finally appears. The face is recognizable. It's Tony Cox, a truly excellent dwarf actor. However, his talents as well as the patience of the audience are completely ignored as Cox is only given a handful of lines in a brief announcer role at a jazz club. This is exploitation of the highest caliber as Cox is only in the movie long enough to show up and disappear soon after. It's as if Eastwood put a dwarf in the movie just for dwarf's sake which, naturally, I wouldn't protest but at least give me a scene with the dwarf. One scene, Mr. Eastwood, is that too much to ask for? And if it's going to be a cameo, at least make it have validity or be of some significance.

We love you Mr. Eastwood. You are America's bad-ass. You also gave Billy Curtis perhaps the greatest dwarf role in Western film history. All we want is for you to continue loving dwarves as much as we do.

142:06 dwarf announces.
Dwarf announcer.

Bitch Slap (2009)

Written by Eric Gruendemann and Rick Jacobson
Directed by Rick Jacobson
Starring Julia Voth, Erin Cummings, America Olivo, Lucy Lawless and Kevin Sorbo
Featured dwarf: Debbie Lee Carrington
"My mom used to say she wished I was born a midget…"

When I saw the trailer for this B movie romp that showed hot, well-endowed girls with big guns, I was very excited. When I heard that little person legend Debbie Lee Carrington was in it, I was even more excited. To my dismay, Carrington does not show up until close to the end as one of many in a gun fight. She does get to hold a large machine gun and run around wildly, going back and forth across the screen firing the gun, but is otherwise wasted. Had Carrington been one of the main three women, this would have been a classic well worth a watch.

Dwarf with machine gun.
Running wild across screen.
No lines for little person.

Black Samurai (1977)

Written by B. Readick
Directed by Al Adamson
Starring Jim Kelly
Featured dwarf: Felix Silla

We'd buy anything *Little Cigars* (1973) alumnus Felix Silla sells.
He has the professionalism of ten tallies.

Dwarf loving director Al Adamson is back with a Jim Kelly starrer where he's an agent asked off his vacation to save a hot Chinese girl who is the daughter of a top ambassador. It's either serve up the ransom, a freeze bomb, or be saved by the Black Samurai! The movie is pure cheese with some fun, bad one-liners delivered by Kelly (several of which sound dubbed), whose acting is in bottom form and has some top of the line hokey fight sequences but it's pushed over the top when it has numerous dwarf actors taking on Kelly. That's right! If you've ever wanted to see dwarves take on a large black man with half-assed fighting talent, this movie gives it to you! It's weird and complete crap but still worth a view even if it's just for Felix Silla swinging through the trees like Tarzan.

> Dwarf with shotgun.
> Dead dwarf.
> Dwarf in cowboy hat.
> Dwarf extras.
> Dwarf hit by Jim Kelly.
> Dwarf called "shorty."
> Dwarves on roof.
> Dwarf jumps off roof.
> Dwarf thrown.
> Dwarf swinging Tarzan style.
> Dwarf laughing.
> Dwarf lassoes large black man.
> Dwarf dead on trees.
> Dwarf flipped.
> Dwarf beaten.
> Dwarf tag team attack.

Blade Runner (1982)

> Screenplay by Hampton Fancher and David Webb Peoples
> Directed by Ridley Scott
> Starring Harrison Ford
> Featured dwarf: Kevin Thompson, John Edward Allen

Considered by many to be a classic science fiction film, this Harrison Ford starrer would not be complete without the participation of little people. Unfortunately, as is the case too often, the first group of little people show up mostly in costume as toys. They aren't given much of anything to do other than seem silly. If anything, they are a distraction from an otherwise dark film. Late in the movie is what feels like a pointless scene where Ford is parked on the street and ends up seeing some street thug dwarves who end up jumping on his car after going through the trash. Both groups feel as if they were just thrown in as a novelty to keep the slow moving movie going. I can't recommend this for dwarf enthusiasts as there was no pay off for either group. I kept waiting for the toys to attack or be of some significance to where people were needed in those costumes but they simply felt unnecessary in all ways.

>Dwarves dressed as toys.
>Dwarf with long nose.
>Dwarf with darting eyes.
>Street thug dwarves.
>Trash-collecting dwarves.
>Thieving dwarves.
>Fighting dwarves.
>Dwarf running into door.

Blankman (1994)

>Written by Damon Wayans and J. F. Lawton
>Directed by Mike Binder
>Starring Damon Wayans, David Alan Grier, Robin Givens and Mike Binder
>Featured dwarf: Tony Cox
>"It's a big world and we all have to do our part."

When super-nerd inventors Darryl Walker (Damon Wayans) and Kevin Walker (David Alan Grier) decide to clean up the streets by becoming homemade superheroes, their actions inspire others. While watching a talk show, Grier's character sees a talk show host (Greg Kinnear) talking to some new superheroes they have inspired, including Midget Man (Tony Cox). Midget Man then tries to demonstrate by picking up a chair and throwing it but falls over, taking part of the set with him. The role is brief and Cox is underused and would have served better as the sidekick.

Dwarf superhero.
Dwarf can't lift chair.
Dwarf knocks over set.

Blind Beast Vs. Killer Dwarf (2004)

Directed by Teruo Ishii
Starring Lily Franky, Shinya Tsukamoto
Featured dwarf: Little Frankie
"He looks just like a dwarf from the circus."

After a night out seeing hot Japanese singer/dancers, a dime novel writer is hanging out in a park filled with prostitutes (not sure why) when he spots a dwarf that he becomes obsessed with. When he sees the dwarf drop a severed arm, he continues to follow him until he disappears into a temple. When Moulin Rouge star Ranko Mizuki disappears, the dime novelist and his detective pal Akechi go in search of solving the mystery.

The late Japanese wrestler Little Frankie gets the part as the killer dwarf. A whole back story is told about how he was mistreated by members of the circus and then he burned it to the ground, starting his killing streak. There is no real "versus" as each spends their time separately when it comes to screen time. While there are plenty of hot Japanese women on display and enough strange violence to keep the cult fans happy, the movie is not the dwarf movie one might hope for. Frankie doesn't get much to do other than "Cut to" shots and "inserts." His final scene is a chase scene on a roof that is the most memorable for me. The movie is for fans of sick weirdo cinema only.

Dwarf walking in smutty park.
Mistaken for a child.
Writer fascinated by dwarf.
Dwarf harassed by drunk.
Dwarf drops his stuff.
Dwarf joins circus.
Dwarf forced to drink.
Tallies play catch with dwarf.
Tallies laugh at dwarf.

Crawling dwarf.
Dwarf uses fake legs to look like a tallie.
Dwarf running on rooftop.
Dwarf thrown off rooftop.

Blood Dolls (1999)

Written and directed by Charles Band
Starring Debra Mayer
Featured dwarf: Phil Fondacaro
"If there happens to be a dwarf or a clown, don't be alarmed."

Mr. Travis "always wears a mask and is very eccentric," as it's explained in the first three minutes of the film. "He might have a clown or a dwarf, a rock band behind bars…he's an eccentric weirdo with a fondness with freaks." The tagline for this winner is "Power…lust…freaks." You can't have a movie with freaks without including a dwarf, in this case Phil Fondacaro donning an eye patch and tuxedo. Unfortunately he doesn't get much to do beyond shocking the girls in the cage, forcing them to play particular songs—he's nothing more than eye candy, a waste of a true talent. When the girls escape, one of them hits Phil with a guitar, sending him flying.

"I didn't see you there."
Tallie runs into dwarf.
Dwarf wears eyepatch.
Angry dwarf.
Dwarf in tuxedo.
"I'm not a dog, you know?"
Yelling dwarf.
Sleeping dwarf.
Ties up tallie woman.
Dwarf crawling.
Hit with a guitar.

Bloodsucking Freaks (1976)

Written and Directed by Joel M. Reed
Starring Seamus O'Brien, Viju Krem, Niles McMaster, Dan Fauci, Alphonso DeNoble
Featured dwarf: Louie De Jesus

Joel M. Reed's *Bloodsucking Freaks* (1976) is one of the most controversial films ever made, and when you see it, you'll know exactly why. It's also one of the greatest dwarfsploitation movies ever made. Dwarf actor Louie De Jesus (aka Ralphus) gleefully serves his master Sardu (Seamus O'Brien) as they both take part in the brutal torture and murder of several naked women. Together the two put on a Grand Guignol-style theatrical show where the crowd believes it's the staged torture and murder of naked women when in reality they're saving budget on special effects and props because they're actually doing it! Yes, it's live theatre snuff and the audience doesn't have a clue.

What really sells this movie is Ralpus the dwarf. He is so ecstatically involved in his performance, the movie transcends from torture porn into bizarre, morbid comedy. Not to mention that Ralphus looks like John Oates from Hall and Oates in a Chucky outfit. The acts he performs are truly loathsome, such as putting women's body parts in vices, plucking out their eyeballs and eating them, frying their eyeballs in a pan, drinking beer with his master while throwing darts at a bulls-eye-painted woman's ass, caning a naked woman, riding a naked woman while dressed in a cowboy outfit, the list goes on. But the gore is so shitty looking in all its red paint-colored 70s glory and the dwarf is so happy at the misery he's creating that you just can't help but laugh at the absurdity of it all, not to mention that every time Ralphus feeds a group of feral women in a cage raw meat, he dances a jig.

Needless to say, I could go on all day explaining how crazy this movie is, but you just have to see it for yourself to believe it. This movie is listed throughout the internet as one of the worst movies ever made but I actually find it to be a fascinating work of S&M performance art unlike anything I've ever seen. The fact Reed was able to get his actors to pull off and commit to film what he did, let alone get his actors to agree to it, and with such vigor, is a truly impressive feat. This film will go down in history as one of the weirdest movies ever made and it earns my vote for the most gleefully enthusiastic, torturing dwarf in film history.

John Oates-looking dwarf.
Crate-opening dwarf.
Dwarf puts woman's finger in vice.
Dwarf puts woman's head in vice.
Dwarf runs around with crowbar raised in the air.
Eyeball-eating dwarf.
Dwarf saws off woman's hand.
Dwarf feeds raw meat to feral, naked women in cage.
Happy, dancing dwarf.
Blowgun-shooting dwarf.
Dwarf rides woman like a horse while dressed in a cowboy outfit.
Cymbal-clashing dwarf.
Beer-drinking dwarf.
Dwarf throws darts at a naked woman's ass.
Dwarf eats popcorn as he watches a woman get tortured on a rack.
Dwarf makes chicken noodle soup.
Dwarf places woman's head in guillotine.
Ass-caning dwarf.
Pipe-smoking dwarf.
Dwarf force feeds critic.
Dwarf cuts off woman's feet.
Barber dwarf.
Dwarf primps himself with makeup.
Dwarf pan-fries eyeballs.
Dwarf kicks tallie in crotch.
Dwarf's head is jammed through door.
Dwarf's severed head part of a buffet arrangement.

Bloodsucking Redneck Vampires (2004)

Written and directed by Mike Hegg and Joe Sherlock
Starring Jeff Dylan Graham
Featured dwarf: Bill Bradford
"Farts are like salmon, they both like to head upstream."

Sub Rosa studios brings us this micro redneck vampire greatness that features everything from a drunken dwarf to an extremely large nude woman to some really bad fart jokes. The film mostly centers on a redneck family, one of whom hangs out with a dwarf. We are introduced to "Clete" while he's peeping through a window at a girl taking a shower. He spends most of the rest of the movie yelling at people and drinking away. He reminded me of a drunken Macho Man Randy Savage. With some restraint, Bill Bradford could be a great actor. He has some talent and is obviously willing to do anything.

I would not recommend this film to just anyone. However, if you have watched micro films in the past then this one has all the ingredients you could ask for from such a small film.

> Dwarf on ladder.
> Peeping Dwarf.
> Dwarf thrown from ladder.
> Dwarf rolls around.
> Dwarf fighting tallie.
> Dwarf running away.
> Dwarf who loves saying "peckerwood."
> Dwarf eats with hands.
> Dwarf yells.
> Shirtless dwarf.
> Beer-drinking shirtless dwarf.
> Dwarf digging through fridge.
> Drunken dwarf.
> Dwarf vampire.
> Dwarf vampire on DVD menu.

Blue Demon (2004)

> Written and directed by Dan Grodnik
> Starring Dedee Pfeiffer, Jeff Fahey
> Featured dwarf: Danny Woodburn

There are movies that are just plain bad and then there those that are bad but they have enough fun elements to them that they are enjoyable. This one falls into the fun category. For instance, just look at how it starts:

- Sorority initiation
- Hot girl gets in underwear.
- Hot girl gets out of water in her soaked underwear

- Hot girl grabs hand of friend and it ends up being a bloody, bitten off arm.

Doesn't that sound like fun? If the answer is "no," then move on. This one is for the people who can find the fun in the above absurdities.

The dwarf in this classic is Danny Woodburn (probably best known for *Seinfeld*). Woodburn plays Lawrence Van Allen, the boss of a group of doctors who are creating a new breed of great white sharks, nicknamed "Project Blue Demon." When sharks attack the above-mentioned sorority girls, Woodburn is put in a tough spot and has to play the tough and angry boss. When we first see Woodburn, he is hilariously placed HIGH above anyone who enters, with his desk on a large platform. In a bit of irony, he is later making a speech but can barely be seen over the podium. Woodburn's character feels poorly written, as he's made out to be a villainous character through most of the movie, but by the end he is being made out more as one of the good guys. Despite the flip-flopping of writing, Woodburn plays the stereotypical angry dwarf flawlessly. Other than the podium and desk incidents, I think it's a role that normally would have been played by a tallie actor but Woodburn definitely brings something different to an otherwise mediocre B film.

> Dwarf higher up.
> Angry dwarf.
> Dwarf has hot secretary.
> Dwarf walking among tallies.
> Dwarf in purple pants.
> Dwarf barely seen over podium.
> Dwarf has to hold tallie's cigar.
> Tallie blows smoke in dwarf's face.
> Yelling dwarf.
> Male dwarf in women's restroom.
> Dwarf with arms crossed.
> Dwarf running.
> Dwarf with gun.
> Dwarf rolling on floor to kick door.

The Bodyguard (2004)

> Written and directed by Petchtai Wongkamlao
> Cast: Petchtai Wongkamlao
> "With my good looks I can find anybody, so get the hell out of here!"

This Thai action film feels like a vanity project for wannabe Fabio Petchtai Wongkamlao. To try and avoid the movie getting boring, Petchtai tries to spice it up along the way with various side characters. For instance, Tony "Ong Bak" Jaa pops up long enough to randomly kick ass. In the same vein, we are treated to a VERY large woman who is getting beaten by her husband. They trade remarks with the camera only showing her back. As she moves from the in front of the camera, an angry Thai dwarf is revealed spitting out fat/slut insults to the oversized wife. It's short and only considered a cameo but worthy viewing.

Reverse dwarfsploitation humor with size proportion visuals and insults.

> Angry dwarf.
> Dwarf whining.

Brain of Blood (1972)

> Directed by Al Adamson
> Written by Kane W. Lynn, Samuel M. Sherman, Joe Van Rodgers
> Starring Grant Williams, Kent Taylor, John Bloom, Regina Carrol, Vicki Volante
> Featured dwarf: Angelo Rossitto
> "I like you just as you are. I wouldn't trust you in a tall body."

Brain of Blood (1972) features a dwarf who looks like the love child of Lloyd Kaufman and Mel Brooks. I hadn't even thought such a thing was possible before seeing this movie, but leave it to dwarf obsessed director Al Adamson to deliver the goods on the dwarf frontier. This is, after all the man who brought us the great *Black Samurai* (1977), a myriad of dwarves and kung fu. *Brain Of Blood* may not have the number of dwarves *Black*

Samurai did, but the Kaufman/Brooks love child dwarf is one of the main characters and intercut throughout the rest of the film.

I was very happy Adamson didn't just use a dwarf in a male nurse outfit to lure us into the first ten minutes, then either cruelly dispose of him or write him out of the story. No sir, when Adamson's at the director's chair, the dwarf stays in the picture! Other dwarf elements we're treated to in this picture are dwarf giggling, dwarf cruelty to humans, evil dwarf laughing at carnage and, my personal favorite: a dwarf in a funny golf hat. Perhaps Tim Conway received his inspiration from *Brain of Blood* when creating *Dorf On Golf* (1987)?

> Dwarf in nurse outfit.
> Dwarf-assisted brain transplant.
> Unseen dwarf activity due to height.
> Dwarf drains blood from young girl.
> Dwarf carries blood to mad scientist.
> Dwarf haunts woman with his maniacal laugh.
> Sunglass-wearing dwarf scatters into forest.
> Dwarf laughs at death and claps his hands at the sight of death.
> Dwarf's head framed over skeleton's crotch.
> Specialized dwarf glasses.
> Dwarf lies over opened hood of car.
> Dwarf attempts to protect mad scientist boss by rushing at his attacker's knee and squeezing it.
> Dwarf drags man down stairs.
> Dwarf jumps off stairs.
> Dwarf stabbed by syringe.
> Dwarf in flashback montage.

Bride of Frankenstein (1935)

> Written by William Hurlbut
> Directed by James Whale
> Featured dwarves: Billy Barty and John George

As it's discovered that the monster lives, chaos ensues. While it's a monster movie classic, it's not a dwarf classic but did employ two legendary dwarf actors—Billy Barty as a baby (again) and John George as one of the many, many villagers. Don't blink or you'll miss them in the madness.

Dwarf extras.
Dwarf as baby.

Bringing Up Baby (1938)

>Written by Dudley Nichols and Hagar Wilde
>Directed by Howard Hawks
>Starring Cary Grant and Katharine Hepburn
>Featured dwarf: Karl "Karchy" Kosiczky

Straight laced paleontologist Dr. Huxley (Cary Grant) has a series of strange encounters with the breezy Susan Vance (Katharine Hepburn). One of the many comical mix ups involves her pet leopard and a bad leopard from the circus. With a brief scene outside a circus tent, it's really not complete without a little person, in this case Karl "Karchy" Kosiczky. Don't blink.

Dwarf extra.
Dwarf in circus.

Bubble Boy (2001)

>Written by Cinco Paul, Ken Daurio
>Directed by Blair Hayes
>Starring Jake Gyllenhaal, Swoosie Kurtz, Marley Shelton, and Danny Trejo
>Featured dwarves: Verne Troyer, Beetlejuice
>"Dear Lord, if thou findest the stealing of this truck offensive in any way, please direct thy wrath upon that midget and not upon us."

Bubble Boy (2001) is about a kid (played by then relatively unknown actor Jake Gyllenhaal) who lives in a bubble and embarks on a road trip to tell the girl of his dreams how much he loves her after she gets engaged to another man. Along the way, BB gets picked up by a sideshow circus. Confused and frightened in the dark confines of a train, he turns the light on and it blasts right in the face of Beetlejuice, the dwarf from *The Howard Stern Show*. It's a pretty humorous sight as Beetlejuice freaks out on him, hands flailing all over the place and screaming like a little girl. BB then discovers he's stuck in a train with a bunch of freaks, run by carnival boss Dr. Phreak (played with a mean spirit by the great Verne Troyer). Beetlejuice sees that Dr. Phreak is headed their way and runs out of the train screaming at the top of his little lungs.

It's then that Verne Troyer appears, dressed like some kind of a tough guy gangster (who would be pretty intimidating if he wasn't 2'8.") Phreak is pissed that someone's distracted his freaks, spots the new tallie in the train (BB) and attempts to bully him into joining his freak show. When Bubble Boy laughs at him and calls him 'mini,' (an obvious reference to Troyer's *Austin Powers* fame) Troyer bashes up a car with his *Walking Tall*-style stick. He's furious, screaming "I'm not mini!" as he continues to trash the car. Then he proceeds to harass BB into exploiting him as one of his freaks. This is one of the things I thought was so funny about the movie, was that the dwarf was notoriously harassing the tallie into working for him. When the tallie refuses, the dwarf jumps on the top of his bubble and acts like an angry pimp, relentless in his pursuit of cheap labor. BB pushes at Troyer from the inside of his bubble and sends him flying into a truck, where Troyer appears to now be dead, lying on the ground not moving a bit. The tallie immediately books it out of there, apparently not too worried about the well being of the dwarf he potentially murdered.

Could this be an accurate depiction of how tallies rarely care about the well being of dwarves? Beetlejuice tosses BB's bags at him on the way out (how did he ever get the bags in the bubble in the first place?) and joins the other freaks following BB, who quickly blows them off and abandons them to look for the girl on his own. Beetlejuice and Troyer show up again through crosscutting sequences where BB's parents team up with Dr. Phreak to help him find his freaks so they can find their son. Lots of comparisons to Troyer as a baby ensue along with maternal tallie/dwarf cuddling and tempting the dwarf with candy. Not a great movie by any means but it fulfills its dwarfsploitation quota and certainly has some memorable moments. Recommended viewing for Troyer in the teamster outfit smashing up a car alone.

Freaked out Beetlejuice dwarf.
Angry dwarf smashes up car with *Walking Tall*-style stick.
Dwarf attempts to exploit tallie into becoming one of his freaks.
Wife beater-wearing dwarf.
Dwarf reaches for candy and falls off train.
Tallie tries to clean off dwarf's face while he eats ice cream like
    a messy baby.
Truck-stealing dwarf.
Tallie mother makes dwarf use hand sanitizer.
Dwarf barely visible in car.
Mom cradles dwarf in her arms like baby and he tries to feel her up.
Tattooed dwarf.
Dwarf thrown out of truck while strapped to a child seat.
Dwarves drink at Bubble Boy's wedding.
"Why are you so mini?"
"Mini? Mini? I'm not mini!"
"One of you two gotta' drive. I can't reach the pedals."

Carnival of Souls (1998)

Written by Adam Grossman
Directed by Adam Grossman, Ian Kessner
Featured dwarf: Joseph S. Griffo

This remake of the Herk Harvey classic is nowhere near as good as the original and certainly could have used much more dwarf screen time to spice the movie up but we're hardly treated to any. In this cornholing of the original, a clown gets out of prison for murdering a young woman's mother and then comes after the daughter. He gets in a car with her and freaks her out so much that she drives the vehicle into the river and starts seeing bizarre things, like a photographer dwarf. Unfortunately, that's all the dwarf we get in this movie. The filmmakers do take the approach of using the scene as a flashback and showing it again later on in the film, but this hardly makes up for the limited amount of dwarf they gave us in the first place.

Not only is this pathetic, it's completely unacceptable especially since the backdrop is a carnival setting! What's wrong with these filmmakers? The setting is ripe for dwarves. The best they could do was give us a dwarf jumping in front of our lead character and taking a bright picture? Boo, Wes Craven and company. You all need to go back home and watch *Freaks* before you attempt to make another movie with dwarves again.

Dwarf flashback.
Dwarf takes picture and runs off.

Casablanca (1942)

Written by Julius Epstein, Philip G. Epstein, and Howard Koch
Directed by Michael Curtiz
Starring Humphrey Bogart

Everyone knows the final scene of Casablanca even if they haven't seen it. The mechanics working around the plane are none other than little people.

Size proportion to plane
No lines
Serving as extras

Cerebral Print: The Secret Files (2005)

Written and Directed by Ford Austin
Starring Ford Austin, Mitchel Auman, Felissa Rose
Featured dwarf: Mighty Mike Murga

Rare movie that is a bunch of shorts about an alien's last few moments alive. There are two different segments featuring Mighty Mike Murga. One has Mighty Mike in his *Slaughter Party* (2005) attire, fighting the alien in a cockfight-type scenario. The other has Mighty Mike playing a child trick or treating, seemingly because they were too scared a child would get hurt.

Dwarf fighting.
Dwarf probing.

Charlie and the Chocolate Factory (2005)

> Written by John August
> Directed by Tim Burton
> Starring Johnny Depp
> Featured dwarf: Deep Roy
> "What is it? It's a little person!"
> "Are they real people?"

In Tim Burton's wonderful remake of *Willy Wonka and the Chocolate Factory* (1971), we get weirdo actor extraordinaire Johnny Depp trying to fill the superior Gene Wilder's shoes. Both films are most notable for the appearances of little people as Oompa Loompas. In this particular film, all of them are played magically by Tim Burton's favorite dwarf actor Deep Roy.

The story is well known. A reclusive master candy maker has decided to place a handful of golden tickets into some candy bar packages. Five lucky children will get to enter into the factory and the one who is the least rotten gets a special prize at the end. As the five get a tour through the factory, they one by one make mistakes that send them to another part of the factory, disappearing till the end of the film. Each time this happens, the Oompa Loompas arrive to sing and dance about the departed.

The Oompa Loompas are definitely the highlight, even going back to the history of how Willy Wonka lured them to the factory. Seeing so many Deep Roys singing and dancing is a sight worthy of a viewing in and of itself but you also see him playing everything from a female secretary to a shrink to a barber—it's quite the sight.

> Dwarf drilling.
> Dwarf throwing candy balls.
> Dwarf squashing worm creatures.
> Dwarf with cocoa bean head.
> Dwarf shakes tallie's finger.
> Dwarf treats tallies to song.
> Dwarves diving into chocolate.
> Dwarves swimming.
> Dwarf answers tallie's call.
> Boat of dwarves.
> Dwarves sing and dance on blueberry girl.

Dwarves with weird glasses.
Dwarf head bobbing.
Dwarf tugs on tallie's coattails.
Dwarves on Fudge Mountain.
Dwarves shearing pink sheep.
Dwarf nurse.
Dwarves taking target practice.
Dwarf watching Oprah.
Dwarf news anchor.
Dwarf playing games.
Dwarf rock stars.
Dwarf sticking out tongue.
Dwarf mimics *Psycho*.
Dwarf cook.
Dwarf on ladder to cut hair.
Dwarf barber.
Dwarf shrink.
Dwarf in oversized chair.

Child's Play (1988)

Written by Don Mancini, John Lafia, Tom Holland
Directed by Tom Holland
Starring Catherine Hicks, Chris Sarandon, Alex Vincent, and Brad Dourif
Featured dwarf: Ed Gale
"Ugly doll."
"Fuck you."

A tallie serial killer is chased into a toy store and possesses a "Good Guy" doll with his evil soul just before death. Sure enough, a tallie kid watches and wishes for a "Good Guy" doll, and what does he get? Chucky. It's a brilliant idea for a movie and well executed to boot. Not too creepy and not taking itself too seriously, the movie walks the line perfectly. Perhaps its greatest testament, though, is how seamlessly they incorporated the shots with an actor in the Chucky suit with the actual puppeteering. Awesome dwarf actor Ed Gale plays the doll's stunt double. Before writing this book I had no idea the film used shots with an actor, and I'd seen the film several times. Talk about making a character come alive! Even after knowing and watching again closely, the movie merges the two perfectly. This undoubtedly played a large part in what made the film so effectively realistic and frightening. The moment where the doll runs behind the babysitter sends a chill up my spine every time.

The idea of something that is safe to us as children, coming alive and attacking us is a powerful universal fear. Gale's performance power brought the movie to legendary status and created a franchise no one is soon to forget. Let's hope they bring Gale back and don't switch over to CGI, which in my opinion has taken all the fun out of hand-crafted cinematic magic.

> Doll dwarf watches news.
> Doll dwarf POV.
> Doll dwarf freakishly runs past babysitter.
> Doll dwarf sits psychotically in chair in little boy's room.
> CU - Doll dwarf shoes.
> Doll dwarf murders with mini hammer.
> Doll dwarf manhandled by numerous tallies.
> Doll dwarf looks creepy lying in bed with young boy.
> Creepy ginger-doll dwarf.
> Doll dwarf POV running.
> Doll dwarf looks even more psychotic in daylight.
> Doll dwarf makes one of his tallie enemies blow himself up.
> Tallie kid attacks doll dwarf.
> Tallie mom cusses out doll dwarf.
> Doll dwarf's head spins around, *Exorcist* (1973) style.
> Doll dwarf wrestles with tallie.
> Doll dwarf bites tallie mom's arm.
> Doll dwarf comes alive when tallie mom discovers batteries are gone.
> Doll dwarf tries to strangle cop.
> Doll dwarf tries to stab cop through car seat.
> Cop puts cigarette lighter in dwarf's eye.
> Cop shoots doll dwarf.
> Doll dwarf makes voodoo doll out of tallie and stabs away at it.
> Breaking and entering-doll dwarf.
> Doll dwarf stabs doctor in ankle and electrocutes him.
> Knife-toting doll dwarf.
> Doll dwarf bashes tallie kid over the head with a mini bat.

Doll dwarf tries to possess little boy.
Doll dwarf stabs cop in ankle.
Doll dwarf bashes tallie cop over the head with mini bat.
Tallie kid burns doll dwarf in fireplace.
Burned doll dwarf attacks, *Shining* (1980) style.

Child's Play 2: Chucky's Back (1990)

Written by Don Mancini
Directed by John Lafia
Featured dwarf: Ed Gale

Chucky's back and trying to get young Andy's soul! Also back is Ed Gale, doing stunts and bringing some life to the psychotic doll! Chucky is what makes this otherwise standard movie good, with his hilarious delivery (the excellent Brad Dourif) and fascinating doll features—when it comes to entertainment, size does matter!

Dwarf toy prodded.
Dwarf doll smashed by trunk.
Dwarf doll on phone.
Dwarf doll with gun.
Dwarf doll maniacally laughs.
Dwarf doll suffocates tallie.
Dwarf doll hand close up.
Dwarf doll hits other dwarf doll.
Dwarf doll buries other dwarf doll.
Dwarf doll on top of kid.
Dwarf legs under bus.
Dwarf doll eye close up.
Dwarf doll kills teacher.
Dwarf doll on people's backs.
Dwarf doll comes out from underneath toy boxes.
Dwarf doll hand smashed.
Dward doll screaming.
Dwarf doll with knife.
Dwarf doll with knife hand.
Dwarf doll explodes.

Chopper Chicks in Zombietown (1989)

>   Written and directed by Dan Hoskins
>   Starring Billy Bob Thornton and Don Calfa
>   Featured dwarf: Ed Gale
>   "If God had wanted me to do normal stuff, he would have made me look like normal people."

Although most people instantly categorize this one as a bad movie, it's not as bad as they may want you to believe. The filmmaker throws in every "bad" movie element he can—zombies, biker babes, mad scientist and even a dwarf—but it's not THAT bad. It's like watching a regular low budget movie but with all these great things thrown in to the mix to make it a little more interesting. It's *Feast 2* (2008) twenty years earlier (*Feast 2* tried to satisfy us by giving us two dwarves instead of just one, different biker babes, a different *Return of the Living Dead* alum and a different monster).

This one is an early "out of the suit" performance for dwarf acting legend Ed Gale, fresh off his stints as "Howard the Duck" and "Chucky." With Don Calfa playing a mad scientist type, he isn't complete without a dwarf sidekick and he gets that with Gale, doing his every request until things start going wrong. If biker chicks fighting off zombies with the help of kids and a dwarf sound like a blast to you, then this one is a home run.

>   Dwarf with ladder.
>   Dwarf with top hat.
>   Dwarf changes population.
>   Dwarf hides under morgue table.
>   Dwarf coughing, smoking, waving.
>   Dwarf picked up by tallie, forced into coffin.
>   Wet dwarf.
>   Dwarf with gun.
>   Dwarf in dumpster.
>   Dwarf throws grenade.
>   Dwarf captures tallie.
>   Dwarf looking over wheel.
>   "He said he could make me small."
>   "We could start a sideshow."

Referred to as dwarf.
Tells tallies how to kill the zombies.
Dwarf shoots zombie in head.
Dwarf wearing "Cycle Sluts" jacket.

Chronicles of Narnia: Prince Caspian (2008)

Written by Andrew Adamson, Christopher Markus, Stephen McFeely
Directed by Andrew Adamson
Starring Ben Barnes
Featured dwarves: Peter Dinklage and Warwick Davis
"That's not at all patronizing now, is it?"

A prince has to flee because his life is endangered. The only chance he has is to go into a forest that his pursuers are supposedly scared of. As he falls from his horse, he ends up meeting characters played by dwarf acting legends Peter Dinklage and Warwick Davis, and the real adventure begins.

I was not excited to see this film until I heard Dinklage and Davis were finally teamed up but it turns into the sort of team-up that *Forbidden Kingdom* (2008) was for Jackie Chan and Jet Li—they deserved better as they are legends.

Their screen time is mixed up with the kids and various other side characters, leaving much to be desired. Sure, I would have rather seen the movie star Dinklage and Davis but we're left to love what we got instead. And what we got, were a few fun moments like when Dinklage and Davis individually get involved in sword fights, are bossed around by a badger, and wage battle.

It is also notable there are many dwarf extras working as Narnians.

With swords.
Dwarf gagged and held captive.
Dwarf slapped.
Drowning dwarf.
Angry, ungrateful dwarf.
Dwarf swordfights kid.
Dwarf sets anchor.
Dwarf shoots bear.
Dwarf running.

Size differential.
"We were expecting someone, um, taller."
Dwarf stabs dwarf.
Hugs child who is taller.

Citizen Toxie: The Toxic Avenger IV (2000)

Written by Patrick Cassidy, Gabriel Friedman, Trent Haaga, Adam Jahnke, Corey Kalman, Lloyd Kaufman, Matt Levin
Directed by Lloyd Kaufman
Starring: David Mattey, Heidi Sjursen, Joe Fleishaker, Ron Jeremy, Corey Feldman, Trent Haaga, James Gunn
Featured dwarf: Hank the Angry Drunken Dwarf.
"And, you tell the pope, stop talking about me, he doesn't know me…"

In *Citizen Toxie: The Toxic Avenger IV* (2000), Stan Lee's narration at the beginning proclaims that two rotten sequels were made and that this is the real sequel. Perhaps that's because the great Lloyd Kaufman cast Hank the Angry Drunken Dwarf from the Howard Stern show in this one. And not only that, Hank plays the biggest role a little person can possibly play: God! Hank resides over Heaven (which has a population of 16 in the movie). I was wondering how many of those were little people since naturally all little people should go to Heaven, but I unfortunately didn't see any dwarves besides Hank. He's only in a cameo scene in the film (possibly because he was too drunk to make it through any extended dialogue), but it's a funny one.

In it a few scantily clad, attractive girls are at his side as he brags about all the great diseases he's made. The Toxic Avenger shows up and asks to go back to Tromaville. Hank obliges as long as Toxie kicks the asses of the all the murderers and child rapists and tells the Pope to stop talking about him and lets him know his hat looks stupid. Then Hank low fives his tallie sidekick and grabs the breasts of a nearby scantily clad tallie female, and he does it all with the innocent smile that made Hank so likeable.

Unfortunately Hank passed in 2001, before his acting career was allowed to flourish. We miss you, Hank. You may have passed on but your role in *Toxie IV* will live on forever.

Dwarf brags about creating disaster.
Cursing dwarf.
Dwarf grabs tallie female breast.

Corky Romano (2001)

Written by David Garrett and Jason Ward
Directed by Rob Pritts
Starring Chris Kattan
Featured dwarf: Martin Klebba
"That's a good little bitch."

Pirates of the Caribbean series star Martin Klebba pops up briefly in this goofy comedy about the idiot family member of a crime family who is sent undercover to get rid of the evidence against his family. Klebba comes into play when Romano is trying to enter an underground casino. When he continues to harass a hot bouncer, Klebba steps up with large shades and bling reminiscent of Mr. T. Not giving up easily, Romano finds an alternate way in. When Klebba finds out, he kicks in the door and makes Bruce Lee-esque noises and stances, with a wild but brief kung fu fight that includes him flying and kicking wildly.

While the movie is full of mediocre stupidity, Klebba's few scenes are awesome and has "future star" written all over them.

Dwarf bouncer.
Dwarf wearing bling/shades.
Dwarf kicks in door.
Dwarf makes kung fu noises.
Dwarf flies and kicks.

The Corpse Vanishes (1942)

Written by Sam Robins, Gerald Schnitzer, and Harvey Gates
Directed by Wallace Fox
Starring Bela Lugosi
Featured dwarf: Angelo Rossitto

62 ✦ Dwarfsploitation

Rossitto rubs his hands maniacally as he toadies up to evil tallie Bela Lugosi.

When a doctor, Bela Lugosi playing Dr. Lorenz, has a sick wife that he wants to keep young, he does what any man would do—he kidnaps brides from weddings and takes a fluid from them that he puts in his wife. It should be no surprise as you read that summary that I tell you this film was on *Mystery Science Theater 3000*.

As is typical for this type of film, the mad doctor can't do all these mad acts without help. Helping him in his madness is a retarded man and a dwarf, played by the great Angelo Rossitto. Angelo doesn't do much more than play the dwarf-bitch to Lugosi and company as he's yelled at, put to work like a servant, and then ends up getting shot in the back and left by Lugosi. It's a pure waste of talent but at least we got to watch Angelo carry a large suitcase up the stairs.

Dwarf on cart.
Dwarf lifted down.
Laughs as hunchback gets beaten.
Dwarf answers door.
Dwarf bows.

Dwarf yelled at.
Referred to as "Little Gargoyle."
Dwarf bossed around.
Dwarf carries large suitcase up stairs.
Dwarf laughing maniacally.
Dwarf in stairwell.
Dwarf shot in back.
Dwarf left by master despite begging.

The Court Jester (1955)

Starring Danny Kaye, Glynis Johns, Basil Rathbone, Angela Lansbury, John Carradine
Featured dwarves: Hermine's Midgets
"Who are these little people?"

When the royal family has been slaughtered, it's discovered that a bandit named "The Black Fox" is caring for a surviving child who is the heir to the throne. During an early number by Kaye, he's singing about how there are multiples of him and then he's singing with four other Black Foxes. Soon enough those four turn into eight, thanks to splitting into dwarves in the Black Fox outfit. We are treated to dwarves singing and dancing, even a large cheerleader-like pyramid wall with Danny Kaye standing on top of the dwarves. As it turns out, Kaye is nothing more than the court jester and has brought his dwarf friends from the carnival along to help out. Unfortunately the real Black Fox doesn't want them to entertain the men, so they are quickly sent away.

It's not until there are ten minutes left in the film, when Danny Kaye is in trouble, that the little people show up again and save the day. The end fight scene is an amazing spectacle with little people all over the place fighting the knights and continuously saving the day. Oddly, the tallies don't show up until the little people have taken out most of the baddies.

The Court Jester (1955) is old fashioned, with lots of goofy comedy, song and dance numbers and is kept clean but whether you're into that or not, it's well worth viewing just for the two major parts the little people play in it.

Tallies turn into dwarves.
Dwarves singing and dancing.
Dwarves in silly costumes.
Drinking dwarves.
Wall of dwarves with Danny Kaye on top.
Two dwarves on top of each other, pretending to be a knight.
Dwarves crawling up ropes.
Dwarves with shields.
Dwarves attacking knights.
Dwarves flip over tallies.
Dwarves beat knights with sticks.
Dwarves lay down and use their legs to push tallies up the stairs.
Dwarves trip up tallie.

The Creeps (1997)

Written by Benjamin Carr
Directed by Charles Band
Featured dwarves: Phil Fondacaro, Jon Simanton, Thomas Wellington and Joe Smith
"We don't want to be three feet tall forever, do we?"

Oh, Full Moon. They filled video shelves with bad movies for years but the one gift they did give us is a Phil Fondacaro filmography beyond just a few costume movies. In this one, a mad scientist brings to life Dracula, the Mummy, Frankenstein and the Wolfman, but there's a problem, causing them all to be three feet tall. That's right, we get more than just Phil in this one—we get four dwarves! Unfortunately everyone but Phil is hidden under heavy amounts of make-up and don't get to do much more than grunt but it's still fun to see them at work!

To top it off, the story is kind of ironic as they spend the majority of the film searching for a way to be a normal size. Of course, it's not as easy to find a virgin and other requirements as one would think.

There are some classic bits, including one about Phil's Dracula using a step stool to bite someone's neck, but the movie overall is filled with bad dialogue, lots of bad acting and quickly outdated effects. If you can forgive that, there's just something special about watching dwarves rip off a bound woman's clothes, or chase around a woman who loses her shirt for no reason in a library.

> Dwarf monsters.
> Dwarf with red eyes.
> Dwarf growling.
> Dwarves trip tallie.
> Dwarf on top of tallie.
> Dwarf rips off tallie's clothes.
> Dwarf with powers.
> Dwarves ride on car.
> Dwarf kicked.
> Dwarf goes through bookcase.
> Dwarves in search of virgins.
> Dwarves forced in.
> Angry dwarf.

Dahmer Vs. Gacy (2010)

> Written by Andrew J. Rausch
> Directed by Ford Austin

Who says clowns and mimes can't get along? Photo courtesy of Ford Austin.

It's hard out here for a dwarf mime.

Starring: Ford Austin, Randal Malone, Harland Williams, Steven Adler, Art LaFleur
Featured dwarf: Jerry Maren

Clones of Dahmer and Gacy escape from a military lab and wreak havoc until they finally face off. While wreaking havoc, Gacy runs into a mime, played by legendary dwarf actor Jerry Maren. At first it's just weird with Gacy (played by B movie staple Randal Malone) standing next to Maren's mime, who is mimicking him. Getting fed up with this, Maren launches into a foul mouthed tirade against the infamous serial killer. Not only is the size difference between Malone and Maren completely exploited but Maren spitting out words that a sailor would find offensive is downright hilarious. This movie is worth a look if only for Maren's classic scene.

> Size differential between dwarf and clown.
> Foul mouthed dwarf.

Darkest Knight (2000)

> Written by Mark Ezra and Harley Cokeliss
> Directed by Terry Marcel
> Starring Ben Pullen, Charlotte Comer
> Featured dwarf: Peter O'Farrell

A great cover for a movie you've never heard of is a near guarantee that the movie will be worse than most you've seen. Instantly upon watching it I realized I was watching what was a TV show trying to be passed off as a real film. The effects were beyond bad, although the costumes were passable. What we're given is the beginning of the adventures of Ivanhoe (Ben Pullen), who meets up not only with a red headed martial artist witch (Charlotte Comer), but also dwarf actor Peter O'Farrell as "Odo." It sounds much better than it is, believe me.

Odo is introduced in a bar of freaks that also includes a few other dwarves playing chess. There are monstrous looking people abound—and dwarves. Insert what the filmmakers were trying to say on your own. As it turns out, Odo is a thieving dwarf trained in magic which comes in handy as Ivanhoe and the ginger try to stop a necromancer from bringing demons from hell.

I would suggest skipping this one. Not only is the movie bad but O'Farrell is given nothing to do but be annoying.

> Dwarves with funny noses playing chess at freak bar.
> Causes bar fight.
> Dwarf thief.
> Referred to as "Little man."
> Dwarf rides donkey.
> Scared dwarf.

Greedy dwarf.
Dwarf in chest.
Dwarf hangs on to tallie for dear life.
Invisible dwarf.

Date Movie (2006)

Written by Jason Friedberg and Aaron Seltzer
Directed by Aaron Seltzer
Starring Alyson Hannigan
Featured dwarf: Tony Cox

Date Movie (2006) has its funny moments but it falls in the "stupid as movies can be" category. The movie is a spoof, mostly of romantic comedies like *Say Anything* (1989) but also goes into the territory of movies like *Kill Bill* (2003). In the case of our dwarf actor, Tony Cox, he is involved mostly in a spoof of the Will Smith film *Hitch* (2003). When Alyson Hannigan's fat girl character wants to get the man of her dreams, she goes to Tony Cox. No one knows love better than the ultra suave Tony Cox. As is par, Tony gets completely immersed in the film, singing and dancing and even making out with the fatty Hannigan. As he always seems to be, Tony is downright hilarious despite subpar material. It made me want to go to him for advice and then take him out for a beer. His part was once again a little blaxploitation meets dwarfsploitation but that may just be what makes all his "name" appearances so damned special. I'd definitely say everyone gets attacked in the movie, especially fat people, so when you take those lame gags plus all the dwarfsploitation moments I think it's safe to call these filmmakers "sizeists."

Dwarf kissing tallie.
Dwarf playing video games randomly.
Dwarf in Yoda face.
Dwarf doing liposuction.
Horny dwarf.
Dwarf dancing.
Dwarf singing.
Dwarf hitting motorcyclist with a bat.
Minister dwarf.

Size proportion shot.
Dwarf comes from behind woman with big butt.

Dead in Love (2009)

Written by David Lawson and Chris Watson
Directed by Chris Watson
Starring Kristin Minter, Eric Edwards, Margaret O'Brien, Randal Malone
Featured dwarf: Mighty Mike Murga

A movie about two guys who go in search of a girl they liked in high school. Not knowing where to find her, they wander around from place to place. One place they stop is a movie theatre showing *Terror Firmer* (1999). After the guys decide to leave, it cuts to a shot of Mighty Mike Murga laughing at the violence on screen. No lines for Mighty Mike Murga, just a featured extra.

Dwarf actor featured without lines.
Dwarf laughs at violence.

Death at a Funeral (2007)

Written by Dean Craig
Directed by Frank Oz
Starring Jane Asher, Peter Egan, Rupert Graves, Peter Vaughan
Featured dwarf: Peter Dinklage

The great Frank Oz (best known as the voice of dwarf puppet Yoda) directs this excellent British production. The story ties together several different subplots of characters that meet up at a funeral. The primary focus is on the two sons of the father who is the corpse of honor. As the tension builds between the two over sibling rivalry and payment for the funeral, a dwarf enters the scene (Peter Dinklage) and throws their already spiraling world into chaos as he awkwardly explains he was the father's gay lover. Hurt and feeling like a cheap man whore after finding out he's been left out of the will, the seemingly benign dwarf attempts to blackmail the family for money or he'll reveal the secrets of his love for the father (complete with photographic evidence) to the members of the funeral party.

Death at a Funeral (2007) offers an amazing role for the always stellar Dinklage. It's certainly a way I've never seen a dwarf used before and piques your curiosity to keep watching in what would otherwise be a clever but more standard comedy. It's dwarfsploitation with A-grade material and British humor that doesn't miss a beat. Now that's a combination I'd love to see more of.

> Gay dwarf.
> Ignored dwarf.
> Scorned dwarf.
> Staring dwarf.
> Dwarf awkwardly attempts to explain to explain how he's the corpse's ex gay lover.
> Blackmailing dwarf.
> Dwarf feels cheap and used.
> Spectacle wearing dwarf.
> Bound and gagged dwarf.
> Dwarf on drugs.
> Hopping dwarf.
> Tallies put dwarf in coffin with ex gay lover.
> Dwarf lies in 69 position over the corpse of his ex gay lover.
> Deranged dwarf springs out of coffin during funeral.

Death to Smoochy (2002)

> Written by Adam Resnick
> Directed by Danny Devito
> Starring Robin Williams, Edward Norton
> Featured dwarves: Danny Woodburn, Martin Klebba

When kids show phenom Rainbow Randolph (played by Robin Williams) is caught trying to sell off spots to kids on his show, he's replaced by Smoochy (played by Edward Norton) who turns the show into an even bigger hit.

As part of dwarf actor Danny Woodburn's character introduction, Robin Williams character is singing about "friends come in all sizes," and then Woodburn appears in a wild pink outfit with feminine pink hair agreeing with him. It then goes into a dance number with multiple little people dancing to the song. When Norton's character takes over, Woodburn tells him "work is work," which says a lot more than it probably meant to. Woodburn gets a decent amount of action in the film as he is the only one who helps out Williams when he's down and out doing everything from housing to feeding him. You get to see several sides to Woodburn as he kicks ass, gets his ass kicked, is sympathetic, coach-esque… However, the rest of the dwarves get to do nothing more than dance around in silly outfits making them nothing more than scenery.

>Dwarf dancing.
>Dwarves in eccentric wear.
>Forced dwarf smiling.
>Dwarves in costumes.
>Dwarf tossing.
>Dwarf reaching to stir pot.
>Dwarf attacked.
>Angry dwarf.
>Ice-skating dwarf.
>Dwarf assaulted and tied up.
>Dwarf announcer.

Decadent Evil (2005)

>Story by Charles Band
>Screenplay by August White
>Directed by Charles Band
>Starring Phil Fondacaro
>"Look, Marvin, your son has grown into a fine young man.
>>Well, not exactly grown. I think I can still bounce you on my knee."

This is one short movie coming in at 75 minutes but one of my fav's, Phil Fondacaro, gets top billing. You'd think with top billing and a short running time that Phil would show up sooner than 30 minutes into the film. It's a damn shame, really, that they went with boobsploitation over more Phil screen time. Imagine the fun we could have had if Phil had popped up at the strip club instead of at some lame guy's apartment! The movie has the Full Moon clichés of a little person, a couple of puppets (doing dirty things), and tons of breasts but it's not as good as it sounds. Phil is great as the bad-ass, ass-kicking, no-nonsense hero but he isn't given much to do and not enough vampires to take out—the body count is very low considering. At first the movie looks like it's trying to avoid being exploitative towards Phil but soon enough everyone gets a line in about him being short. While I commend them for giving Phil top billing, they should have given him more screen time and more to do, it felt way too much like they were shooting around him.

> Big-hat-wearing dwarf.
> Dwarf in bushes.
> Dwarf behind curtain.
> Dwarf hero.
> Dwarf carries heavy bag.
> Referred to as "Shorty."

Deuce Bigalow: European Gigolo (2005)

> Written by Rob Schneider, David Garrett, Jason Ward
> Directed by Mike Bigelow
> Starring Rob Schneider, Eddie Griffin, and Til Schweiger
> Featured dwarf: Edwin Alofs (as Edwin Adolfs)
> "Hey, I agreed to one midget, not two!"

Deuce is called back for another display of perversion and man whoring when he has to help his old pal T.J. Hicks (Eddie Griffin) out of a jam in Amsterdam. During his adventure, Deuce is under the impression that the woman he loves works in porn as she tells him she has to go to work. A dwarf in a sailor outfit greets her before walking inside and compliments her on her great work the day before.

Shortly after, she walks into a building with a bunch of dudes standing around outside in various costumes; this includes men in robes, soccer players and a man holding a donkey. Deuce fights his way into the set and discovers the dwarf in the sailor outfit kissing what appears to be his woman right below the boobs. He tosses the dwarf out the window, where he lands in a river. When he lands, he makes the sound of a little drop of water instead of a big splash, even though he creates one. Schneider quickly discovers the dwarf was making out with a porn star and not his girlfriend, who's painting the set in the same room. When the porn star sees Schneider she says, "Hey, I agreed to one midget, not two." The dwarf storms back in sans sailor hat and Schneider embarrassingly says, "Hey little friend. I guess I owe you a big…" right before the dwarf head butts him in the crotch and walks away pissed, cursing him on the way out.

It's a funny bit but the movie would have been strongly enhanced if Schneider had a dwarf sidekick who he passed the man whoring ropes onto, instead of the usual quick cameo by a dwarf that's disposable to the plot.

Dwarf in sailor outfit.
Dwarf gets it on with tallie.
Dwarf tossing.
Angry dwarf head butts Schneider in the crotch.

Dirty Work (1998)

Written by Frank Sebastiano, Norm MacDonald, Fred Wolf
Directed by Bob Saget
Starring Norm MacDonald, Artie Lange, Jack Warden, Traylor Howard, Don Rickles
Featured dwarf: Arturo Gil

In Bob Saget's classic, *Dirty Work* (1998), a movie that's both filthy and funny, Norm MacDonald and Artie Lange start their own revenge-for-hire business after taking a stand and deciding not to take crap from anyone ever again. Their business starts up after they set a trap for the boss of MacDonald's love interest while he's shooting a commercial for the car dealership he presides over. MacDonald and Lange hire a bunch of prostitutes and position them in the trunks of the cars displayed for the commercial and have them play dead so that when the actual commercial begins, our heroes crash the commercial and ask the a-hole boss why he has a bunch of dead hookers in the cars he's trying to sell. Then they proceed to open all the trunks during the filming of the commercial and reveal a bunch of what looks to be dead hookers. The revenge plan ends up working and the a-hole boss has to sell the dealership due to his lost reputation. However, it doesn't fare too well with the girl that Norm's trying to bang as she bursts into the Dirty Work offices and yells at him, explaining how his little stunt cost her her job.

At this point, a tacky-suit-wearing dwarf enters and completely contradicts the girl's statement by praising Norm and Artie for the dead hooker stunt. The girl storms off, pissed. However, not all is lost because he and Artie have gained the adoration of the dwarf, who has gone ahead and hired them both for his own revenge gig. In prime exploitative fashion, the dwarf works at the circus and has problems with what he describes as a "classic dwarf hater." The hater in question is played by tallie Rebecca Romijn, a bearded lady at the circus where the dwarf works, who is constantly pushing him around. Norm and Artie watch with disgust as she disrespects the dwarf right in front of their eyes. They instantly agree to help him. The next thing you know, Romijn wakes up without a beard (which doesn't seem like much of a punishment because she's pretty damn hot without one… for a tallie, that is) and the dwarf is standing on a tallie's shoulders spraying out the bearded part of the bearded lady sign on the outside of Romijn's trailer. It's a funny scene that adds to a very underrated comedy.

> Tacky suit wearing dwarf.
> Mulleted dwarf.
> Circus dwarf.
> Dwarf stands on suit case to talk to tallies.
> High angle on circus dwarf.
> Bearded woman pushes dwarf off suit case.
> Dwarf stands on tallie's shoulders and sprays out the word bearded in the bearded lady sign.

Dollman Vs. Demonic Toys (1993)

> Written by Charles Band, Craig Hamann
> Directed by Charles Band
> Starring Tim Thomerson, Melissa Behr, R.C. Bates, and Phil Brock
> Featured dwarf: Phil Fondacaro
> "I can get you all the hookers you want."

Full Moon brings several of its regulars together, including the legendary Phil Fondacaro. At toy warehouse Arcadia, Phil is a perverted, cigar chomping security guard who not only misses a cop entering, but also a drunken homeless man who is making a large racket. He also seems to miss a bunch of toys coming to life. Why? He's too busy looking at porn and pounding his head to loud music. This movie certainly fills its quota of horny dwarfsploitation as well as evil dwarfsploitation when Fondacaro teams up with the Demonic Toys to do battle with Dollman. It's also an unusual movie since the enemies of the dwarf are smaller than he is. Phil is great in a limited role, offering up hookers to the demonic toys was the highlight for me. I wouldn't recommend it to anyone but if it's sitting around your house and you have nothing better to do, why not check out a legend in action?

> Head banging dwarf security guard.
> Cigar smoking dwarf.
> Dwarf security guard thumbs through a nudie mag.
> Dwarf enters behind other tallie cops after the demonic toys are unleashed, holding gun and ready for action.
> Dwarf hands tallie cop the tallie girl cop's gun.
> Dwarf talks up his security prowess to a tallie cop.
> Dwarf framed next to tallie cop's leg.
> Baby doll freaks out dwarf security guard and makes him fall over.
> Dwarf prepares tallie sacrificial victim for demonic toys.
> Dwarf makes deal with demonic toys to protect them until they can summon the master.
> Horny dwarf continues to thumb through smutty pics of scantily clad tallie chicks while at work.
> Tallie cop slips in past horny dwarf as he browses through porn.
> Dwarf faces off against Dollman and Dollgirl to protect the demonic toys.
> Dwarf referred to as "half pint."
> Dwarf security guard shot by tallie female cop.
> Dead dwarf.

Dolly Dearest (1991)

> Written and directed by Maria Lease
> Starring Denise Crosby, Sam Bottoms, Rip Torn
> Featured dwarf: Ed Gale

When I mentioned this movie to Ed Gale, he referred to it as "Chucky in drag" and that's exactly what it wants to be. It begins with a family moving to Mexico to make dolls — yep, really. Oh, but they have the factory right next to a devil child from a satanic Mayan-esque group. Of course, the dolls become possessed and start messing with the family's young daughter and knocking off supporting characters. It ends in a rampage of doll corpses as the tallies take them on.

When the dolls are on screen, the movie excels and is extremely entertaining. Unfortunately, their screen time is extremely short considering it's the advertised character. Worth a look for some fun moments as you watch the doll attack and then get blown away.

> Daddy is making dolls in Mexico.
> Dwarf doll hand and feet close up.
> Dwarf doll stabs.
> Dwarf doll runs away.
> Dwarf doll shadow.
> Dwarf doll electrocutes housekeeper.
> Dwarf doll on shelf.
> Dwarf doll sews tallie.
> Dwarf doll waving.
> Dwarf doll maniacal laughing.
> Dwarf doll climbing.
> Dwarf doll shot.
> Dwarf dolls blown up.

Dracula Vs. Frankenstein (1971)

> Written by William Pugsley and Samuel M. Sherman
> Directed by Al Adamson
> Starring Lon Chaney Jr., Greydon Clark
> Featured dwarf: Angelo Rossitto
> "I'm a little man of no use to anyone."

This trash epic by Al Adamson has a mesh of a couple premises. First, out in the hippie heavy Venice Beach area is Dr. Frankenstein, working as "Dr. Durray." Dr. Durray has been performing experiments on the victims of Lon Chaney, Jr.'s "Gorton." Of course, this leads to a group of youngsters looking for their lost siblings. Dr. Durray also runs a house of horrors and the ticket taker is none other than dwarf extraordinaire Angelo Rossitto as "Grazbo." Rossitto's part looked as if he was shot out in a day but nonetheless it was fun to have him there yelling about how the tallie could pick on him now but he wouldn't be little for much longer. The movie is a cult classic without a doubt and deserves to be seen by those that can appreciate a good bad flick but is definitely low on dwarf screen time even though they cut to him a couple of times in the trailer I watched for it.

> Dwarf sales pitch.
> Dwarf laughing maniacally.
> Dwarf eating a dollar.
> More maniacal laughing.
> Dwarf sneaking around.

Dune Warriors (1990)

> Written by Thomas McKelvey Cleaver
> Directed by Cirio H. Santiago
> Starring David Carradine

In New California 2040 A.D., water is in shortage and the warlords want it. In a strange futuristic *Seven Samurai* (1954) type story, a woman gets five warriors (one of which is the great David Carradine) to help defend the village. As good as this may sound, dwarf enthusiast Santiago uses his stock dwarf army even less than usual, appearing in only one scene. Sure, they are great chasing the woman until Carradine shoos them away but I was hoping for the dwarves to join the battle. So much potential wasted.

> Army of dwarves chase after woman.
> Carradine shoos away dwarf army.

Dungeons and Dragons (2000)

> Written by Topper Lilien, Carroll Cartwright
> Directed by Courtney Solomon
> Starring Jeremy Irons, Bruce Payne, Justin Whalin, Marlon
>   Wayans, Thora Birch
> "The problem with elves is they ain't got no meat on their

bones. You've gotta' get yourself a nice, 250-pound dwarf, hair on her chin you can hang onto."

In *Dungeons and Dragons* (2000) the movie, it's not exactly what a fan of the series would be looking forward to. However, they did get one thing right. They cast a dwarf character. Yet, the filmmakers once again failed to have faith in dwarves and gave the dwarf Elwood's (who of course has one of the main roles) part to a tallie. The actor who played the dwarf in this movie is named Lee Arenberg and is 5'4" which is short for a tallie but clearly out of real dwarf range. Both this film and *Tiptoes* (2003) are responsible for stealing the lead roles away from dwarves. I find this highly insulting for both dwarf enthusiasts and dwarves alike. And what's even more bizarre is the filmmakers did go so far as to cast several real dwarves in this film.

As in so many other fantasy movies, there is a scene where the heroes go into a tavern that is much akin to the Mos Eisley cantina from *Star Wars* (1977) (creatures everywhere, etc.) The bar is filled with drunken dwarves, which is nothing short of awesome, but it just makes it that much weirder that they would hire several dwarves for a scene but not for a lead role. Bunch of sizeists, if you ask me. So clearly what was going on in this movie was the filmmakers weren't afraid to hire several dwarf actors for the bar scene so that we could watch them get sloppy drunk, picked up and manhandled for the sake of a visual sight gag, but when it came down to actually casting a part that blatantly called for a dwarf, the filmmakers once again failed to have any faith in the acting ability of dwarves and hired a tallie to shamelessly impersonate a real dwarf. Others may be blind, Courtney Solomon and company, but we are not. Your crimes against dwarves need to be accounted for. Insulting… just plain insulting. And if all the above weren't enough nails in the already-sealed coffin, this film contains the most insulting line I've ever heard before. During the bar scene, when the fake tallie dwarf eats like a glutton, the female mage turns to him and says, "Why don't you try and rise above being a dwarf?" Need I say any more?

> Fake tallie dwarf stands in armor in front of sign that says "Dwarfs Not Allowed."
> Fake tallie dwarf's armored hat and part of his hair shot off.
> Angry fake tallie dwarf swings battleaxe at villain tallie with blue lipstick and sweep kicks him, then runs away, grabs hat and slips into the sewer.

Hooded fake tallie dwarf tries to merge with common folk.
Dwarf sits high on a support beam in the bar and drinks.
Dwarf on second level of bar drinks.
Fake tallie dwarf eats giant bird with meat sticking out of his mouth as he speaks.
War story-telling fake tallie dwarf.
Tallie picks up dwarf and lifts him out of the way to talk to an elf.
Bar filled with drunken dwarves.
Fake tallie dwarf sits in tree.
Mage insults fake tallie dwarf.
Fake tallie dwarf hangs off horse, demanding to walk instead.
Crying fake tallie dwarf.
Fake tallie dwarf runs into invisible force field.
Fake tallie dwarf repelled by magic.

D'Wild Wild Weng (1982)

Written by Cora Caballes
Directed by Eddie Nicart
Starring Weng Weng
Featured dwarf: Weng Weng
"How could a child kill a full grown man?"

Oh, Weng Weng. If only he were alive today, continuing to make beautiful art like this one. You know a movie is great when it begins with a dwarf in kung fu-wear. You know it's brilliant when said dwarf gets in a fight, runs between a tallie's legs, kicks him and ends up with his knee against the fallen tallie's neck. Then, you know a movie is at dwarfgasm status when said dwarf meets a dwarf Native American, complete with loin cloth and bow, in the middle of nowhere and this is just in the first ten minutes.

After we learn the mayor of Santa Monica (I would assume in its original language it was something different but hearing them say this over and over again is hilarious) was killed, Weng Weng (inside a bag, no less) and his tallie friend are revealed to be agents of the government. They are there to set things straight but they're going to have some obstacles along the way—like ninjas! Yes, in true exploitation form, ninjas for no reason show up to take on our heroes! Personally it has been a dream of mine to see a dwarf take on ninjas and this film was kind enough to make that a reality. Thank you *D'Wild Wild Weng* (1982). Thank you.

In one classic scenario, Weng Weng is taken prisoner. His tallie buddy enters in a monk-like outfit with the brilliant guards letting him through without hesitation. When he gets to where Weng Weng is being kept, he crawls inside the monk-like outfit, making the tallie look like he's now pregnant. It works until they see the guards. The guards let him through but then we see Weng Weng's little legs slipping out at the bottom of the robe. When the guard lifts the robe, he gets a kick to the face and then a shot to the crotch courtesy of our dwarf friend. Pure brilliance. In another part of the escape, Weng Weng slides across the floor, landing between a tallie guard's legs. He hits the guard in the calves and then treats him like a punching bag. Awesome.

Oh, but wait. Weng Weng turns himself over to the baddies so they won't kill a bunch of kids—he's kindhearted like that. Weng Weng is tied by all fours and elevated in the middle of the desert. Of course, half the guys who are supposed to be guarding him leave for no reason. Soon after, they are attacked by Weng Weng's dwarf Native American and tallie friend. When his legs are freed, Weng Weng starts flipping around, kicking tallies while the Native American dwarf fires arrows into the baddies. When Weng Weng is lowered, he grabs a large gun that blows him back each time he fires it. It's a battle scene as it should be.

As if they are trying to top the rest of the film, the final fight scene features Weng Weng on the back of the Jeep blowing away tallies Audie Murphy-style, an army of Native American dwarves (at least that's what I think they're supposed to be), Weng Weng vs. a ninja, Weng Weng using a large gun that blows him back every time he shoots, Weng Weng being passed dynamite to kick, and so on.

The movie is nothing short of brilliant. It's a guaranteed dwarfgasm.

> Walking down rocks next to tallie.
> Running.
> Kicking.
> Runs between legs.
> Kneels on tallie.
> Patted on head.

Dwarf Native American.
Dwarf stomps on tallie's foot.
Bare dwarf butt.
Dwarf hides in bag.
Steal banana and eats it from inside bag.
Consoles tallie.
Pats stomach.
Lifted up by tallie.
Shirtless, practicing kung fu.
Practices shooting.
Referred to as "small boy."
Climbs on car.
Dwarf takes out ninjas.
Dwarf commits crotch violence.
Dwarf carried by tallie.
Dwarf serenades tallie woman.
Dwarf strangles ninja.
Dwarf kicks ninja in face.
Dwarf shoots ninjas.
Dwarf at bar.
"Young and tiny."
Dwarf under robe.
Dwarf with gun larger than he is.
Dwarf jumps down stairs.
Dwarf jumps from high window.
Dwarf shooting from back of Jeep.
Dwarf jumps on tallie.
Dwarf hides under sombrero.
Grabs ceiling, lifts self, and kicks tallie in face.
Dwarf jumps on tallie's back.
Dwarf jumps off cliff.
Dwarf hanging.
Dwarf shooting arrows.
Dwarf falls back after firing gun.
Weng Weng tossed by tallie friend onto wall of mansion.
Fires huge machine gun.
Army of dwarves.

Eating Raoul (1982)

> Written by Paul Bartel, Richard Blackburn
> Directed by Paul Bartel
> Starring Robert Beltran, Mary Woronov, Pamela Carter, Vernon Demetrius
> Featured dwarf: Billy Curtis
> "Oh, great! Trigger likes you already."

Paul Bartel's classic is about a prude couple (Paul Bartel and Mary Woronov) who are constantly annoyed with all the crazy swingers in their apartment. Plus, they've got several more problems of their own. They're broke as hell and unable to afford to open their own restaurant, let alone buy the house of their dreams. They're on the brink of selling several bottles of their prized wine collection just to make ends meet when a sleazy swinger comes on a little too strongly to Mary Woronov and Bartel accidentally kills him. That's when genius inspiration occurs. Mary takes on the role of a dominatrix and entertains several clients before hubby Bartel whacks each one of the degenerate perverts over the head, kills them, and then takes their money.

One of the clients Paul and Mary entertain is classic dwarf actor Billy Curtis. Mary opens the door and the camera tilts down to reveal the dwarf in a cowboy outfit standing next to a large dog. The dwarf is instantly happy after he pets the dog and notices man's best friend has taken a liking to Mary as well. What is strange is that the filmmakers clearly dubbed over the dwarf's real voice with a much lower one. Now, this is a classic movie that holds up incredibly well over time, but I kept getting disturbed while watching it, not being able to get over the fact that a movie about swingers would be absolutely perfect for a variety of dwarf roles. Unfortunately the great Paul Bartel has passed on which means a sequel is out of the question. Unless, that is, Hollywood does a remake, which is very likely in this day and age.

> Camera tilts down to reveal dwarf.
> Dwarf in cowboy outfit.
> Horny dwarf.
> Deep-voiced dwarf.

The Elephant Man (1980)

> Written by Christopher De Vore, Eric Bergren, and David Lynch
> Directed by David Lynch
> Starring Anthony Hopkins, John Hurt
> Featured dwarf: Kenny Baker
> "Luck, my friend. Luck. Who needs it more than we?"

The Elephant Man (1980) is the story of a doctor (Anthony Hopkins) who discovers an odd, ugly man with special characteristics at a freak show. What's a freak show without some little people? At first we only see them as extras. Then, when the Elephant Man has been caged up with rabid monkeys, some random freaks, led by a dwarf (played by Kenny Baker), free the elephant man and lead him to freedom. The movie is considered by most to be a classic so it's worth seeing for that reason alone. However, if you're watching it in hopes of lots of screen time for Baker and company, you will be disappointed. Baker has a nice little role but it could have easily been a larger part, and much deserved.

> Dwarf turning player.
> Dwarves at table.
> Dwarf in costume.
> Dwarves with toys.
> Dwarf leader.

Elf (2003)

> Written by David Berenbaum
> Directed by Jon Favreau
> Starring Will Ferrell, James Caan, Kyle Gass, Andy Richter, and Bob Newhart
> Featured Dwarf: Peter Dinklage

The story of a human raised as an elf (played by Will Ferrell) who leaves the North Pole to go to New York City in search of his father. When his father (played by James Caan) is looking for a children's book to be published immediately, two of his writers (Kyle Gass and Andy Richter) suggest Miles Finch, a celebrated Children's book author. Finch is played by dwarf acting legend

Peter Dinklage, giving a knowledgeable and manic performance as the childish Ferrell mistakes Dinklage for an elf. As the Dink becomes more and more enraged, he ends up attacking Ferrell's elf but then exits after just a few minutes of screen time. Between this and *Living in Oblivion* (1985), one wonders if Dinklage isn't living out every dwarf's dream by insulting and assaulting everyone who goes after the little people clichés. His attack on Ferrell almost feels like he's enjoying the moment too much. He is, as always, perfect.

What makes this film odd is that it's a movie about a human who doesn't know he's an elf yet all the elves are played by normal sized actors. While the shots make them look smaller than Santa and Ferrell's character, I think it would have worked much better had they been played by natural little people, not to mention giving little people some work. It's movies like these that could have been so much better had they just gone to the trouble of hiring a dozen dwarf actors for a few days.

Elevator door opens with camera behind desk but nothing but footsteps are heard.

> Mistaken for elf.
> Angry elf.
> Little feet close up on table.
> Dwarf kicking.

El Topo (1970)

> Written and Directed by Alejandro Jodorowsky
> Starring Alejandro Jodorowsky and Brontis Jodorowsky
> "Too much perfection is a mistake."

This has got to be one of the weirdest movies ever made. I would not recommend watching it on drugs, especially if you're prone to having bad trips. It's disturbing enough on its own. Before we even get to the dwarf, a gunslinger rides into a town overtaken by seriously degenerate thugs with a naked little boy on the back of his horse. Much death, carnage, perversion and all around weirdness ensues until after an hour and fifteen minutes into the film when our hero is in a cave with a bunch of little boys stuck in barrels. It's there he meets a sexy dwarf female who cares for him by giving him a shoulder massage followed by a hot application of eyeliner to the face. The two quickly fall in love and they combine forces to survive in the brutal outside world. This includes vaudeville-like skits in front of crowds where the dwarf climbs a little ladder to kiss our hero on the lips. They're also forced to have sex in front of several degenerates at an extremely freaky party and it's at this moment that our hero truly falls head over heels for the ultimate girl next door that used to live in a cave.

Our hero commits to marriage because not only does his dwarf lover exhibit wonderful caring maternal traits, she also buries every normal sized woman in the film in the looks department. Allow me to throw out the disclaimer once again. Don't rent this movie just to see hot dwarf nudity. You'll get it but you'll also be severely disturbed by the rest of what's going on in the madness that ensues. Artistic madness, but complete insanity that even the hottest of dwarves can't erase from the damaged subconscious. But, I guess that's a compliment to Jodorowsky. I have a feeling this movie is going to stay in my head for quite some time.

> 117:52 dwarf applies eyeliner.
> Dwarf rubs tallie's shoulder.
> Dwarf kisses tallie.
> Dwarf mistakes tallie for diety.
> Dwarf gives man tour through hell.
> Dwarf barber.
> Crawls with dwarf on back.
> Dwarf piggyback ride.
> Dwarf holds hand with hero in robe.
> Horn-blowing dwarf.
> Ladder-holding dwarf.
> Dwarf climbs ladder to kiss man.
> Panhandling dwarf.
> Dwarf rides donkey.
> Toilet-cleaning dwarf.
> Musical dwarf.
> Hero carries dwarf down ladder.
> Dwarf nudity and consensual sex with tallie.
> Dwarf hottest woman in movie.
> Man beats hiding dwarf.
> Man runs off with dwarf under arms.
> Dwarf protects hero from death.
> Dwarf lifted up to clean sign.
> Sweat-cleaning dwarf.

Post-cleaning dwarf.
Cave-escaping dwarf.

The Empire Strikes Back (1980)

Written by Leigh Brackett, Lawrence Kasdan
Directed by Irvin Kirshner
Starring Mark Hamill, Harrison Ford, Carrie Fisher, Billy Dee Williams
Featured dwarf: Kenny Baker

With *Empire*, dwarf appreciators Lucas and Kirshner give us the best sequel ever. Now, I'm not saying the film specifically used dwarves to make it the greatest sequel of all time. The dwarves were instead used like an extra ingredient in a good soup that makes it win awards at carnivals across the country. R2-D2 gives us the usual head turning and light blinking after arguing with C-3PO. He does fix the hyperdrive which proves to be a major asset to the rebellion, but other than that and a few humorous bickering scenes with Yoda, dwarf actor Kenny Baker's role is more of a backdrop in this installment.

However, we are treated to some excellent, skulleted pig-looking dwarf guards later on in the film. After C-3PO is blown to pieces at Bespin, the dwarf guards in a factory pick up his head and play catch with it, pissing Chewie off. The evil little bastards are even the ones responsible for freezing Han Solo in carbonite! They rappel into the chamber, secure Han's straps, lower him into the pit and for the coup de grace... tip Solo over after he's frozen. Those bastards! They give good dwarves everywhere a bad name. I can only hope they were under Vader's influence and weren't actually born that evil. *For an example of good, happy dwarf role models, see our write up on *Return of the Jedi* (1983).

Pig guard dwarves play catch with C-3PO's head.
Pig guard dwarf looks official while carrying pages.
Pig guard dwarf repels into foggy pit in carbon freezing chamber.
Pig guards with boar fangs secure Han's strap onto the carbon freezing chamber.
Pig guard lowers Han into pit for carbon freezing.
Pig guards push over frozen Solo.

Employee of the Month (2006)

Written by Don Calame, Chris Conroy, Greg Coolidge
Directed by Greg Coolidge
Starring Dane Cook, Jessica Simpson, Harland Williams
Featured dwarf: Danny Woodburn

Dane Cook really wants to win the affection of Jessica Simpson, who supposedly loves the employees of the month. In a strange subplot, the manager's brother, Glen from corporate, drops by to do a surprise audit. Apparently it's supposed to surprise us that this intimidating character that is talked about in the scenes before he arrives sets him up as a large, menacing figure. Instead, we get the talented Danny Woodburn, swinging a cane and giving his tallie brother a noogie. He comes off like a mean boss, not wanting to see even a speck of dust and making constant gay cracks against his brother.

Woodburn continues to show up, this time at a baseball game against a rival store Maxi-Mart. When they are losing, Woodburn is tossing his mitt and throwing a fit, falling in the clichéd angry dwarf category. Of course, once they start winning, he gets happy.

While it's good to see a dwarf represent a person in power, it's pure exploitation to have him set up as the mean boss and to only be a dwarf. Toss onto that a few clichés and you have a film that tries to sneak in dwarfsploitation without us noticing—it's like they killed the black guy first.

> Dwarf with cane.
> Dwarf with one white glove.
> Dwarf is mean boss.
> Dwarf gives tallie a noogie.
> Angry dwarf.
> Dwarf pointing stick.
> Dwarf makes gay remarks.
> Dwarf throws cane.
> Dwarf runs into catcher.
> Dwarf argues with umpire.
> Dwarf shooting champagne.
> Dwarf yelling.

Enchanted (2007)

> Written by Bill Kelly
> Directed by Kevin Lima
> Starring Amy Adams, Patrick Dempsey
> Featured dwarf: William Huntley

In this Disney movie, Amy Adams' Cinderella/Snow White mesh of a character has been transported from the cartoon world to New York City. As she's freaking out being in this new land, she runs into a crowd. Wearing an overly large gown, we suddenly see the bottom part shaking—a dwarf is under there. She mistakes him for one of the seven dwarves but not just anyone—Grumpy, keeping with the angry dwarf stereotype. It's brief but complete dwarfsploitation.

> Dwarf under dress.
> Dwarf referred to as "grumpy."
> Dwarf in tallie crowd.
> Dwarf chased.

The Enigma of Kaspar Hauser (1974)

> Written by Werner Herzog and Jacob Wassermann
> Directed by Werner Herzog
> Starring Helmut Doring

Helmut Doring made two movies and both were by the great dwarf appreciator Werner Herzog. The first of which was the classic *Even Dwarfs Started Small* (1970) where he memorably laughed maniacally for a long, long time. In this film, Helmut shows up during a circus scene sitting on a throne in a king's outfit—he is the "Little King." A story is told where he's supposedly the last in the line of giants, the kings of Punt, each one smaller than the last. During this story, Helmut seems noticeably nervous and uncomfortable, like he doesn't understand what's going on. It's very unfortunate that Helmut shows up late into the film, doesn't get to say anything and then is gone—he's essentially a featured extra. It seems too common in dwarf cinema.

Dwarf king.
Uncomfortable dwarf.
Dwarf extra.

Epic Movie (2007)

Written by Jason Friedberg, Aaron Seltzer
Directed by Jason Friedberg, Aaron Seltzer
Starring Kal Penn, Jennifer Coolidge, Fred Willard, Adam Campbell
Featured dwarves: Tony Cox, Mighty Mike Murga

It's pretty much a given with everyone who's seen the other films of Jason Friedberg and Aaron Seltzer that their movies contain large amounts of highly unfunny shit. But what all their movies do have in common is the dwarf factor. The decision to add a dwarf in all the films Friedberg and Seltzer have made is arguably, hands down the most intelligent decision either one has ever made. I mean, let's face it. These movies are so horrendously shitty that for them to have any form of redemption whatsoever it's not going to take just any dwarf to solve the problem. No, my friends. It's going to take a very special dwarf. Very special indeed. It's going to take Tony Cox! And thank God for Tony Cox too because without him, nearly 95% of this movie would be completely unwatchable. Fortunately for us, the dwarf appears to breathe life into the abortion of a script they were using, and he does an amazing job. Seeing Cox in the movie harkened me back to the days of *Bad Santa* (2003) where the dwarf was also dressed as an elf. He's really the only bit of light and joy in this movie as he plays Jennifer Coolidge's elf sidekick. Dwarfsploitative elements abound as she uses her wand to spin him through the air, etc. Cox is also very amusing in a medieval battle outfit complete with a little axe in the parody battle scene from The *Lion, the Witch, and the Wardrobe*. This movie also solidifies the stereotype that dwarves just absolutely love to punch tallies in the crotch. It must have something to do with them being at just the perfect height to do it.

Epic Movie (2007) also adds other dwarves to the film, which helps but they're not given enough screen time. They show up during the parody segment of Tim Burton's version of *Charlie and the Chocolate Factory* (2005) but instead of using one dwarf and essentially cloning him to give off the effect of having multiple dwarves like Burton did with Deep Roy, *Epic Movie* (2007), in its best decision next to casting Cox actually casts a multiple amount of dwarves (the key here being a bunch of different dwarves) to play Oompa Loompas. Now, it doesn't look like they cast all that many different dwarves because we do see a lot of the same ones being recycled, but it's still better than having only one dwarf in the movie when the budget would clearly allow for several.

Shame on you, Tim Burton! In a twist that allows for an evil dwarfsploitative twist, this movie's Willy Wonka, played by the always creepy Crispin Glover, reveals to the kids who get the winning tickets to his chocolate factory that his goodies are made out of human body parts. The movie then springs forward into a montage where the dwarves assist Glover in his *Saw*-style torture porn experiments on the kids, which the kids strangely live through after they've been hacked up, but that's beside the point. The evil dwarf stereotypes seemed to work here really well as the dwarves were indeed creepy as hell in this movie. It kind of erased all those childhood dreams I had about actually wanting to step foot into Willy Wonka's chocolate factory.

> Dwarf Oompa-Loompas.
> Dwarf Oompa-Loompa landscapers.
> Dwarf Oompa-Loompas walk out from behind pillars and corral humans.
> Dwarf smashes human's nuts into candy mold with sledgehammer.
> Dwarf Oompa-Loompas help Glover torture people and get their parts into his special candy mold.
> Dwarf Oompa Loompa puts severed human head into "Willy's Genuine Jumbo Sour Yellow Head" candy.
> Dwarf elf drives white tallie queen's sled to metal music with the license place DRIFT.
> Dwarf elf punches Kal Penn in the crotch and tells him to kneel before the queen.
> Dwarf elf blasted by witch's wand and flies through the air.
> Dwarf elf hits Kal Penn's legs with bat.
> Dwarf elf in armor during Narnia battle.
> Dwarf elf dances to squid-faced DJ's music.
> Dwarf elf stabs Kal Penn in gut.
> Kal Penn body slams dwarf frozen in time.

Ernest Saves Christmas (1988)

>Written by B. Kline and Ed Turner
>Directed by John Cherry
>Starring Jim Varney, Noelle Parker
>Featured dwarves: Buddy Douglas, Patty Maloney

Part of the series of movies spawned from the infamous Jim Varney character "Ernest", this time with a Christmas back drop. And what's a Christmas movie without elves? Unfortunately the elves don't show up until a little after an hour into the movie. It's almost like they ran out of ideas and just threw them in. When first introduced, we see several tallies pass by before we see the elves for the first time, dressed in overcoats and wearing large sunglasses. They go on to give banter to Ernest, who they seem to detest. Other than that, they're not given anything to do and are wasted. It's great to see Buddy and Patty working but I wish they would have given them more to do than complain about Ernest.

>Tallies walk by before Elves walk up.
>Elf smaller than boxes.

Even Dwarfs Started Small (1970)

>Written by Werner Herzog
>Directed by Werner Herzog
>Featured dwarves: Helmut Döring, Paul Glauer, Gisela Hertwig, Hertel Minkner, Gertrud Piccini
>"It wrinkles its ass!"

This is easily one of the most bizarre dwarf movies ever made. Its tone is one of complete insanity, which makes sense because it is about dwarves who take over a mental institution. And, like *The Terror of Tiny Town* (1938), *Even Dwarfs Started Small* (1970) features an all-dwarf cast. The film seems to have a completely unscripted plot throughout. It's as if Herzog got all liquored up and created weird scenarios which the dwarves improvised like some kind of a psychotic version of an underground comedy troupe. And indeed there are several hilarious moments, such as when an older dwarf is peer pressured into marrying a female dwarf he's clearly not interested in. She makes it onto the bed and waits for him to consummate their marriage while he tries and tries but is unable to make it to the top of the bed. After several attempts fail, including putting magazines on the ground to act as a launching pad, the two dwarves end up looking at pictures together instead.

The odd humor of *Even Dwarfs Started Small* (1970) is counterbalanced by a weird tone which you're not sure you should be laughing at and creepy moments like dwarves parading a spider monkey around on a cross, a laughing dwarf in a rocking chair and a laughing dwarf who giggles like a child and twitches his arms spastically around. You may not be able to tell why what's happening is happening while you watch this film but you most certainly won't forget it.

> Annoying dwarves sing over opening credits.
> Weird sign-holding dwarf.
> Dwarf crawls on top of roof.
> Gun-toting dwarf.
> Motorcycle-riding dwarf.
> Dwarves throw rocks at one of their own.
> Dwarf stands on chair to open door.
> Old laughing dwarf.
> Dwarf struggles to reach door handle.
> Goggle wearing, sight impaired dwarves.
> Dwarves work together to pull down tree (aka dwarves vs. nature).
> Nonstop laughing dwarf.
> Dwarves forcing dwarves to marry and have sex.
> Dwarf unable to jump on top of bed.
> Dwarf passed out in chair.
> Dwarves own spider monkey.
> Dwarves fascinated by entomology.
> Dwarves chase around baby pigs.
> Dwarf stands on a car to fix it.
> Dwarves team up to push car and get it started.
> Dwarves climb on top of moving car and screw around.
> Blind dwarves poke dead pig.
> Arguing dwarves.
> Blindly swinging blind dwarf.
> Dwarves throw plates at revolving truck.
> Dwarf drinks out of oversized wine bottle.

Jumping/celebrating dwarves.
Dwarves initiate cockfight.
Dwarves parade spider money around on cross.
Chicken-wrangling dwarf.
Chicken tossing dwarves.
Frantic roof dwarf.
Dwarves knock camel on its knees.

Evil Bong (2006)

Written by August White
Directed by Charles Band
Starring Tommy Chong
Featured dwarf: Phil Fondacaro

If you're a stoner and you're looking for a few cheap laughs you may get a handful out of this movie. However, if you're a dwarf enthusiast you will be severely disappointed by Full Moon veteran Phil Fondacaro's incredibly short appearance (pun intended, it *is* a book about dwarves) in this cheap attempt to take all your hard earned pot money by having a catchy title, a stoner celebrity (Tommy Chong) and a dwarf celebrity (Fondacaro). The fact that Fondacaro's appearance is right next to a hot stripper who kills a man with her fanged bra does not excuse the fact Fondacaro is not in this movie longer. The fact that it's also next to a little voodoo doll who appears to be pleasuring himself while watching the horny teenager leave this world at the hands of a killer bra does earn points for effort but just doesn't cut the mustard when it comes to dwarf screen time. It is somewhat excusable and would have been completely forgiven if the scene took place in a club of dwarf strippers. That didn't happen so I reserve the right to protest this movie.

Boycott the incredibly dwarf-light *Evil Bong* (2006) and check out one of Fondacaro's many other films instead. You know, like the ones where he actually has a role.

Dwarf in stripper club.
Hat-wearing dwarf.
Dwarf in stoner movie.

E.T.: The Extra Terrestrial (1982)

Written by Melissa Mathison
Directed by Steven Spielberg
Starring Henry Thomas, Drew Barrymore, Peter Coyote, Erika Eleniak, Dee Wallace
Featured dwarf: Tamara De Treaux

Steven Spielberg's classic movie plays like a love letter to a boy and his dwarf alien. It's also one of the very few movies that made me cry in the theatre. At first I thought it was just because it was a sad and emotional movie, but upon recent viewing, I re-examined my analysis and discovered it was because it was so hard to watch a dwarf alien suffer. And indeed, as an adult watching this film again I felt the same way. Why did those evil government bastards torture E.T? Why couldn't they just let him run around and explore the human tallie world and eat Reese's Pieces? Why couldn't they let the boy and his dwarf be?

Three-foot, one-inch dwarf actress Tamara De Treaux helped portray E.T. and there are indeed moments when it's clearly obvious that there is a dwarf inside the suit (like at the very beginning of the movie when E.T. gets off the ship and waddles around in the forest). In other shots such as the craning of the neck, puppetry was obviously involved. Indeed, though, the most impressive thing about E.T. is how Spielberg uses a dwarf to inspire compassion from the other characters via an alien suit. It must have been a very special dwarf indeed to break through that suit and reach the hearts of tallies everywhere because only a very little person with a very big personality could make the world love them as much as the world has grown to love *E.T.* (1982) Spielberg took dwarfsploitation to a groundbreaking, emotional level that hasn't quite been duplicated again. It remains to be seen if we'll get another film like this from him in the future. I'm certainly keeping my fingers crossed.

> Dwarf alien leaves spaceship.
> Dwarf alien walks amongst giant trees.
> Dwarf alien POV
> Dwarf alien immersed in shadow.
> Reese's Pieces eating dwarf alien.
> Dwarf waddles to Elliot.
> Close up of dwarf alien feet.
> Dwarf alien head framed by desk.
> Confused dwarf alien eats car.

Barking dog scares dwarf alien.
Dwarf alien opens umbrella.
Dwarf alien hides amongst stuffed animals.
Neck-extending dwarf alien.
Drew Barrymore scares dwarf alien.
Telekinetic dwarf alien.
Dwarf alien places its fingers on Elliot's back.
Reading dwarf alien.
Plant-healing dwarf alien.
Drunk dwarf alien.
Shirt-wearing dwarf alien.
Fridge-raiding dwarf alien.
Beer-drinking dwarf alien.
Dwarf alien gets kid drunk.
TV-watching dwarf alien.
Dwarf alien hit by fridge.
Dwarf alien learns to talk from TV show.
Cross-dressing dwarf alien.
Spying dwarf alien.
Fingertip-healing dwarf alien.
Object-levitating dwarf alien.
Dwarf alien collapses from flashbulb.
Dwarf alien makes bike fly.
Dwarf MacGyver's his own phone out of random household items.
A boy and his dwarf alien.
Dying dwarf alien.
Bike-riding dwarf alien.
Glowing heart dwarf alien.
Dwarf/tallie hug.
Botanist dwarf alien.
Dwarf spaceship leaves behind rainbow.

Evil Ever After (2006)

Story by Brad Paulson and Chris Watson
Screenplay and directed by Brad Paulson
Starring Randal Malone, Joe Bob Briggs, Ford Austin, Rebekah Brandes and Felissa Rose

Evil Ever After (2006) is the story of a reformed cannibal who has to get back in the game when he's wrongfully accused of rape, beaten, and left for dead.

In true exploitation form, there's a random dwarf, played by Mighty Mike Murga. We see him for the first time in a dog cage, making dog whimpers, being fed raw flesh by the hero of the story, "Bernie." There's no explanation, just narration saying

Jerry and Elizabeth Maren give in to the author's groveling and hold up the *Evil Ever After* (2006) poster at the Dark Delicacies signing.

"That's a story for another time." Mighty Mike doesn't show up again until the brutal end where a group of kids who thought they left Bernie for dead go to his house to party. When Bernie comes back in drag with a samurai sword to take out the kids, he unleashes his dwarf sidekick, leading to some bloody anarchy.

In the anarchy, we get to see the dwarf strip and be masturbated to, jump on the back of a tallie while gnawing on his neck, and jump up excitedly over a naked girl. Good times.

> Dwarf making noises.
> Dwarf without lines.
> Dwarf in dog cage.
> Dwarf eating body parts.
> Dwarf on tallie's back.
> Dwarf killer.
> Dwarf stripping.
> Dwarf clapping excitedly.

Factotum (2005)

Written by Bent Hamer, Jim Stark
Directed by Bent Hamer

Starring Matt Dillon, Lili Taylor, Fisher Stevens, Adrienne Shelley, Marisa Tomei

Matt Dillon, who is way too good looking to be playing Bukowski, plays Bukowski anyway and does a pretty good job of it, except for the fact he's way too good looking to be doing it. I've read "Ham on Rye." The man was covered with boils, for crying out loud! At least Mickey Rourke went a few weeks without a shower (or at least looked like it) and packed on several pounds of sloth before taking on the role. The movie is based off the novel by the same name and the main character is called Hank Chinaski even though it's blatantly obvious it's Bukowski.

A dwarf pops in during a scene where Hank Chinaski works one of his many shitty jobs and asks him to get back to work. The dwarf tries his hardest to get Bukowski to stop slacking off, but Chinaski refuses and says he's going to go out and get a drink. The dwarf insists he get back to work and Bukowski wrestles the dwarf and manhandles him, spinning him around the room. After something that looks like an odd dwarf/tallie dance, Chinaski leaves the dwarf on the ground defeated and humiliated. A tallie attempts to come to the dwarf's aid after Chinaski puts him down, but the dwarf both protests and resists his aid. The dwarf bullying does not make Chinaski's character likeable. The Bukowski we all know and love can be seen in Barbet Schroeder's masterpiece, *Barfly* (1987). Sadly, though, that film doesn't contain dwarves.

Hardhat-wearing dwarf.
Dwarf bosses tallie around.
Dwarf/tallie struggle.
Tallie bullies dwarf.
Defeated, humiliated dwarf.

Fear and Loathing in Las Vegas (1998)

Written by Terry Gilliam, Alex Cox, Tod Davies, and Tony Grisoni
Directed by Terry Gilliam
Starring Johnny Depp and Benicio Del Toro
Featured dwarves: Verne Troyer (as Verne J. Troya) and Michael Lee Gogin

If you're not familiar with Hunter S. Thompson's classic book about searching for the "American Dream" while tripping on every drug imaginable then you're not in touch and you're missing out. In this adaptation of the book, dwarf lover Terry Gilliam has Thompson (played by Johnny Depp) and his lawyer (Benecio Del Toro) tripping out and seeing various dwarves on their various misadventures. I suppose they thought a person is on even more of a trip if they're constantly seeing dwarves. The movie being good is a matter of taste but it's definitely garnered a cult following and does contain multiple dwarves, even if their parts aren't much more than eye candy. Notable is Michael Lee Gogin, who also appeared in another Thompson adaptation *Where the Buffalo Roam* (1980).

> Dwarf waiter.
> Throws coins on floor for dwarf waiter.
> Dwarf waiter stiffed.
> Dwarf waiter runs into door.
> Circus act.
> Dwarf with hammer.
> Dwarf with scissors.
> Dwarf artist.
> Dwarf with money.
> Dwarf Thompson can't see without looking down.
> Dwarf in silly hat.

Feast 2: Sloppy Seconds (2008)

> Written by Patrick Melton and Marcus Dunstan
> Directed by John Gulager
> Starring Clu Gulager, Jenny Wade
> Featured dwarves: Martin Klebba and Juan Longoria Garcia
> "It's little people, mother fucker!"

When a few of the survivors from the first *Feast* (2005) end up in a small town, they just give the alien monsters a larger venue of humans to chomp down on. To bring something different to the sequel, two wrestling dwarves, "Thunder" and "Lightning," are introduced into the mix. And what an introduction they get when they are first seen! Lightning is wearing a wrestling mask while getting laid. Thunder is pissed off he's so loud. Then they are attacked, one of the monsters ripping the chick to shreds. Freaked out, both dwarves take off running where we have to watch Lightning's penis flap around as he runs off. Apparently the filmmakers were not happy enough just having dwarves to look at, they had to show us they were better endowed than your regular tallie.

When the dwarves join up with the tallies, it's nothing but trouble for them. First they are sent on a mission to make a key (they make keys for a living). The dwarves are forced to risk their lives only to have Lightning's grandmother's killed by a thoughtless tallie. Then they end up on a rooftop where the tallies create a machine where they can flip the dwarves across to another building. It doesn't work, of course, and we have to watch the great Martin Klebba, as Thunder, get ripped in half by one of the monsters and the other dwarf get blown to pieces.

In my world, the dwarves would be the heroes and the tallies would have died off by their own stupidity. This film is worth seeing for the dwarves but be prepared to be pissed off.

"Not politically correct to kill a little person, let alone two."

> Beer-drinking dwarf.
> Dwarf knocked over.
> Dwarf makes racist remark.
> Dwarf wearing mask.
> Dwarf penis.
> Dwarf wrestling.
> Dwarves open "Tiny Keys" store.
> Dwarf jumps over alien carcass.
> Dwarf stabs alien in ass.
> Dwarf taunts alien.
> Dwarf wearing goggles.
> Dwarves make key.
> Dwarves risk life for tallies.
> Dwarves carry woman in bag.
> Dwarves in nightvision.
> Dwarves push each other.
> Dwarves attack tallie.
> Referred to as "little farts."
> Dwarf pushed out of way.
> Dwarf gives two legged kick.

Dwarf hitting with sledge.
Referred to as midgets.
Dwarves fight.
Dwarf puking.
Dwarf crying.
Referred to as "little cocksucker."
Dwarf catapulted.
Dwarf torn to pieces.
Dwarf with trash can over him.
Referred to as "Slippery midget."
Referred to as "tiny people."

Feast 3: The Happy Finish (2009)

Written by Patrick Melton and Marcus Dunstan
Directed by John Gulager
Starring Clu Gulager, Chelsea Richards, Dianne Ayala Goldner
Featured dwarves: Juan Longoria Garcia and Martin Klebba

Part 3 picks up right where 2 left off, complete with massive carnage archive footage. Included in the footage is the death of Martin Klebba, where he's poorly catapulted and ends up in the street where he's ripped to shreds by one of the beasts. The big change in this one is that we were left thinking Juan Longoria Garcia's wrestler character was dead by explosion. As it turns out, he's alive and kicking and nothing more than tired from being involved in the explosion. He eventually joins up with the rest of the ensemble to fight off the beasts. Meanwhile, we are treated to a few brief moments with Klebba, whom we are left to assume dies since the last time we see him he's only got half his body left (although still talking).

There are some fun moments in the film, such as when a tired Juan gets a piggy back ride from a hottie. If you look closely, there are a couple of shots where he appears to be holding on by gripping onto her breasts. In the same series of scenes, he also slaps her like he's riding a horse. Another fun moment is when a man who sacrificed a baby earlier in the movie becomes senile and begins thinking Juan is the baby.

The movie is obviously trying to capitalize on "freaks." In part 2 we had dwarves and in part 3 they throw in a "special" person, who at times is protected by Juan's character. On some levels this works but I think they went a bit overboard by throwing the "special" person in.

> Archive footage.
> Dwarf catapulted.
> Dwarf bleeding.
> Dwarf gutted.
> Dwarf in trash can.
> Referred to as "Slippery midget."
> Referred to as "midget."
> Dwarf survives explosion.
> Dwarf talks when ripped in half.
> Referred to as "Tattoo."
> Referred to as "little tiny people."
> Dwarf given piggy back ride, holds onto boobs.
> Dwarf reaching.
> Dwarf swats woman's ass.
> Dwarf throws flashlight.
> Dwarf crawls through sewer drain.
> Dwarf smells fart.
> Dwarf with shotgun.
> Dwarf protects special person.
> Dwarf confused with baby.
> Dwarf chewing on beast flesh.
> Dwarf pushes dirt bike.
> Dwarf stomped by robot.

Find Me Guilty (2006)

> Written by Sidney Lumet, T.J. Mancini, Robert J. McCrea
> Directed by Sidney Lumet
> Starring Vin Diesel, Peter Dinklage, Linus Roache, Ron Silver, Annabella Sciorra, Alex Rocco
> Featured dwarf: Peter Dinklage

Powerhouse acting dwarf Peter Dinklage once again nails a role dwarf actors across the world would kill for. After each viewing of a Dinklage movie, I keep asking myself whether he sold his soul to Satan or killed someone to get such excellent roles. It's either that or he has a great agent or… perhaps, he's just a great actor. No, that couldn't be. It must be related to the supernatural, that's how Hollywood operates, right? Regardless, Dinklage certainly must have the envy and adoration of every acting and wannabe actor dwarf out there. He is a powerhouse and once again proves himself to be quite possibly the finest dwarf actor ever with another magnificent, stereotype-defying performance in which he plays an attorney representing several alleged mafia members in an extremely lengthy, real life trial while forming a friendship with Vin Diesel's character as sort of an everyman thug who represents himself in court.

This film is incredibly light on dwarfsploitation. Aside from the typical overhead shots which draw attention to the dwarf's vertical challenge, there are a couple of bits where an elevated podium is rolled into the courtroom for the dwarf to stand up on and address the jury. Other than that, *Find Me Guilty* (2006) is a movie that defies dwarfsploitation stereotypes. Dinklage is featured in almost the entire movie and is hardly ever used as the butt of a joke. Lumet has complete confidence in his acting abilities and it certainly pays off here as Dinklage delivers several eloquent monologues and elevates dwarf cinema to potentially unseen heights. A must see.

> Dwarf lawyer.
> Dwarf attempts to counsel out of control tallie.
> Dwarf stands on podium to address jury.
> Dramatic zoom in on dwarf.
> Dwarf yells at Jackie, separates him from potential fight with prosecuting attorney tallie.
> Cool-headed dwarf.
> Special podium once again rolled out for dwarf.
> Dwarf/tallie friendship blossoms.

Firecracker (2005)

> Written and Directed by Steve Balderson
> Starring Karen Black
> Featured dwarf: Selene Luna
> "No one wants to see someone so low to the ground."

From filmmaker Steve Balderson comes this excellent arthouse film chronicling a murder in a small town while a circus is in town. As we all

The beautiful Selene Luna makes us want to buy a circus membership. Courtesy of Steve Balderson.

know, a circus in a film is not complete without the inclusion of a dwarf. In this case, we get Selene Luna. The highlight scene from Selene starts off with her in a baby outfit lying in a baby carriage. As she's helped out, she begins dancing and stripping and going down to just her nipples being covered. Selene is nothing short of beautiful in the scene and makes you wish this circus would come to your town.

The downside is that Selene's screen time is mostly background work as part of a larger group. While this is a shame, the movie is a great independent flick that should be seen anyway, so Selene's inclusion ends up being a cherry on top.

Tallie steals dwarf's hat.
Dwarf in baby outfit.
Dwarf stripper.
Dwarf accomplice.

Forbidden Zone (1982)

Written by Richard Elfman, Matthew Bright, Nick L. Martinson, Nick James
Directed by Richard Elfman
Starring Susan Tyrell
Featured dwarf: Herve Villechaize
"He may be a little man, but he carries a big stick."

I guess this is sort of Richard Elfman's answer to *The Rocky Horror Picture Show* (1975). Except with the dwarf from *Fantasy Island* (Herve Villecaize), in black and white, and a lot more sexually confused, and to be more

Every girl's crazy 'bout a sharp dressed dwarf.

sexually confused than *The Rocky Horror Picture Show* (1975) is to be really, really sexually confused. Not unlike Eflman's other attempted masterpiece, *Shrunken Heads* (1994), there are not only flying heads but flying heads and dwarves, which definitely earns extra points in my book.

The plot revolves around a woman named Frenchy (Marie-Pascal Elfman/pretty hot for a tallie), who falls into the phantasmagorical Sixth Dimension by accident. The place turns out to be something out of a horny crackhead's vision, where visitors are shat out of a large Monty Python style cutout of a sphincter. While there, Frenchy meets King Fausto (Herve Villechaize). His character goes down in history as one of the horniest on-screen dwarves (falling just short of dwarves in porn and Torben Bille). He wears a funny crown, holds a little scepter and repeatedly confesses his overwhelming love for Frenchy, not really giving much of a damn how much it pisses off his wife Queen Doris (Susan Tyrell). In fact, Villechaize is so horny in this movie, he doesn't really seem to care about how Frenchy feels about his banging other tallie women behind her back either. The little guy is pretty much led around by his wang throughout the entire movie, which makes things pretty entertaining (especially during the love scenes) and Villechaize leading a parade while marching and waving his scepter in the air is priceless.

Forbidden Zone (1982) is certainly not for everyone but it's so incredibly weird it's a must see. After watching, I guarantee you'll never, ever look at *Fantasy Island* the same way again.

Trumpet-playing dwarf.
Crown-wearing, feasting and drinking dwarf.
Dwarf watches woman eat giant sausage.
Dwarf walks across table.
Sex-magnet dwarf.
King dwarf.
Smoking, dice sitting dwarf.
Dwarf air conducts woman's song.
Pervert dwarf looks through telescope at woman.
Dwarf chased by wife.
Dwarf stands on table to argue with wife.
Dwarf makes out with tall woman.
Dwarf/tallie sex.
Painting dwarf.
Promiscuous dwarf.
Dwarf steps on oversized dice to talk to a hot tallie woman.

Having a gun pointed at his dome poses no threat to this battle hardened dwarf.

>Dwarf talks to severed head.
>Breast-grabbing dwarf.
>Plastic-sword-wielding dwarf.
>Sobbing dwarf consoled by flying severed head with wings.
>Dwarf leads parade in musical number.

For Y'ur Height Only (1981)

>Written by Cora Ridon Caballes
>Directed by Eddie Nicart
>Starring Weng Weng, Anna Marie Gutierrez, Tony Ferrer, Yehlen Catral, Carmi Martin, Beth Sandoval, and Mike Cohen
>Featured dwarf: Weng Weng

For Y'ur Height Only (1981) is a pure classic dwarf exploitation film from the Philippines, starring 2 ½ feet tall Weng Weng as Agent 00, a cross between James Bond and Chuck Norris—he can make love to all the beautiful women while throwing a kick to the face of the baddies. Weng Weng is every dwarf enthusiast's wet dream come true. We get to see him as an action star—kicking, running, jumping, using very large guns, flying through the air in his jet pack, the works. Then we get to see him making out with every beautiful woman he comes across and the women are enthralled with him.

In this tale, "Mr. Giant" has not only kidnapped a doctor but also Weng Weng's love interest, Irma, who had infiltrated his gang of drug dealing slavers. The movie gives Weng Weng many adventures, some that stop awkwardly and suddenly but not before we get a few bits of fun. It's basically a movie with a VERY thin plot that is based around getting to see Weng Weng do his various bits. The best moments are definitely a combination of seeing Weng Weng do stunts that would normally be reserved for an action star and seeing Weng Weng have such good luck with the women. However, the most memorable moment may be at the end when it's revealed that "Mr. Giant" is actually a dwarf himself, leading to a classic dwarf versus dwarf fighting match.

This movie is an absolute must see, as are any of the sequels that you can get your hands on.

If one were watching this movie and looking for a drinking game, here's a suggestion: drink every time Weng Weng looks at the camera. We don't think you should (you'll get severely intoxicated) but if you're looking…

> Weng Weng like James Bond credits.
> Tallies walk in front of Weng Weng before he's revealed for the first time.
> Weng Weng with large gun.
> Weng Weng jumping off building followed by freeze frame.
> Weng Weng in big glasses, surrounded by bikini girls.
> Close up of Weng Weng's hand.
> Weng Weng saves beautiful woman.
> Weng Weng shooting at assassin with mini gun.
> Weng Weng sitting at a table that's too tall for him.
> Weng Weng hiding behind tree.
> Weng Weng kicks tallie multiple times in crotch.
> Weng Weng hides in wall.
> Weng Weng trips baddie.
> Baddie keeps punching too high.
> Weng Weng goes between baddie's legs.
> Weng Weng kicks baddie in the butt.

Weng Weng does handstand to kick baddie in face.
Weng Weng going up ladder.
Weng Weng jumps on table.
Weng Weng puts knee on tallie to keep him down.
Weng Weng jumps off table and forces man to talk.
Weng Weng says, "Talk or you'll eat lead!"
Weng Weng on oversized phone.
Weng Weng enters room secretly between Lola's legs.
Weng Weng sliding across floor firing his gun.
Weng Weng says, "Oh, my little head."
Weng Weng saluting.
Weng Weng in silly hat.
Weng Weng puts on see through glasses to see hot secretaries nude—makes funny kid face when he sees them nude.
Weng Weng blows kiss.
Weng Weng flips over railing using a tallie.
Takes tallie to ground to kick him in face.
Weng Weng sliding down wire.
Weng Weng claps for waiter.
Woman says, "I like 'em little,"
Weng Weng's hand on large glass.
Weng Weng shirtless.
Weng Weng blowing darts.
Weng Weng ducking as he walks.
Weng Weng confuses tallies by hitting them on the feet.
Weng Weng hanging on to top of table to hide.
Referred to as "midget."
Weng Weng stands on gate so he can talk face to face.
Weng Weng holds hands with tallie.
"You're such a little guy, though. Very petite, like a potato."—Irma, a hot chick
"Yeah, let's go." —Weng Weng
Weng Weng throws slicing hat.
"He's a one man army." –Baddie
"He's a mass killer, that double OO, who will be next to go?"—Baddie
Referred to as "twerp."
Weng Weng running with girl in tow.
"What about you?"—Irma, a hot chick

"Don't worry, I'll see you later at the disco dance."—Weng Weng

Weng Weng hides UNDER a bush.

Kicks multiple guys in crotch.

Weng Weng leaps onto baddies from above.

Weng Weng sits on baddie.

Weng Weng pops head through stairs.

Chased on stairs by baddie with umbrella gun.

Weng Weng thrown onto baddies.

Weng Weng kicks more baddies in crotch.

Weng Weng constantly looking up.

Weng Weng sliding across floor and firing gun again.

Weng Weng kisses hot beautiful woman who is a stranger before jumping off building.

Woman likes Weng Weng's kiss.

Weng Weng jumps off building using an umbrella.

Weng Weng lands on jeep, sits on it and waves at bad guys.

Weng Weng laughs after shooting three bad guys, then he goes to the disco.

Weng Weng disco dancing.

"Where's that little midget?"—Baddie

"Probably hiding in her handbag,"—Baddie

Weng Weng kissed by Irma.

Shot of Weng Weng through baddie's legs.

Weng Weng held like a baby by baddie.

Weng Weng tied up and put into trunk.

Weng Weng punches hole through trunk and then crawls through.

Weng Weng kicking baddies with dagger boot.

Referred to as "little stinker."

Weng Weng jumping when firing his gun.

Weng Weng hides in hole, comes out of hole between guards legs and kicks him in the crotch.

Weng Weng leaps up using a gun the baddie is holding to kick him in the face.

Weng Weng uses foot to cock gun, flies back when he fires it.

Weng Weng hiding amongst plants.

When he pops up, a weird sound effect plays.

Referred to as "Stupid, little runt."

Referred to as "half pint."

Swings under table to kick baddie.
Stands on table to kick baddies in the face.
Hot woman swings Weng Weng around to kick bad guys.
Weng Weng claps between slapping baddie.
Weng Weng turns on hottie who requests sex.
"That midget nearly did me in."—Baddie
Weng Weng smoking.
Close up of Weng Weng's foot on wound.
Flirtatious Weng Weng.
Weng Weng walks behind gate, pulls down baddie and knocks him out.
Weng Weng climbs wall.
Weng Weng jumps on tallie, knocks him down and hits him on top of the head.
Weng Weng on baddie's back is flipped over.
Weng Weng climbs over fence.
Weng Weng in sword fight.
"I have to walk on my little feet!"—Weng Weng to taxi driver
Referred to as "little man."
Can just see the top of Weng Weng's head when sitting in car.
Weng Weng kisses random black woman.
Weng Weng jumping off a bridge.
Weng Weng amused by his own reflection in mirror.
Weng Weng sliding down handrail.
Weng Weng jet packing.
Mr. Giant is a dwarf.
Dwarf crawling.
Dwarf vs. dwarf fight.
Dwarf kicked in crotch.
Dwarves roll around on floor.
Weng Weng loses love interest.

Foul Play (1978)

Written by Colin Higgins
Directed by Colin Higgins
Starring Goldie Hawn, Chevy Chase, Don Calfa and Dudley Moore

Featured dwarf: Billy Barty
"Beware of the dwarf."

An innocent, beautiful woman (Goldie Hawn) picks up a random stranger whose car has broken down. It turns out this guy is an undercover cop who has uncovered an assassination plot by the biggest hitman, known as "The Dwarf." When the cop meets her at the theatre for their 'date,' he's bleeding. His last words to her are "beware of the dwarf." This leads to the audience and Goldie Hawn's character expecting a dwarf assassin. In steps Billy Barty as a door-to-door bible salesman, mistaken by Goldie for the dwarf assassin. Mayhem ensues as Goldie fights off what she thinks is an assassin, pushing him with a chair, knocking him out the window where he hangs on as he's beaten by her, finally falling in a trash can that rolls and rolls (with him screaming the whole way) until it hits and he flies out and into a manhole. The next time we see Billy he is injured horribly and scared to death of Goldie.

The movie is funny; however, while Billy's part is hilarious, especially after you're let in on the gag, it begs the question of whether it would be funny if a tallie had been mistaken for an assassin.

Referred to as "elf."
Referred to as "little man."
Referred to as "midget."
Dwarf standing on box.
Dwarf pushed by chair.
Dwarf hit over head with flower pot.
Dwarf hanging out window.
Dwarf lands in trash can.
Dwarf rolling down steps in trash can.
Dwarf screaming.
Dwarf flies through manhole.
"That's right, honey. You've attacked an innocent dwarf."—
    Chevy Chase
Dwarf in bandages and casts in hospital.

Frankenstein's Castle of Freaks (1974)

Written by Roberto Spano, Mark Smith, William Rose and Mario Francini
Directed by Robert H. Oliver
Starring Rossano Brazzi
Featured dwarf: Michael Dunn
"You necrophile!"

Oh, what a beautiful work this is. Right off the bat we are introduced to "Genz," played by the legend Michael Dunn, playing with a corpse's breast. Not long after, Genz is going through the house spying on tallies making love. This was one horny little guy. Eventually, he causes too much trouble and gets booted from the house. Ostracized, he ends up finding friendship with a couple of monsters, which eventually takes the chaos to a new level as they fight each other. This guy just wanted to get laid and have some tallie friends but it just wasn't meant to be.

Highlights include dwarf necro action and a dwarf raping a tallie woman with the help of a monster.

Oversees grave digging.
Plays with corpse breast.
Dwarf with mustache.
Peeping tom dwarf.
Dwarf commanded to sit in corner.
Referred to as "rat".
Dwarf crying.
Dwarf camping with Neanderthal man.
Dwarf rapist.
Dwarf lifted up by moaning tallie.
Dwarf pushed down.
Referred to as "little monster".
Dwarf with torch.

Frankie Starlight (1995)

    Written by Ronan O'Leary and Chet Raymo
    Directed by Michael Lindsay-Hogg
    "Do you guys fuck?"—random woman
    "Dwarves or writers?"—Frankie
    Starring Gabriel Byrne and Matt Dillon
    Featured Dwarf: Corban Walker

Based on "The Dork of Cork" by Chet Raymo, this feels similar to *The Station Agent* (2003) in that it's a classy movie that ties in dwarfism. To top it off, they cast Corban Walker, a well known artist, as the dwarf writer, Frank, who is the wrap-around as he tries to sell the story of his mom from his conception to him being raised. We see his mother on a troop ship with a group of soldiers, who she apparently did several of and doesn't know which one is the father. She ends up running into Gabriel Byrne, an officer from that ship, who tries to help her out but also makes her his mistress. Byrne ends up igniting an interest in astronomy in the young dwarf as his contribution to his childhood. Just when Byrne leaves, we get a drifter (played by Matt Dillon) who seems to have memories of her on that ship as well (who could forget her?), and who takes them to Texas. They don't end up staying there long, and it almost feels like a forced side story until the mother ends up pregnant again. Towards the end, the movie mostly focuses on the wraparound story and the should-have-been-a-star Corban Walker and I'm very thankful for this. I found Walker to be very reminiscent of Peter Dinklage. His calm, yet depressed nature and overall presence is what makes this film special. It's a shame that Walker has only appeared in one other film but he is a very talented and successful artist off-screen that more than likely accounts for his absence. As for the film itself, it's a definite for a fan of dwarves but falls short in general (no pun intended) with its cheesy light nature and waste-of-time side characters.

    Checks out hot chicks.
    Gets hidden behind hot chicks.
    Referred to as little man.
    Referred to as little fella.
    Referred to as wee kid.
    Referred to as dwarf.
    Dwarf lives in dump.
    Dwarf child.

Dwarf child looking at dwarf art.
Dwarf child walks out of tallie classmate crowd.
Dwarf child running upstairs.
Dwarf drinking.
Dwarf on motorcycle.
Dwarf holding Dillon's hand.
Dwarf walking next to Dillon.
Dwarf on roof.
Dwarf mimics Dillon.
Dwarf pissing off cliff.
Dillon lifts dwarf onto motorcycle.
Dwarf feeling sorry for himself.
Dwarf turned down by hooker.
Drunken dwarf.
Dwarf doesn't like himself.
Dwarf overflows liquor glass.
Dwarf throwing table.
Dwarf crying.
Dwarf with shades on.
Dwarf with football.
Dwarf jumping out of truck.
Dwarf playing football.
Dwarf running after girl.
Dwarf looking up at girl he's talking to.
Dwarf referred to as "sexy."
Dwarf kissing tallie.

Freaked (1993)

Written by Tim Burns, Tom Stern, Alex Winter
Directed by Tom Stern, Alex Winter
Starring: Brian Brophy, Henry Carbo, Jaime Cardriche, Nicholas Cohn, Morgan Fairchild
Featured dwarf: Deep Roy

Whoa, dude! Alex Winter directs a movie with dwarves! Within the first ten minutes of this bizarre and highly underrated cult movie, the great Deep Roy appears. Winter plays an egomaniacal actor known mostly for his "Bill and Ted" style roles, who is approached by an evil corporation to be their spokesman for a highly suspicious toxic fertilizer. Bill Sadler plays a corporate slime who tells Winter the product is completely safe and to prove it Sadler brings forward the head of the South American research facility, George Ramirez, to calm Winter's nerves. Ramirez is a tall, heavily mustached Mexican man who tells Winter he's been working closely with the product for some time and there is nothing to worry about. Right in the middle of his speech, the once-tall Mexican man shrinks into the much smaller-in-stature dwarf actor, Deep Roy. Roy wears a thick mustache much like his large Mexican counterpart and fits very well into the image of what Ramirez would look like as a dwarf version of himself.

Other than the appearance of Deep Roy in the movie, and even though this film has a million opportunities to cast dwarves (think of the brilliant movie "Freaks") doesn't do so. But we are, however, treated to a brief cameo with a dwarf once Winter stumbles across a freak show and becomes a part of it. During one of the freak show performances, the camera focuses on a dwarf who wears a clown outfit and stands on a barrel next to a sign that proclaims "ASK ME I'LL FART YOUR WATE!" (And yes, the sign is intentionally misspelled). The clown dwarf looks at a slender, smoking girl next to him and guesses her weight of 107 just before placing a large bullhorn against his ass and farting through it. There are also two dwarves who show up intermittently in the film that are in eyeball suits and who serve as gun-toting guards that speak with Jamaican accents. The eyes are played by dwarf actors Michael Gilden and Joseph S. Griffo. So there are technically dwarves throughout the entire movie, I just would have preferred them to have larger roles and/or actually show their faces with the dialogue.

Dammit, Hollywood, when are you going to stop neglecting all the great dwarf actors we have out there?! Just think, if you would have actually hired more dwarves for this film or actually make at least one of them a lead character maybe *Freaked* would have a status closer to the 1930's masterpiece which featured several dwarves as leads.

    Tallie transforms into dwarf.
    Dwarf in oversized suit.
    Dwarf clown stands on barrel.
    Dwarf clown farts through a bullhorn.

Freaks (1932)

> Written by Al Boasberg, Charles MacArthur, Clarence Aaron 'Tod' Robbins, Edgar Allan Woolf, Leon Gordon
> Directed by Tod Browning
> Starring Wallace Ford, Leila Hyams, Olga Baclanova, Roscoe Ates, Henry Victor
> Featured dwarf: Angelo Rossitto

The Tod Browning classic and one of the greatest dwarfsploitation movies ever made. Except in this one, the dwarves get their revenge and they get it good by turning one of their tormentors into a human/duck woman. I know what you're thinking, and yes, it is that weird. In fact, it's easily one of the weirdest movies I've ever seen. The plot revolves around the performers in a carnival sideshow. Its focus is on a married dwarf named Hans who has feelings for an Amazon woman. Behind his back, she teams up with the circus strongman to try and scam him out of his inheritance. The sexual tension between the dwarf and Amazon woman is awkward and bizarrely fascinating (especially considering the time in which the film was made). Why Hans would ever want to leave his hot dwarf wife for a boring, gold-digging Amazon woman is beyond me, but aside from my own personal issue, it's a really fantastic film.

On the surface, it appears to be 100% dwarfsploitation, but a closer look reveals multidimensional characters for whom you, as an audience member, have a great deal of compassion for. They become empowered by the end when they take their vengeance out on their transgressors and we cheer for them every step of the way. *Freaks* is a must see for dwarfsploitation completists and fans alike.

Dwarf in love with Amazon woman. The two of them having sex would be visually along the lines of someone getting lucky with a 50 year old baby.

> Dwarf's wife rides around on Shetland pony.
> Dwarf with no legs, walks around on hands. (Don't quote me on this, it's hard to tell whether this one's a dwarf or not.)
> Dwarf who hangs out with deformed groupies.
> Dwarf being taken advantage of by Amazon woman. She flirts

with him because he lends her money. Clearly, the bitch has no intention of paying it back.

Angry Dwarf.

Dwarf stands up and yells with his fists clenched like a little kid throwing a temper tantrum.

Freakshow (2007)

Written by Keith Leopard
Directed by Drew Bell
Featured dwarf: Mighty Mike Murga

The Asylum, the company that is best known for 'mockbusters' such as *Transmorphers* (2007), brings us this modernized knock off of the classic *Freaks* (1932). When a group of criminals join the security team of the freakshow, they are in for more than hiding out—they also want to steal some ticket sales. Things get bad when the youngest member of the freakshow family turns up dead. The freaks then team up and take out the criminals the only way they know how, including turning one of them.

As is typical for freakshows in cinema, it's not complete without the inclusion of a dwarf. In this case, it's dwarf actor Mighty Mike Murga (credited only as "Mighty Mike"). Unfortunately, he's mostly relegated to background work and the occasional one or two lines. They also try and remind us that he's there by cutting to him once in a while. In pure dwarfsploitation form, the movie could have been fine without the dwarf actor but they had him there for the occasional sight gag. The movie is crap and the dwarf role is not worth watching this one for.

Dwarf circus act.
Dwarf drinking beer.
Flame juggling.
Dwarf eating fire.
Dwarf killing.

Fred Claus (2007)

>Written by Dan Fogelman
>Directed by David Dobkin
>Starring Vince Vaughn, John Michael Higgins, and
>   Ludacris

This generally unfunny, wannabe Christmas classic falls flat by giving the role of the elf with the most lines to John Michael Higgins—A tallie made to look like a dwarf. The movie gets its first laughs when real dwarves show up and attack Vince Vaughn for what I'm going to pretend is vengeance for bad improv. As if Higgins playing an elf isn't bad enough, we then get Ludacris (ironic, I know) playing a DJ elf. I wouldn't mind if there were no little people who could do it but Tony Cox would have knocked this part out of the park, unlike Ludacris who is making us forget his decent turn in *Crash* (2004) and remember he's just another rapper turned wannabe actor. I wonder how Ludacris would feel if the producers of *Crash* (2004) had put Peter Dinklage in black face and let him play "Anthony" in place of him? Skip this one.

>Tallies' superimposed heads on dwarf bodies.
>Ninja dwarves attack super tallie Vince Vaughn.
>Skilled attack elves go after Vince Vaughn.
>Elf dancing with tallie.

Freshman Orientation (2004)

>Written and directed by Ryan Shiraki
>Starring Sam Huntington

You know the romantic comedy cliché where the guy gets forced on stage to perform? This one has that too when Sam Huntington's straight-guy-pretending-to-be-gay character is forced to perform on stage at "Queer Slam." Perhaps it's because the scene is so unoriginal that the director decided to go to the crowd to make it "original." When Huntington's character turns his performance into a crowd pleaser where the crowd—why we don't know—suddenly starts clapping and singing along. Out of nowhere comes a shot of two little hands and then the camera moves revealing a little person. The little person becomes the most frequent shot for absolutely no reason. She never gets a line and is never seen again in the film. I can only imagine how much better this film would have been had they used this actress instead of the many untalented ones that got lines. This scene is pure dwarfsploitation, with the actress being nothing more than a sight gag.

> Close up of little hands clapping.
> Little person dancing.
> No lines for little person actress.

Friday (1995)

> Written by DJ Pooh and Ice Cube
> Directed by F. Gary Gray
> Starring Ice Cube, Chris Tucker, Bernie Mac
> Featured dwarf: Tony Cox

In this black pot comedy, Ice Cube and Chris Tucker have a hot neighbor across the street who is getting banged by Bernie Mac. When the husband comes home early, he discovers the hot wife and Mac in bed together and chases him out, ending by throwing a brick through the window of his car. As it turns out, the husband is a dwarf (played beautifully by Tony Cox). He comes back later in the film to throw her clothes on the lawn and kick her out. While Cox does spend his few scenes angry, we do get to see him smiling at the end of the film. Cox is only one of many side characters, qualifying him as nothing more than a cameo.

> Angry dwarf.
> Dwarf with hot wife.
> Dwarf getting cheated on.
> Dwarf throws brick.
> Dwarf throws clothes.

From a Whisper to a Scream (1987)

Written by Jeff Burr, C.Courtney Joyner, Darin Scott
Directed by Jeff Burr
Starring Vincent Price, Clu Gulager
Featured dwarf: Angelo Rossitto
"Now I'm bigger than you are!"

Also known as *The Offspring*, this surprisingly good horror anthology stars Vincent Price telling three stories of people who have been corrupted by a hell spawn of a town. The final segment involves a carnival, so of course there must be dwarves. Led by the legendary Angelo Rossitto, a few dwarves appear in the segment where Angelo seems to be revisiting his role in *Dracula vs. Frankenstein* (1971). Donning his top hat and cane, he's trying to sell passersby on a freakshow. He doesn't get a whole lot to do in the segment and they're all there more for show, getting an unexplained scene where they talk about why they can't leave the carnival. Angelo does get one short scene where he gets to stab a tallie but is nowhere as good as it could have been if Angelo was the Fabio-male lead.

Dwarves at Carnival.
Dwarf with glasses.
Dwarf with stuffed doll.
Dwarf freakshow host.
Dwarf on table, lifted off.
Angry dwarf.
Dwarf kissed on top of head.
Scared dwarf.
Dwarf stabs tallie.

Fur: An Imaginary Portrait of Diane Arbus (2006)

Written by Erin Cressida Wilson
Directed by Steven Shainberg
Starring Nicole Kidman, Robert Downey Jr.
Featured dwarf: David Joseph Steinberg

It's impossible for Hollywood to make a film about people who are unique (commonly referred to in cinema as "freaks") without the inclusion of dwarves and this film is no different. An imaginary story indeed about photographer Diane Arbus (played by Nicole Kidman) follows her as she discovers her new neighbor, played by Robert Downey Jr., covered in hair; lots and lots of hair. As a freak of nature, he has freak friends including a woman with no arms, a giant, Siamese twins and a bunch of dwarves. Not much originality here.

The best dwarf scene comes in a party scene where Arbus is taken by the wolf man to a party that consists mostly of dwarves. We are treated to David Joseph Steinberg singing a tune while the lady dwarves swoon over him and see another dwarf play with a tranny's hair. Why is it dwarves get these roles but rarely seem to even get elf roles anymore?

> Dwarf smoking.
> Dwarf walking between tallies.
> Dwarf at freakshow.
> Singing dwarf.
> Dwarves toasting.
> Dwarf extras.
> Dwarf musician.

Future Hunters (1986)

> Written by J. Lee Thompson
> Directed by Cirio H. Santiago
> Starring Robert Patrick, Ed Crick, Elizabeth Oropesa, Bruce Le (as Bruce Li), Richard Norton
> Featured dwarves: the same fighting dwarves from *Raiders of the Sun* (1992)

In *Future Hunters* (1986), Santiago recycles the fighting dwarf army he used in *Raiders of the Sun* (1992). I'm not sure what to say about this film other than it does contain certain magical and watchable elements such as Richard Norton, a Bruce Lee impersonator and an army of fighting dwarves who are basically like the Ewoks without the teddy bear outfits. The plot is pretty fast forward able but it is worth stopping when the dwarves show up to assist the great Robert Patrick on his quest. The dwarves wisely make Patrick and his female sidekick help them first before they return the favor. And as well they should. After all, a dwarf's trust isn't given, it's earned. And indeed, once Patrick and co. have earned the full trust of the dwarves, they reap the full rewards of having the little bad-asses as friends (the one with the samurai-style haircut was my personal favorite). It's great to see the dwarves work as a team so efficiently to attack and booby trap evil tallies.

There's a very valuable lesson to this film: if you are battling evil tallies in the forest, odds are you're doomed. But, if you manage to earn the trust of forest dwarves and you are pure of heart, they have the power to save your life.

> Cave dwarves.
> Warrior dwarves.
> Headband-wearing dwarves.
> Dwarf in jawa-esque robe.
> Dwarves feed Robert Patrick.
> Mouth stuffed dwarves.
> Heroes must help dwarves before dwarves help heroes.
> Dwarf pokes horse with stick.
> Dwarf with samurai hair.
> Crawling stealth dwarf.
> Multiple dwarves attack tallie.
> Dwarf jumps off several dwarves' backs to attack tallie.
> Munitions-carrying dwarves.
> Dwarves throw rocks at tallie and swing from rope.
> Dwarf lights dynamite.
> Cheering dwarves.
> Dwarves dig out trapped tallies.

Galaxina (1980)

> Written and directed by William Sachs
> Starring Stephen Macht, Avery Schreiber, J.D. Hinton, and Dorothy Stratten
> Featured dwarf: Angelo Rossitto

Starring *Playboy* Playmate Dorothy Stratten (who's pretty hot for a tallie), *Galaxina* (1980) is about a space babe who falls in love with a human.

Not much to see here dwarf-wise, but there is a bit where the film parodies the original *Alien* (1979), where a man becomes more or less impregnated by a tiny alien that grows into a dwarf in an alien suit and thinks the human it came out of is its mommy. The dwarf alien doesn't show up until the very end of the movie. From a dwarfsploitation point of view, it's worth a fast-forward to the end to see the dwarf in the alien outfit, but that's about it. The talents of classic dwarf actor Angelo Rossitto are wasted here.

Dwarf in alien outfit.

Gamer (2009)

Written and directed by Mark Neveldine and Brian Taylor
Starring Gerard Butler

This action flick about prisoners fighting battles with others controlling them is filled with oddities and weird characters. Standing alongside an Oprah-style host is a dwarf. The dwarf is only seen blurred out in an early scene and then briefly helping Gerard Butler's character get in a van. It's not worth checking out for the dwarf but is a fun action movie made better by the brief appearance.

Notably, the film also briefly features a cameo by dwarf enthusiast director Lloyd Kaufman.

Dwarf cameraman.
Dwarf extra.

Games of Survival (1989)

Written by Armand Gazarian and Lindsay Norgard
Directed by Armand Gazarian
Starring Nikki Hill, Cindy Coatman and Roosevelt Miller Jr
"Small but deadly!"

You know when the box cover says "Game of Survival" but then the movie itself says "Games of Survival" that you're in for a real treat and this one is no exception. Zane is captured in the opening scene and then sent to Earth where he is to battle six of the most brutal warriors in the galaxy. Instead of fighting it out anywhere else in the galaxy, they decide to fight it out in Hollywood. What it boils down to is a couple of guys fighting in silly outfits in all the clichéd locations—a bar, train depot, etc. And they're all guys and they're looking for balls. Really big black balls, to be precise.

As luck would have it, five of the six most brutal warriors in the galaxy are the typical Conan types but the last one happens to be a dwarf! He looks ridiculous with feathers as his outfit and a toy bow and arrow set as his weapon, but it's an absolute blast when he's on screen. The filmmaker takes every advantage of the fact that he's a dwarf with constant close ups of every dwarf body part.

My favorite part is a random scene where the dwarf hears something and sneaks around. He sees it's a dog. He stops. He shoots it anyway. "Food!" he yells as he walks towards it but then it cuts to him doing something else. To top it off, the end fight scene for OUR hero is extremely laughable, but so is the whole film. I can't believe I hadn't heard of this film before starting on this book, and I declare it a Beer Classic. Absolute must-see for the sheer ridiculousness of it all—yes, it's bad, but it's so bad it's brilliant.

> Dwarf transported.
> Dwarf in front of dumpster.
> Dwarf with feathers.
> Dwarf and tallies are the baddest of the galaxy.
> Dwarf crawls under door.
> Dwarf with beer bottle.
> Dwarf knocks out large black man.
> Dwarf running.
> Dwarf hit by car.
> Dwarf with broken leg runs off fine.
> Dwarf climbing.
> Dwarf leg close up.
> Dwarf shooting bow and arrow poorly.
> Dwarf jumping.
> Dwarf feet close up.
> Dwarf kicking dead body.
> Dwarf eye close up.
> Dwarf ducking.
> Dwarf falling.

Dwarf choked.
Dwarf stabbed.
Dwarf fight scene.

Ghoulies (1985)

Written by Luca Bercovici and Jefrey Levy
Directed by Luca Bercovici
Starring Peter Liapis, Lisa Pelikan, Keith Joe Dick
"They call me Dick, but you can call me Dick."

The movie that started the puppet craze around the nation was not *Ghoulies* (1985), but rather *Gremlins* (1984). *Ghoulies* (1985) is the cheaper version of a 'puppets gone mad' movie, but it is a fun series. The puppets are very well designed, and unlike many other movies with puppets, this one finally realized that puppets alone weren't enough. For a puppet movie to truly work, it needs puppets and dwarves. Wouldn't it be great if Hollywood started to adapt this theory? One can only dream. *Ghoulies* (1985) is a puppet/dwarf movie with catchy marketing. After all, who doesn't remember that puppet with overalls coming out of the toilet on the box art?

The plot revolves around a man who inherits the house of his dead father and unleashes demon puppets (aka, the Ghoulies) in order to acquire more power and knowledge. To complete this wish, he brilliantly also conjures up a demonic dwarf couple who looks like they came right out of the medieval days. They're dirty and scruffy, with rat teeth and wearing those armor head caps Merlin donned in *Excalibur*. The guy's girlfriend isn't too happy he's f'ing around with black magic, let alone that he's conjured up a bunch of killer puppets and dwarves. However, he could care less—he's having far too much fun spending time with his killer puppets and dwarves. At first, the dwarf couple from Hell acts like a traditional nagging married couple. Then, they bicker between themselves about who their true master is. Is it the man who's just conjured them, or is it his dead warlock father whom they served before? The issue isn't really resolved but the female dwarf beats the crap out of her partner and they serve their new master anyway.

What ensues is puppet and dwarf madness, several people die at their hands and the movie ends setting itself up for a sequel. The filmmakers must have had a clear vision of how much cash they'd make in the future by making more sequels with more killer puppets and dwarves. And even though the medieval dwarf couple doesn't share the same spotlight as their puppet peers, the filmmakers did have enough sense to include them throughout the entire movie so the audience doesn't get cheated on their Merlin-capped dwarf good times.

> Black magic ceremony produces two dwarves with bald, Merlin-style armour helmets and ratlike faces.
> Male and female dwarf.
> Dwarves appear through smoke in an overhead shot.
> Back to back standing dwarves.
> Pouting dwarves.
> Rat-toothed dwarves.
> Cautionary dwarves warn their new master of the dangers of the ritual he wants to perform.
> Medieval dwarves help their master get laid.
> Candle-carrying medieval dwarves.
> Screaming, summoning, medieval dwarves.
> Medieval dwarf scatters across hall.
> Medieval dwarf stealth-attacks man with baseball bat.
> Two Medieval dwarves struggle to move man across floor.
> Medieval dwarves tag-team beat-down a ghoulie.
> Medieval female dwarf smacks around medieval male dwarf.
> Medieval dwarves fight over who their real master is.
> Medieval dwarf tosses ghoulie at man.
> Men fight over the dwarves.
> Medieval dwarves stand by their real master.
> Father tricks son into resurrecting him, then steals his dwarf guardians back. And all this accomplished while in zombie form. Impressive!
> Dwarves wave goodbye to fleeing kids like they've just left a theme park instead of a portal to Hell filled with demonic puppets.

Ghoulies 2 (1988)

> Written by Dennis Paoli
> Directed by Albert Band
> Starring Damon Martin, Royal Dano, J. Downing and Kerry Remsen
> Featured dwarf: Phil Fondacaro
> "What are you, a member of the dwarf's union or what?"

In *Ghoulies 2* (1988), the great dwarf actor Phil Fondacaro, who not unlike the dwarf from *"Bloodsucking Freaks* (1976) also looks like John Oates from the band Hall and Oates and wears suspenders. Maybe the filmmakers were giving a nod to the formerly mentioned classic. Fondacaro plays a very meaty role as a sideshow carnival employee. In one of the most bizarre dwarfsploitation twists ever, Fondacaro continuously quotes Shakespeare, dresses up in a little horned gorilla outfit and runs around scaring children and others that come to check out the show at the attraction he works, aptly called "Satan's Den."

His character also has an incredibly pretentious name to boot: Sir Nigel Penneyweight. As soon as I heard that name I instantly laughed out loud. Now how did such a brilliant Shakespearean actor get stuck working as a carnie who dresses in a little gorilla outfit with horns? We can only assume it's due to the usual ignorance of a tallie-dominated society that rejects the always-understated brilliance of the dwarves it lives amongst. Moving on, when Satan's Den is in jeopardy of shutting down due to lack of funds, the ghoulies find their way inside and the attraction suddenly gets a lot more frightening.

There are several dwarfsploitation elements in this film, including Fondacaro's introduction by way of walking down a tall ladder, being repelled by the ghoulies (who are much smaller than he is), hiding in a trunk, being picked up and bossed around by multiple tallies. Sir Nigel is not exactly one of the bravest dwarves in cinema history but he does redeem himself by, bizarrely enough, having a comprehensive understanding of the Latin language which he uses to transcribe a magic book to fight the ghoulies, who as I mentioned before are at least twice as dwarfish as he is. Points to the filmmakers for their dwarfsploitation originality and keeping the dwarf in the movie for its entire duration.

Pretentious dwarf actor.

Dwarf makes entrance climbing down a tall ladder.
Diva dwarf.
Shakespeare-quoting dwarf.
Flipping-off-the-man dwarf.
Schoolboy hat-wearing dwarf.
High angle on dwarf holding coffee.
Painting of dwarf couple on carnival wall.
Carnie dwarf.
Dwarf in mini monster outfit.
Dwarf lives in trailer where everything is sized down to meet his needs.
Dwarf framed next to giant tractor.
Dwarf frightened of creatures at least half his size.
Tripping and falling dwarf.
Dwarf hides in trunk from ghoulies.
Dwarfed picked up by metalhead teenagers with bad attitudes.
Latin-transcribing dwarf.
Failed magician dwarf.
Man and woman pick up dwarf and run to safety.
Dwarf decoy.

Ghoulies IV (1994)

Written by Mark Sevi
Directed by Jim Wynorski
Starring: Pete Liapis, Barbara Alyn Woods, Stacie Randall, Raquel Krelle, Bobby Di Cicco
Featured dwarves: Arturo Gil, Tony Cox

This one is very strange because it somehow trades dwarves for puppets. In the first *Ghoulies* (1985), there were dwarves and puppets. Same thing with *Ghoulies II* (1988). *Ghoulies III* (1991) took a break from dwarves and featured only puppets. *Ghoulies IV* (1994) did the flip side of *Ghoulies III* (1991) and features dwarves and no puppets. That is, unless you count the flashback scenes from *Ghoulies* (1985). The point is, they had a heavenly thing going on with dwarves and puppets so why didn't they keep the winning combination going? My guess is they didn't want to spend the money or the time on the puppeteering.

B-movie legend Jim Wynorski directs this installment, which begins with a really hot chick (for a tallie) in sexy superhero garb screwing up a ceremony to bring back an evil hell spawn from crossing over into the earthy realm and what takes his place are dwarves in ghoulie outfits. The ghoulie dwarves are credited as Ghoulie Lite and Ghoulie Dark (yes, this does reflect their skin color). The first thing Ghoulie Dark says to Ghoulie Lite is, "You know, man. I don't think we're in Oz anymore." Ghoulie Lite promptly responds by bitch slapping him and the pair run off like frightened little imps who have just angered their master, and thus sets the tone for the rest of the film, where the ghoulie dwarves end up acting like two of the Three Stooges throughout the duration of their screen time.

Brilliant dwarf actors Tony Cox and Arturo Gil are not to blame here, it's clearly the material. The movie does contain a few laughs (unfortunately not out loud) for the dwarf-curious and as always, Wynorski has a great eye for packing it with hot female eye candy, but it's a definite pass unless you're a completist of the work of Cox and Gil. What I kept trying to wrap my head around, even after viewing, was why they kept cutting back to shots of the ghoulie puppets from the first movie. Why, besides filling screen time, did the filmmakers keep reminding us of puppets that weren't in the fourth installment? Like many decisions made in this earthly realm, it most likely had to do with saving money.

> Dwarf ghoulies appear in pentagram.
> Dwarf ghoulie bitchslaps his toadie.
> Dwarf ghoulies hide from tallies in picture frames.
> Dwarf ghoulies escape from warehouse by walking out in giant cans.
> Dwarf ghoulies hide in the back of tallie detective's car.
> Dwarf ghoulies accidentally discharge detective's shotgun while trying to steal his car.
> Tallie cop mistakes dwarf ghoulies for kids as they run away from his car after they shoot it up.
> Dwarf ghoulies hide from tallies on top of liquor store.
> Dwarf ghoulie picks up an ad to be a movie extra.
> Dwarf ghoulie bashes tallie over the head after he tries to mug a tallie girl.
> Dwarf ghoulies identify themselves to female tallie as Sears and Roebuck.
> Dwarf ghoulies stare at female tallie's boobs.
> Dwarf ghoulies steal key from Asian janitor.

Dwarf ghoulie reads nudie magazine.
Dwarf ghoulie steals chicken leg from tallie's fridge.
Dwarf ghoulies hide under the bed from tallie.
Dwarf ghoulies mistake a can of mace for food.
Dwarf ghoulies blast tallie in the eye with mace.
Dwarf ghoulies jump over homeless man.
Dwarf ghoulies jump into the back of tallie's truck.
Dwarf ghoulies slip down little set of stairs.
Dwarf ghoulies steal jewel from sacrificial victim.
Dwarf ghoulies announce their return in a sequel right before jumping into a portal. Thank God they left and thank God the sequel never came.

Grind (2003)

Written by Ralph Sall
Directed by Casey La Scala
Starring Adam Brody, Mike Vogel, and Jennifer Morrison
"I'm not a little kid."

A slacker skateboarding tale of some guys that set out on a road trip to try to get into professional skateboarding, meeting various oddball characters along the way. When the skateboarders need to get into a competition, they try to pass off a random dwarf as a kid whose head is going to explode soon so they're trying to give him his last wish. The part isn't really funny, is very random and gives the dwarf actor next to nothing to do. It's short and not worth watching.

Skateboarders try to pass off dwarf as kid.
Angry dwarf.

Gummo (1997)

Written and Directed by Harmony Korine
Starring: Wendall Carr, Charles Matthew Coatney, Bryant L. Crenshaw, Darby Dougherty
Featured dwarf: Bryant L. Crenshaw
"I can't shoot ball like Michael Jordan. But it's okay. I'm also gay."

Remember how disturbing *Kids* was? (*Note to couples: not a good date movie) Well, *Gummo* is by the same writer (Harmony Korine). Basically it's *Kids* (1995) that feels like it's set in the Dirty South but actually takes place in Ohio. The kids here are even more vicious than they were in the formerly mentioned Korine film, and not just to humans. Let's just say if you're a cat lover, you may find yourself up in arms over this one. This is one movie that definitely makes you want to take a shower after you watch. Fortunately, a dwarf appears before too long, clearly with the filmmaker's intent to make the movie watchable to the masses. The addition of a dwarf is even more interesting in this case because it's a gay, black dwarf with a really weird, alien-shaped forehead.

The movie feels a lot like a series of unconnected vignettes, sort of like a trailer trash version of a Jim Jarmusch movie. I'm not sure how a gay, black dwarf ended up in this mix, but it's interesting nonetheless. After some truly disturbing scenes with redneck kids, the film cuts to the gay black dwarf in question. He sits on a couch in a wife beater, next to a drunk kid (played by director Harmony Korine, who I'm assuming went Method for his role). Korine blathers on for a while while the dwarf listens patiently. Then, the drunk kid gets some liquid courage and hits on the dwarf. However, even though the dwarf admits he's gay, he pushes the drunk kid away and clearly isn't interested. The dwarf's rejection doesn't sink through to the drunk kid though as he's clearly on a mission to have sex with the bald, gay dwarf. He continues harassing the dwarf by rubbing his man boobs on the outside of his wife beater and asking to kiss him over and over again. Finally, accepting the fact that the gay dwarf is just not that into him, the drunk kid settles for a hug, then blathers on about his shitty childhood. Clearly the dwarf had higher standards in his gay taste than just the slobbering, blathering drunk kid on the couch. The question is, if the dwarf was drunk himself, would he have let the slobbering drunk bang him? We may never know.

Moving on, the next dwarf scene occurs when the trailer trash kids have gotten themselves all liquored up and have decided to take their shirts off to expose their true manliness. Then, in an idea that could only be fueled by too many Mountain Dews and VHS viewings of *Over the Top* (1987), the rednecks come up with the brilliant idea to have themselves a good old fashioned arm wrestling competition! A hairy ape of a man who bears a resemblance to Ogre from *Revenge of the Nerds* (1984), loses to the sheer, brutal strength of the dwarf's arms of steel! Clearly pissed that he's been defeated by a dwarf, the hairy tallie protests with wild fury by upending the table they arm wrestled on and ripping out its legs. The other tallies calm their hairy friend down by reminding him he's a spoilsport and the dwarf raises his arms in victory. With the situation now calmed down to a moderate state of chaos, the tallies proceed to bond by wrestling chairs as if they're in a rodeo as the dwarf-curiously watches in the background, most likely trying to figure out what's wrong with all those crazy, cracker tallies.

To say the least, this movie needs to be seen to be believed. Just explaining it to someone doesn't give anywhere near the full effect. A definite recommend for the dwarf-curious but prepare to be disturbed long after watching.

> Gay bald dwarf with arms around drunk tallie.
> Gay dwarf with alien shaped forehead.
> Wife beater wearing gay dwarf.
> Tallie rubs gay dwarf's nipple on the outside of his wife beater.
> Gay dwarf refuses to kiss drunk, babbling tallie.
> Gay dwarf in background during shirtless arm wrestling.
> Gay dwarf acts as referee.
> Gay dwarf arm wrestles hairy tallie.
> Triumphant gay dwarf.
> Gay dwarf in background as tallies wrestle chairs.

Happy Gilmore (1996)

> Written by Tim Herlihy and Adam Sandler
> Directed by Dennis Dugan
> Starring Adam Sandler, Christopher McDonald, Julie Bowen, Frances Bay, Carl Weathers

Happy Gilmore (1996) is about an extremely temperamental ex-hockey player (Adam Sandler) who discovers he has a talent for golf and uses it to enter a tournament in the hopes of winning and saving his grandmother's house from foreclosure. It's not easy for him, though. He has a formidable adversary in Shooter McGavin (Christopher McDonald). Fortunately for Sandler he's got Carl Weathers on his side as his trainer, and when things get rough all he has to do is close his eyes and get himself in the zone by dreaming he's in a happy place: one with Julie

Bowen holding pitchers of beer and wearing sexy lingerie, and a waving dwarf in a cowboy outfit who slaps his own ass. If only more of us allowed ourselves to visit this heavenly zone on a regular basis, just imagine what a wonderful world it would truly be. Say what you want about Adam Sandler, no one can accuse him of not being a dwarf enthusiast.

>Ass slapping dwarf.
>Cowboy dwarf.
>Waving dwarf.
>Happy dwarf.

Hard Cash (2002)

>Written by Willie Dreyfus
>Directed by Predrag Antonijevic
>Starring Christian Slater
>Featured dwarf: Verne Troyer

Who can fault a movie that opens with a heist involving a "pregnant" woman who is really carrying Verne Troyer? The movie starts out looking like an exploitation classic with this stunt followed by Troyer popping out of a toilet with his mini gun. The downside is that Troyer then disappears until the end. The movie sinks without him in what would otherwise be my vote for worst movie of all time. When Troyer pops up back up, it's supposed to be a surprise he's in the bag. He jumps out and spices up the movie with some cheesy one liners and lame pervert talk that is amusing only because it's Verne Troyer delivering the lines. Worth watching but skip anything without Troyer.

>Dwarf in toilet.
>Mini gun for dwarf.
>Tallies carry dwarf around.
>Dwarf in water uses tallie body as lifeboat.
>Horny dwarf.
>Dwarf on weight balance.

Harry Potter and the Half-Blood Prince (2009)

>Written by Steve Kloves
>Directed by David Yates
>Starring Daniel Radcliffe, Rupert Grint, Emma Watson, Jim Broadbent
>Featured dwarf: Warwick Davis

Unfortunately there's barely anything to report here as far as dwarfsploitation is concerned. Warwick Davis only shows up long enough to walk past the students and utter only a few meaningless lines. It's an utter waste of an excellent dwarf.

>Dwarf with Hitler haircut and 'stache.
>Dwarf with weird black coat that covers his entire body.

Harry Potter and the Prisoner of Azkaban (2004)

>Written by Steve Kloves
>Directed by Alfonso Cuaron
>Featured dwarf: Warwick Davis

Unfortunately for this *Harry Potter*, series regular Warwick Davis gets even less screen time than usual. We get to see him only sparsely; once is a big entrance scene into Hogwarts where he's conducting the kids in song. His appearance is completely different from the look he had in the first installment, where he looked more like an old wizard. This time he looks more like a mini Charlie Chaplin with a bad haircut. We get nothing more than an ADR line over a scene where he is part of a group of teachers checking the school out for safety. There is one scene that doesn't involve Warwick's character but does feature other little people. Harry Potter is wearing an invisible cloak so that he can listen in on a conversation, and he ends up overhearing details about his parents' death. Upset, Harry runs outside and ends up busting through a group of little people who were out caroling. His friends see this and run after him. None of the three stop to check on the little people who were knocked over. Why couldn't these carolers be tallies? Why couldn't the little people be the ones who looked at the tallies on the ground in shock? Pure dwarfsploitation.

Dwarf carolers.
One line checking safety of school.
Dwarf conductor.
Dwarves knocked over by hero.
Hurt dwarves ignored.

Harry Potter and the Sorcerer's Stone (2001)

Screenplay by Steve Kloves
Directed by Chris Columbus
Starring Daniel Radcliffe, Emma Watson
Featured dwarves: Warwick Davis and Verne Troyer

There are very few fantasy films that can get by without employing a little person and the Harry Potter series is no exception. In this first installment, Harry is being taken into a bank where his parents have stashed piles of gold for him. The bank is run by "goblins" that mostly appear to be played by little people. The actual bank teller is played by Warwick Davis, in the first of two 1/2 roles. His goblin make up makes him unrecognizable other than by voice. Harry is then led by "Griphook," played by Verne Troyer, by railway to his locked away treasure. Troyer's "Griphook" is also weirdly dubbed over by Warwick Davis in a very Leprechaun-esque voice. Once Harry arrives at Hogwarts, we start to meet his fellow classmates and teachers. Among the teachers is Professor Flitwick, also played by Warwick Davis. We get one scene of Davis teaching spells, but otherwise he's relegated to crowd scenes, most commonly in the lunch room. At first look, I wasn't ready to call this dwarfsploitation but then the scene where Professor Flitwick is putting up the star on this MASSIVE Christmas tree came up and it somehow led to me thinking about the fact that none of these dwarf actors will be recognized for their work but for a few—may we make it more.

Dwarves in heavy make up.
Dwarf putting up ornaments.

Haunted Mansion (2003)

> Written by David Berenbaum
> Directed by Rob Minkoff
> Starring Eddie Murphy
> Featured dwarf: Deep Roy

When a husband and wife real estate team get a creepy message to come out and see an estate, they think nothing of it. When they see the place is attached to a cemetery and is insanely creepy looking, they think nothing of it. As punishment for being stupid, the place is haunted and their world is turned upside down. In one scene, Eddie and his kids are being taken by stagecoach through the cemetery and see ghosts galore. Oddly, with nearly every shot of ghosts there is at least one dwarf. There's no real reason to have more than one dwarf appearance but they give us plenty and they serve as nothing more than eye candy and adding to the weirdness of the moment.

> Dwarf drinking.
> Dwarf extras.

Hawk the Slayer (1980)

> Written by Harry Robertson and Terry Marcel
> Directed by Terry Marcel
> Starring Jack Palance
> Featured dwarf: Peter O'Farrell
> "Be still, ugly one."

At the time of writing this, IMDB actually has a decent rating for *Hawk*, but it may be my least favorite of all the movies I have sat through for this book. It could also be because Peter O'Farrell has become my least favorite dwarf actor. To the common man, they would likely not even realize O'Farrell is a dwarf. As if that wasn't enough, he does his typical shtick acting like a goofball. Granted, no one in this film does a good job acting-wise, even award winner Palance.

O'Farrell only gets a few scenes where he gets to do anything, but several scenes as scenery. I would not suggest this movie to anyone.

Tied up.
Shot at with burning arrows.
Diving into water.
Eats live fish.
Dwarf eating.
Dwarf fighting.
Dwarf on table.
Dwarf stabbed.

The Hebrew Hammer (2003)

Written and directed by Jonathan Kesselman
Starring Adam Goldberg, Andy Dick, Mario Van Peebles, Melvin Van Peebles
Featured dwarf: Tony Cox
"What are you little fucking midgets looking at?!"

This film is a Jewish version of the old blaxploitation films. It plays on everything from shots, to sound effects, to music, to even actors. The plot is simple. The heir to the Santa Claus throne (played by Andy Dick) has killed the current Santa Claus and is out to put an end to Chanukah. With Santa Claus, we of course get several little people playing the parts of elves. Right off the bat they are insulted by Andy Dick's character calling them midgets and little bitches, not to mention the fact we are treated to one little person who laughs at everything Andy Dick does (obviously, he's acting). Ah, but to make up for it all is the wonderful Tony Cox whose first line is, "What's up?" as he's dressed in casual elf wear with cool shades, smoking weed and a hot woman on each side. I think Tony's part would be considered more Blaxploitation than Dwarfsploitation but it certainly wouldn't be the same if it were a tallie playing his part (today they'd probably cast Ludacris). Tony is nothing short of hilarious as he drops the "N" word profusely and plays the womanizing, pot-smoking, black elf with ease. Tony's main goal in the movie is to be an elf but racist Andy Dick doesn't want any "colored midgets." Ironically they placed a dark skinned extra doing work behind Tony so the scene comes off more as a head scratcher. The movie has some real funny moments, but Tony Cox is the real stand out. It's worth checking out for any exploitation fan, but you will probably scoff at the jokes more than you'll laugh.

Elf giggling.
Referred to as midgets.
Referred to as little bitches.
Referred to as little brother.
Elf sweat shop.
Elf strike.
Referred to as little green fuck nuts.
Elves replaced by Taiwanese children.

The Hitchhiker's Guide to the Galaxy (2005)

Written by Douglas Adams and Karey Kirkpatrick
Directed by Garth Jennings
Starring Sam Rockwell, Martin Freeman, Mos Def and Alan Rickman
Featured dwarf: Warwick Davis

Based upon the classic book, this one features "Marvin," a robotic sidekick who is maniacally depressed. Bringing Marvin to life is Warwick Davis. Unfortunately for film fans everywhere, the voice is dubbed over by Alan Rickman. Although Rickman is a good choice, it's one of those things where it's obvious the actor is acting. Warwick does his best, slumping around but in the end it had me yearning for Warwick out of costume and saying the lines himself.

Dwarf in costume.
Dwarf without lines.

Hood of Horror (2006)

Written by Jacob Hair, Tim Sullivan, Chris Kobin, Jonathan McHugh
Directed by Stacy Title
Starring Snoop Dogg, Ernie Hudson, Danny Trejo
Featured dwarf: Gabriel Pimentel

A horror anthology brought to us by rapper Snoop Dogg would not be complete without the inclusion of a dwarf. Three "horror" tales are introduced by Snoop Dogg and as he introduces the first tale, he talks about how the place is filled with freaks, introducing a dwarf right before he introduces a guy without legs. Referring to the dwarf as "half pint," Snoop Dogg rambles on with some dialogue that looks like it's being read from cue cards, while the dwarf vomits off to the side. When Half Pint shows up again it's at Snoop Dogg's side, like his sidekick. Maybe the filmmakers figured out that one dwarf makes a better sidekick than two models? Nonetheless, in his second scene Half Pint vomits again. I'm still unclear about the purpose of the vomiting but it was so random and stupid that I kind of found myself liking it. During the end credits, Snoop Dogg does the equivalent of a music video with Half Pint now looking like the devil.

While it's great to see Gabriel Pimentel (from the Dwarfgasm of a film, *The Mini's* (2008)), the movie is just as bad as the title suggests.

> Referred to as "Half Pint."
> Dwarf flips off Snoop Dogg.
> Dwarf vomits.
> Referred to as "nasty little dude."
> Dwarf tugging on tallie's pants.
> Devil dwarf.

Howard the Duck (1986)

> Written by Willard Huyck, Gloria Katz
> Directed by Willard Huyck
> Starring Lea Thompson, Tim Robbins, Jeffery Jones
> Featured dwarf: Ed Gale
> "This is obviously no place for an intelligent, sensitive duck."

Don't believe the haters. And believe me, there's plenty of them out there. Every year there are at least a handful I have to defend this movie against whenever it's brought up in conversation. But I never hesitate to vocalize my affection for this movie. I still retain the fond memories I have of riding my bike to the theatre multiple times, traveling across miles of danger to see this movie. Even for all the haters and pretentious fucks out there, there are many reasons to watch this film.

The first, of course, would be the dwarf inside the duck suit. Among the many other reasons are the ultra-hot Lea Thompson crawling around in

The legendary Ed Gale (*Howard the Duck*, 1986), stands tall next to co-author Chris Watson.

her underwear, getting to see how Tim Robbins has grown as an actor over the years by seeing his performance in this film, Jeffrey Jones as the creepy villain (well that certainly fits), space creatures, duck boobs, a duck rock and roll show, the list goes on. Sure, *Howard the Duck* (1986) was a bomb financially and it's a cheese fest, but it still to this day remains incredibly enjoyable, and I'm proud to say I've talked to several other fans out there who feel the same way. I believe, as of now, I've met just about as many

Howard the Duck (1986) supporters as I have haters. As with many movies, people either love or hate; there are very few in-between opinions.

As for myself, I remain a fan of the cigar-chomping, beer-swilling, human female skirt-chasing little guy.

- Parody posters of famous Hollywood movies featuring duck dwarves.
- Silhouette of duck dwarf drinking beer.
- Playboy parody magazine featuring a naked duck dwarf.
- Topless duck dwarf nudity in bathtub.
- Duck dwarf smokes cigar.
- Exploitative commercials featuring duck dwarves (my favorite stars Crazy Webbie).
- Planet of duck dwarves.
- Duck dwarf flies through space in his lounging chair.
- Duck dwarf thrown out of bar.
- Duck dwarf beaten by homeless woman.
- Duck dwarf feels up woman's thigh in alley.
- Duck dwarf chased by butch biker gang.
- Duck dwarf bitch-slapped by butch biker.
- Duck dwarf hides in barrel.
- Duck dwarf unleashes quack-fu on street thugs.
- Duck dwarf being taken into Lea Thompson's place like a pet after being left out in the rain.
- Lea Thompson tries to feed duck dwarf milk out of a bowl.
- Human beer looks massive in duck dwarf's hands.
- Snoring duck dwarf.
- Lea Thompson finds mini, opened condom in duck dwarf's wallet.
- Duck dwarf carried around in garbage bag.
- Duck dwarf scares children.
- Duck dwarf is discriminated against while applying for a job.
- Duck dwarf works as a towel duck in a smut spa.
- Duck dwarf is thrown into a dirty hot tub at the smut spa and told to clean out a plugged jet.
- Duck dwarf plays the piano and dances around like an idiot.
- Duck dwarf sexually harassed by Lea Thompson.
- Duck dwarf is stripped down to his underwear by the police.
- Duck dwarf referred to as a pet.

Waitress at restaurant attempts to serve duck dwarf fried eggs.
Duck dwarf threatens rowdy bar patrons with space rabies.
Duck dwarf hoisted in the air and carried by a hungry diner mob.
Duck dwarf almost loses his duck balls to meat cleaver.
Duck dwarf framed next to a giant fowl statue in "Kiddieland."
Duck dwarf flies a mini-plane.
Duck dwarf opens door with a roundhouse kick.
Duck dwarf fires giant laser at dark overlord and his peers.
Duck dwarf does a shitty impression of a dark overlord.
Duck dwarf plays guitar to a packed concert, rocks out and rips off Chuck Berry with his dance moves.

Hundra (1983)

Written by John F. Goff and Jose Truchado
Directed by Matt Cimber
Starring Laurene Landon
"I have no purpose with you, little man."

Hundra (1983) starts out like a replica female "Conan," just a tad stranger. We're introduced to her village, which is filled with women. One woman has just given birth, but to another damned female. Luckily for the village, they have one manly woman in Hundra, who goes out to provide food for them, but she has no interest in men. However, while she's out hunting, the village is attacked (remember *Conan the Barbarian* (1982) and *Beastmaster* (1982) and numerous others?) and she ends up the only one left from her village. At the beginning of her journey she goes to see an old, wise woman. It's very odd because the woman welcomes Hundra but outside the cave, conveniently sitting are a bunch of dwarves who don't seem to like Hundra. One is sitting on a small pony, eyeing her. Others are sitting on rocks. When she leaves the cave, there is a faceoff with one dwarf who has a strange, devil-like pitch fork. After getting into an unwanted fight with that unnecessarily angry dwarf, another one literally jumps her.

The movie begins very normal despite its *Hell Comes to Frogtown* (1988) subplot of impregnating women. However, once the dwarves show up, it's all downhill. The filmmakers actually go straight from her fighting the dwarves to an unnecessary scene of the beautiful Hundra sunbathing. Given that this movie is frequently shot in a very artistic way makes me think the filmmakers thought they were making something wonderful, but anything wonderful goes downhill once the dwarves show up. It is not that it's the dwarves fault—it's obviously in the writing, which is non-existent.

> Dwarf on pony.
> Dwarves sitting on rocks.
> Dwarf grunting noises.
> Angry dwarf.
> Dwarf falls off pony.
> Dwarf arms in air.
> Dwarf spared.
> Dwarf jumps off cliff, slides down rocks.

The Hunting Party (2007)

> Written and directed by Richard Shepard
> Starring Richard Gere, Terrence Howard
> Featured dwarf: Zdravko Kocevar
> "Oh, shit, I'm staring at the midget!"

In this underrated film, Richard Gere is a down-on-his-luck reporter who goes in search of a war criminal no one else can find. When they see his supposed trademark line of orange cars, they take off after them. Unfortunately, it's not only not who they are looking for, but other guys with large guns. As they are about to shoot the reporters, one of them recognizes Gere as an old friend. After they exchange some banter, Gere walks over to Terrence Howard and tells him, "Whatever you do, don't stare at the midget." Soon enough, a little person steps out of a car and goes up to greet Gere by grabbing his crotch.

The little person scene is short, no pun intended, but livens up a very good film. The little person has enough of an effect that at the end of the film, they have to point out that he was a real person.

> Dwarf greets by grabbing balls.
> Greedy dwarf.
> Gere twice dwarf's size.
> Referred to as "Midget."
> "Fucking greedy midget."

The Ice Pirates (1984)

Written by Stewart Raffill and Standford Sherman
Directed by Stewart Raffill
Starring Robert Urich, Mary Crosby, Michael D. Roberts, Anjelica Huston, John Matuszak
"Will somebody please tell me that what I think just happened really did?"

In space, water is more precious than booze to broke writers obsessed with dwarves in cinema. Apparently, it's also more important than giving dwarves a sizeable role. I had to wait nearly halfway through the film before I saw a dwarf and even then it just turned out to be a glorified cameo. I was thinking of counting the little robots in the movie as dwarf robots but that would be cheating the reader. This movie is just downright piss-poor in its lack of dwarf screen time. So much potential and all of it wasted. Think how great the movie would have been as "Mini Ice Pirates." The film's not a total wash, I guess. There's Angelica Houston in a crazy-ass bondage outfit; I haven't decided whether that's a good thing or a bad thing, but it certainly satisfies a curiosity to see it, and then there's Ron Perlman as a space pirate. First *Quest For Fire,* and now this? How old is that guy anyway? And then there's the classic scene with the metal gonad remover with huge jaws. I remember being freaked out by the ball-removing machine the same way I was the first time I saw the *Serpent and the Rainbow* (1988) and that evil bastard put a spike through Bill Pullman's sack. Truly, one of the most disturbing scenes preserved in celluloid.

Ice Pirates (1984) is an okay film with some funny moments but as dwarfsploitation it's inexcusable. Wake up, producers. It's a space movie. There are limitless possibilities for dwarves. Oh well, maybe in the sequel…

> Dwarf waitress carried oversized serving tray.
> Dwarf waitress exploited by working in crappy space restaurant.
> That's it. I know. Sad isn't it?

I Hope They Serve Beer In Hell (2009)

>Written by Tucker Max, Nils Parker
>Directed by Bob Gosse
>Starring Matt Czuchry, Geoff Stults, Jesse Bradford, and Keri Lynn Pratt
>Featured dwarf: Bridget Powers
>"He sacrificed his line in the sand for you and you couldn't sacrifice a midget vagina for him?"

I was not expecting the dwarf treats I got from this one. In fact, I wasn't expecting to see any dwarves at all. I hadn't planned on doing any work on this book the night I watched this film. I simply planned on relaxing and checking out a smaller scale, quirky movie I had heard some good things about. The positive comments on the film were well deserved but I did not see the dwarf curve ball that was about to be thrown my way later on in the film.

Toward the film's climax, a dwarf stripper played by porn star "Bridget the Midget" aka Bridget Powers (as she's credited here) treats us to a topless strip show. This is an absolute must-see for both the dwarf-curious and the dwarf completist alike, although more for the dwarf-curious, if you get my drift. Powers clearly got a boob job before this movie was filmed and I'd personally like to shake the hand of the doctor who performed the surgery because the twins look amazing here. Struggling to pull myself back from dwarfgasm, little did I know another surprise was about to be in store for me: dwarf/tallie sex with circus music playing in the background. Brilliant, absolutely brilliant. The film even brought a tear to my eye as, after the tallie convinced the dwarf to take him home with her, she wraps her dwarf fingers around his pinkie and walks him to the exit in what has to be one of the most beautiful moments since the walking into the sunset shot at the end of *Casablanca* (1942). You'll have to stick it out for most of the film before these cinematic gems are revealed, but it's certainly worth it. That is, if you're a guy and you're watching it alone or with your guy friends.

Do not even attempt to watch this with your girlfriend as it contains some of the most misogynistic one-liners ever committed to film, which the lead tallie hero of course gets away with because women find him attractive. Even though the film seems to apologize for itself halfway through (most likely the deciding factor in the film getting financed and finished), your girlfriend will still most likely be pissed at you for showing it to her. You single guys can feel free to laugh your asses off, though. Kudos to dwarf-obsessed writer Tucker Max for bringing the sex appeal of dwarves to Hollywood in strong form. We salute you and hope your love of dwarves spreads to the masses.

> Memorable lines from dwarf obsessed tallie:
> "How many people do you know who have fucked a midget? Don't you think that's awesome?"
> "The beer bottle looked massive in her tiny little hands and all I could think about was how big those hands would make my penis look."
> Tallie refers to dwarf stripper as a midget princess.
> Gap toothed dwarf.
> Madonna-looking dwarf.
> Tattooed dwarf.
> Dwarf takes tallie's pinkie in her hand and guides him out the door.
> Drinking dwarf.
> Pigtailed dwarf.
> Dwarf in hot stripper outfit.
> Topless dwarf.
> Tallie/dwarf sex.
> Circus music plays during tallie/dwarf sex.
> Dwarf stripper referred to as having sausage fingers.

The Imaginarium of Dr. Parnassus (2009)

> Written by Terry Gilliam and Charles McKeown
> Directed by Terry Gilliam
> Starring Heath Ledger, Johnny Depp, Jude Law, and Christopher Plummer
> Featured dwarf: Verne Troyer
> "I certainly don't know what that is!"

Dr. Parnassus travels around with his imaginarium to the delight of others as he guides selected audience members' imaginations. The set up is very circus-like and made more so by the inclusion of dwarf actor Verne Troyer as Percy.

While the movie drags on, the highlight is definitely Troyer. The conversations between Percy and Parnassus about how he should get a midget are priceless. However, it's not nearly as priceless as the scene where they are performing and Troyer is in black face. A sympathetic woman runs towards the stage, wanting to take care of the little black boy.

It's great that Gilliam brought Troyer back after his near-extra role in *Fear and Loathing in Las Vegas* (1998) to play a much larger and substantial role. Through most of the film, Troyer is the Dr. Parnassus' confidant, almost as if they were intentionally trying to make up for the dwarfsploitation they were doing. Kudos to a well balanced dwarf role!

> Fart noises.
> Dwarf in stupid outfit.
> Tossed dwarf.
> Referred to as "wee man."
> Dwarf kicks tallie.
> Dwarf growls.
> Dwarf driver.
> Dwarf acting like monkey.
> Dwarf has small bed.
> Dwarf with cane.
> Dwarf muted.
> Dwarf in basket.
> Describing midget.
> Dwarf fires cannon.
> Dwarf whips tallie.
> Dwarf in black face.
> Dwarf patted on head.
> Dwarf on stairs.
> "Perhaps you'll find a midget, if you're lucky."—Percy
> "What would I do without you?"—Parnassus
> "Get a midget?"—Percy

The Impossible Kid (1982)

Story by Cora Caballes
Screenplay by Greg Macabenta
Directed by Eddie Nicart

Starring Weng Weng, Nina Sara, Rene Romero
Featured dwarf: Weng Weng

Foreign terrorists continuously kidnap people and try to get a ransom—if they don't get the ransom, they kill them. They run into a problem when Interpol Agent 00 takes the case. He not only solves the case, but kicks ass along the way.

The Impossible Kid (1982) is one of those movies that would be horrible if it weren't for the fact a little person was playing the lead. It's a simple and thin action movie plot that offers us the chance to see the legendary Weng Weng in action. What we see is Weng Weng doing most of the things that I have dreamed of seeing a little person do; make out with hot nude women, doing stunts with a small motorcycle, firing a large machine gun, jumping off buildings, repeatedly committing crotch violence, etc.

While it doesn't have nearly as many great dialogue moments as *For Y'ur Height Only* (1981), it's got better visuals than that flick. Beyond-classic moments in this film include a fight scene with Weng Weng trying to practice Karate, a mini-motorcycle chase scene, the villain's maniacal laughing, a shoot out with Weng Weng using a large machine gun and a miniature boat explosion. However, the jumping off the building scene is better in *For Y'ur Height Only* (1981) due to the fact Weng Weng kisses the girl before jumping—in this one, he just leaves her topless.

This is a dwarf film that can't be missed by any means. You must see this. It is a prerequisite in Dwarf Movies 101.

Weng Weng walking down street.
Weng Weng hides behind fire hydrant.
Weng Weng looking up.
Weng Weng lowered down building by rope.
Weng Weng sees showering woman through glass.
Weng Weng smiles when he sees nude couple.
Weng Weng kisses nude stranger.
A bed is enough cover for Weng Weng.
Weng Weng trips baddie.
Weng Weng kicks baddie in the crotch.
Weng Weng on mini-motorcycle.
Weng Weng on mini-motorcycle telling baddies to "Pull over."

Weng Weng leaps off of truck onto baddies.
Weng Weng does double crotch stomp.
Weng Weng hides under truck nearly standing up.
Weng Weng comes up to the doorknob on door.
Secretary grabs and kisses Weng Weng.
Weng Weng has to reach high for elevator button.
"What the hell is this boy doing in here?"
Weng Weng tossed by multiple tallies.
Weng Weng flips over.
Weng Weng continues his crotch violence streak.
Weng Weng hides in cart.
Weng Weng sits on desktop.
Weng Weng hides in trash can.
Weng Weng looking out of trash can.
Weng Weng comes out of "bag of money."
Weng Weng commits more crotch violence.
Weng Weng hides behind trash can.
Weng Weng kisses and then winks at hot secretary.
Weng Weng leaning against counter.
Weng Weng leaps off building onto man in dress.
Weng Weng knocked over by man in dress.
Weng Weng beats up man in dress.
Weng Weng ducks from grenade explosion.
Weng Weng doing karate exercises.
Weng Weng attacked while doing karate exercises—fights woman, crotch shots, thrown across the floor, rolls.
Weng Weng jumps on table.
Weng Weng steals sheet from naked woman and uses it as a parachute to jump off building.
Weng Weng scooped up by fat hairy guy who calls him a "Pretty boy."
Weng Weng climbs up using a branch.
Weng Weng uses a wire to get across.
Snake thrown on Weng Weng.
Weng Weng at shooting range.
Weng Weng leaning against table.
Referred to as "midget."
Weng Weng waving at bad guys.
Weng Weng drinking Coke at bar.

Weng Weng kissed by waitress.
Weng Weng hides behind vehicle.
Massage girls enamored with Weng Weng.
"Hey, minors aren't allowed in here."
"Sorry, sir. I didn't know you were an adult."
Weng Weng uses pole to fight.
Weng Weng uses pole to hit tallies in the crotch.
Weng Weng uses pole to pole vault to next level.
Weng Weng walks on high wire.
Comes out of shoot onto motorcycle.
Leaps onto bug to start fight.
Kicks baddie in the face from on top of car.
Weng Weng caged up.
"What are we going to do with the midget?"
Referred to as "pet canary."
Wet Weng Weng.
Weng Weng using large machine gun.
Weng Weng jumping on table while firing machine gun.
Weng Weng kicks woman and then kisses her.
Weng Weng beats up woman and leave her to burn.
Weng Weng hiding in suitcase.
Last crotch violence.
Weng Weng jumps on car to make out with hottie.
Weng Weng waving and kissing.

In Bruges (2007)

Written and Directed by Martin McDonagh
Starring Colin Farrell, Brendan Gleeson and Ralph Fiennes
Featured dwarf: Jordan Prentice
"What are they doing over there? They're filming something… they're filming midgets!"

When Colin Farrell and Brendan Gleeson are told to take it easy in Bruges, Belgium after Farrell's character accidentally kills a young boy during a hit gone bad, they run into an American Dwarf actor (Jordan Prentice) who is also an angry racist. From there on out, things just keep getting crazier and crazier. Farell won a Golden Globe for his performance and is responsible for several of the film's memorable midget insults, which include, "Would you ever think about killing yourself because you're a midget?," "Back off, shorty," and "Short ass!" And that's just what he says in front of the dwarf!

In Bruges (2007) is not only a fine piece of filmmaking but also a prime piece of dwarfsploitation. Earning Colin Farell the Golden Globe, *In Bruges* (2007) is a landmark in dwarfsploitation history alone for how it explores the topic of why dwarves commit suicide and features a lengthy speech given by a coked-out dwarf about how all the blacks and whites will be in a race war one day, topped off by how all the white midgets and blacks midgets will also be in that same race war one day.

> Dwarf drinks with both hands around giant cup.
> Reinforcing of the angry dwarf stereotype.
> Dwarf under the table grabbing drinks as his head is barely visible over the top of the bar.
> Dwarf jumps down from table in a long shot.
> Dwarf has arguably the most racist line in the movie, "You don't know how much shit I've had to take off of black midgets, man!"
> Dwarf has epic monologue about black and white midgets being in a race war with each other one day.
> Dwarf wears funny little schoolboy outfit.
> Dwarf's character is cast in a movie specifically for a dream sequence.

In the Soup (1992)

> Written by Alexandre Rockwell and Sollace Mitchell
> Directed by Alexandre Rockwell
> Starring Steve Buscemi
> Featured Dwarf: Michael J. Anderson
> "You see a gorilla, you see a midget…"

Winner of the Grand Jury Price at 1992's Sundance Film Festival, this one is a black and white film starring Steve Buscemi as a wannabe filmmaker. He ends up hooking up with a crooked producer who at one point starts saying, "You see a gorilla, you see a midget…," and then we see Buscemi in a scene with a gorilla and a dwarf in clown makeup. Much like *The Hunting Party* (2007), the dwarf grabs the crotch of Steve Buscemi (I guess that's what they'd reach). The scene is too short and the *Twin Peaks* star is wasted.

> Dwarf in clown make-up.
> Referred to as a "midget."
> Dwarf grabs balls.

Invaders from Mars (1986)

> Story by Richard Blake
> Screenplay by Dan O'Bannon and Don Jakoby
> Directed by Tobe Hooper
> Starring Karen Black and Timothy Bottoms
> Featured dwarves: Tony Cox, Debbie Lee Carrington, Salvatore Fondacaro, Margarita Fernandez, Phil Fondacaro

Through the eyes of a kid, we see aliens slowly take over a town. With the aid of a nurse, played by Karen Black, and his dad's General friend, they try to put an end to it. In it, we get several dwarf actors playing "drones."

Why is it that all of the all-star dwarf films have the actors in costumes? Why couldn't Tony Cox play the General and Debbie Lee Carrington play the nurse? It's a waste of talent. Wouldn't it be a classic film if Tony Cox had blown away some aliens? How did they see all these talented actors show up and no one thought to give them an additional role? Potential dwarfgasm wasted.

> Dwarves without lines.
> Dwarves in costumes.

Island of Dr. Moreau (1996)

> Written by Richard Stanley and Ron Hutchinson
> Directed by John Frankenheimer
> Starring Marlon Brando

Featured dwarf: Nelson de la Rosa
"Look at him!"

Ratman's Nelson de la Rosa, weighing in at 22 pounds at the time of filming, plays Marlon Brando's sidekick "Majai" in this infamously bad film. As if Brando's over the top performance weren't enough, they threw Nelson into most of the shots featuring Brando. The size differential of the bloated Brando wearing mostly muumuu outfits and the smallest man alive (at the time) is breathtaking. We are introduced to Nelson as he strangely washes Dr. Moreau's head, perhaps setting up all the weirdness to come. In another strange yet beautiful moment, we are treated to Brando playing a grand piano with Nelson and a mini piano on top of that one. The shots are perfect for this fascinating yet pointless scene. It's there just for the pure weirdness of it all. While Nelson and Brando's moments are priceless, the movie is pure crap. It is worth fast forwarding to any scene featuring Nelson but not worth a watch for any other reason.

Size differential.
Slave dwarf.
Tallie doesn't want to shake dwarf hand.
Smaller piano.
Smaller glass at dinner table.
Dwarf nudity.

Kill Bill: Volume 2 (2004)

Written and Directed by Quentin Tarantino
Starring Uma Thurman, David Carradine, Michael Madsen,
    Daryl Hannah
Featured dwarf: Clark Middleton
"Get me out of this hole!"

You would think that for as eccentric as he is, Tarantino would make more use of dwarves, but unfortunately, a dwarf is only given a short role as Michael Madsen's buddy who helps him bury "The Bride" alive. In true dwarfsploitation fashion, we don't see the dwarf when he first appears. All we see instead is a shovel digging in a grave and dirt flying out of it. Then, we hear the voice of the dwarf in question (Clark Middleton) complaining and yelling at Michael Madsen to help get him out of the hole he's dug for Uma Thurman. The next scene with the dwarf is where he and Michael Madsen stand over the defeated Uma Thurman as they're about to bury her. Madsen asks his dwarf buddy in a vulgar way if she's the hottest blond girl he's ever seen and the dwarf is quick to disagree as he drinks from an oversized beer, oozing of redneck degeneracy. And of course, the dwarf in question is right.

Uma is attractive, especially in that spandex, superhero-style outfit of hers she wears when slaying people, but the hottest blond woman out there would have to be Debbie Lee Carrington. True dwarf enthusiasts know that there is nothing hotter than when she wore that sexy hooker outfit in *Total Recall* (1990) and blasted away at the Mars Colony troopers with a Franchi LF57. Clearly, this is what was running through dwarf actor Clark Middleton's mind as he was looking down at Uma Thurman and thinking about just who the hottest blond really was. The dwarf adds a lot of personality and life to *Kill Bill Volume 2* (2004), which is why it's such a shame he isn't in more of the movie. I really would have loved to have seen the movie revolve around Madsen and his dwarf buddy for at least a few more scenes. But I guess this was just the dwarf working that great dwarf magic for me.

> Dwarf unseen as he digs grave.
> Dwarf stuck in grave.
> Tallie lifts dwarf out of grave.
> Dwarf senses "The Bride's" anger.
> Dwarf drinks oversized beer.
> Redneck dwarf.
> Dwarf mocks "The Bride" before her burial.
> "Get me out of this hole!'

Killer Klowns From Outer Space (1988)

> Written by Charles Chiodo, Stephen Chiodo
> Directed by Stephen Chiodo
> Starring Grant Cramer, Suzanne Snyder, John Allen Nelson, Rayal Dano, John Vernon
> "What are you gonna do with those pies, boys?"

This is a classic B-movie made back in the day when low budget was considered to be in the low couple of millions. This is a great, fun B-movie and I'm surprised they haven't gotten around to making a sequel yet. It ages well and makes me yearn for the heyday of the 80's B-movie. Unfortunately, it wasn't *Killer Dwarf Clowns from Outer Space*, but the filmmakers were smart enough to include a killer dwarf clown as one of the ensemble.

The killer dwarf clown has a couple of great scenes. There's one where he walks into a pharmacy and plays with all the supplies. He sprays shaving cream on a tallie killer clown's face then inhales a powder right in front of the pharmacist on duty who stares on in great confusion. The killer clowns also sound like Ewoks when they talk to each other (I wonder if this was meant as a nod to George Lucas' Ewok dwarves). However, the greatest scene with the killer dwarf clown occurs when he's confronted by a biker gang while riding a mini bicycle with large handlebars. The gang reinforces the frightening biker stereotype as they insult and mock the dwarf killer clown, followed by smashing up his bike. The killer dwarf clown fights off a tear and composes himself long enough to punch the tallie responsible's head clean off his shoulders. And all while wearing boxing gloves! What a powerful, killer dwarf clown! Other killer dwarf clown scenes include the little guy holding a trampoline below a hot girl's window and being one of many killer clowns to exit a car.

The two scenes that really won me over though, included the killer dwarf clown using a pie as a deadly throwing weapon as well as a little, yellow bat. There was just something about seeing that killer dwarf clown go after tallies while wielding that bat that reminded me of a dwarfish Jack Nicholson during his axe-wielding rage in *The Shining*. Brilliant, Chiodo brothers, brilliant! Now, please give us the sequel, "*Killer Dwarf Clowns From Outer Space.*" That's not too much to ask for, is it?

>Killer clowns talk like Ewoks.
>Killer dwarf clown plays in pharmacy.
>Sneezing killer dwarf clown.
>Killer dwarf clown rides mini bike.
>Biker gang messes with killer dwarf clown.
>Killer dwarf clown cries over smashed mini bike.
>Killer dwarf clown punches tallie biker's head off.
>Killer dwarf clown holds trampoline at the bottom of hot chick's house.

> Killer dwarf clown gets out of clown car.
> Deadly pie throwing dwarf clown.
> Killer dwarf clown closes in on tallie human wielding yellow baseball bat.
> Dwarf clown laughs at death.

Kiltro (2006)

> Written and directed by Ernesto Diaz Espinoza
> Starring Marko Zaror
> Featured dwarf: Roberto Avendano
> "I'm old and I'm a dwarf."

When I first started watching *Kiltro* (2006) it was mere curiosity. I wasn't planning on watching the entire film but in the very beginning of the film there's a dwarf master type who comes out with a cane, a wise man's beard and a mask. It seemed so pointless I had to stick around and watch some more. He shows back up briefly about 30 minutes in and by that time I was sold—*Kiltro* (2006) is a Chilean martial arts movie that is a lot of fun, both humorous and action packed. Sure, it has cheesy moments but it packs an entertaining punch.

When the hero of the film (played by Marko Zaror) is beaten senseless, the wise dwarf (reminiscent of a samurai master or Yoda) approaches and touches his head. Cut to the next scene and the dwarf, "Nik Nak," explains everything—how he was the master of his father and so on.

The highlight of the film comes as the baddies attack the dwarf shack that is built amongst the rocks. As one baddie moves near, dwarf legs come out of nowhere to kick him in the head. It's brief and that's literally all you get but it's a hoot to watch, just like the whole film. Dwarf time is sparse but it's worth a look.

> Dwarf with cane.
> Dwarf with makeup.
> Dwarf walking with cane.
> Dwarf master.
> Dwarf plays with fire.
> Dwarf throws bag.
> Dwarf in hammock.

Kiss of the Vampire (2009)

>Written by Kat Hawks
>Directed by Joe Tornatore
>Starring Gary Daniels, Matthias Hues, Martin Kove
>Featured dwarf: Phil Fondacaro

I found *Kiss of the Vampire* (2009) as part of a massive research hunt for dwarf films. I did not realize it was a movie that I had heard of, but under the title *Immortally Yours*. The reason this film had stuck in my mind is its awesome cast, a real film geek's wet dream; Martin Kove, Gary Daniels, Matthias Hues and little person legend Phil Fondacaro. With a cast like that, it has to at least be fun, right? What went from excitement quickly fell to pure dread—this movie is beyond awful. They play the filming of the movie very, very safe—meaning there's lots of motionless dialogue scenes. The scenery is nice with some good locations but everything else about it stinks. It's rare that I feel sorry for actors but I even felt sorry for the amateur actors on this one. I'm guessing they paid well and I hope they all paid their rent but I would avoid this one despite the great cast.

Fondacaro plays a tallie's bitch as he tags along with the "good" vampire. When Fondacaro is threatened, a woman defends him by saying, "Don't treat him like he's some sort of animal," and she goes to say that he shouldn't do this because he's a decent, loyal friend to the tallie. I guess if he weren't it would be okay since he's small? This movie is a waste of talent and your time.

>Dwarf with torch.
>Dwarf going down stairs.
>Dwarf has hard time looking over hospital bed.
>Dwarf stands on chair.
>Dwarf sits at tallie's side.
>Dwarf sleeping.
>"Who and what is this?"—Tallie asking about dwarf.
>Dwarf referred to as "Little creature."
>Dwarf running.
>Dwarf lifted up by the tallies because he's too slow.
>Dwarf headbutts tallie.
>Dwarf sits on desk.

Kung Fu Killer (2008)

Written by David Seidler, John Mandel, Jacqueline Feather
Directed by Philip Spink
Starring David Carradine, Cheng Pei Pei

The main reason to watch this made-for-TV movie is to see legends David Carradine and Cheng Pei Pei share screen time. While it is unfortunately brief, it was worth it. To make this one better is the addition of a dwarf actor! While he isn't given much to do, he does get a brief dance number that helps keep the movie going. It's a rather strange addition to a kung fu TV movie, but how often do you get to see David Carradine act while a dwarf in the background screws in lightbulbs?

> Given high five.
> Has to get the girls ready.
> Dwarf does handstand.
> Dwarf with fake mustache.
> Dwarf laughed at.
> Dwarf doing dance.
> Dwarf without lines.
> Dwarf screws in lightbulbs.
> Dwarf with bow tie.

Labyrinth (1986)

Written by Terry Jones
Directed by Jim Henson
Starring David Bowie, Jennifer Connelly, Shelley Thompson, Christopher Malcolm
Featured dwarf: Shari Weiser

Contrary to several rumors that have been floating around throughout the years, it was not a dwarf that was stuffed in David Bowie's pants for this film. But whatever was jammed in there was about that size of the dwarf from *The Island of Doctor Moreau* (1996). And whatever it was, it certainly was creepy, especially for a kids' movie. All creepiness aside, this is a great movie and one that employed several dwarves yet refused to show their faces. This is a crime several other dwarf movies are sadly guilty of as well. In *Labyrinth* (1986), dwarf appreciators George Lucas and Jim Henson teamed up to create a fantasy movie with Jennifer Connelly, where several dwarves play part of the goblin corps as well as the self-loathing dwarf-goblin Hoggle, who is played by Shari Weiser. She's listed as a suit performer and the end result is very similar to what we saw in the *The Garbage Pail Kids Movie* (1987): a dwarf inside of a suit which appears to be a large, freakish puppet and yet moves in a more natural, human fashion.

In the movie, Connelly plays a spoiled rich kid who feels neglected and summons the help of goblins (some played by dwarves and some puppets) to get rid of her baby brother. The goblins are more than happy to oblige, and cast her into the goblin kingdom (the ruler of which is played by the formerly-mentioned, makeup-drenched, pants-stuffed David Bowie). The first time we see dwarf-goblin Hoggle he's urinating. Connelly asks for his help to navigate the labyrinth and he instead ignores her and shoots innocent looking fairies (which are actually evil, biting little bastards) with a spray gun, keeping a body count as he goes along. The other dwarves in the film are part of Bowie's goblin corps. All have visually interesting outfits and some ride on crazy-looking dragon puppets. The goblin corps' dwarves are mixed with puppets in the film.

Henson does a good job of mixing dwarves and puppets in the movie and giving everything a sense of visual cohesion. Such a seamless combining of technology hasn't been seen since Peter Jackson's *Lord of the Rings* trilogy where CGI was mixed with practical effects. However, this *Labyrinth* (1986) gives us a much more impressive product because there are actually real dwarves here instead of Fabio actors shrunk down via post only to serve as cheap impressions of the real and much better thing.

> Goblin dwarves under Connelly's bed.
> Urinating dwarf goblin.
> Fairy-killing dwarf-goblin.
> Singing and dancing dwarves.
> Dwarf-goblin distracted by crappy, plastic jewelry.
> Dwarf-goblin grovels at tallie master's knees.
> Coward dwarf-goblin.
> Horned creature fights goblin corps dwarves.
> Dwarf-goblin kissed by Jennifer Connelly.
> Horned creature sits on dwarf-goblin.

Betraying dwarf-goblin.
Self loathing dwarf-goblin.
Dwarf-goblin jumps on metal guard.
Dragon puppet riding dwarves.
Dancing dwarf-goblins.

Land of the Dead (2005)

Written and Directed by George A. Romero
Starring John Leguizamo, Asia Argento, Simon Baker, and Dennis Hopper
Featured dwarf: Phil Fondacaro
"You'll be my friend when you get my car back or I'll have to carry you outside of here in that fucking hat!"

George Romero makes his zombie comeback with an okay movie that's not nearly the classic *Night of the Living Dead* (1968) or *Dawn of the Dead* (1978). *Land of the Dead* (2005) is filled with lots of zombie clichés and Romero wears his politics on his sleeve with his Dennis Hopper character and his approach to greed and zombie control. There is some great gore and some cool concepts though, and tallie Asia Argento is at her prime here as well. As soon as legendary dwarf actor Phil Fondacaro showed up, a brand new enthusiasm swept through my body. "This movie could really be something," I thought to myself. After all, here was a scene where there was illegal fighting with humans against zombies and then on the other side of the club, there was a dwarf dressed to the nines in what appeared to be a pimp outfit with a flashy purple suit complete with a feather in the cap. There are few things more awesome than seeing a dwarf dressed to the nines in a pimp suit, complete with a feather in the cap.

Unfortunately, our little friend is hardly even in the movie at all. The main character, a tallie played by Simon Baker, comes into the shady club and finds our pimp dwarf, who he's clearly had bad dealings with in the past. The tallie bullies and threatens the pimp dwarf in attempts to get his car back. Yeah, try that against Chucky, pal! The tallie even goes so far as to hoist Fondacaro up in the air so as to put on display the fact that he means business. Clearly this doesn't register very well with pimp dwarf, because as soon as the tallie walks away, pimp dwarf finds his gun, and he finds it very fast. Pimp dwarf is pretty cold blooded and doesn't wait very long after the tallie turns his back before taking a shot at him. Perhaps this adverse reaction was because of the way the tallie threatened the pimp dwarf at the club and diminished his street cred in front of everyone. Chaos ensues, and one of the tallie's friends, a slow minded sharpshooter, sets his sights on the dwarf.

Then, we get the best dwarfsploitation moment in the film as we see the dwarf's head running behind a fence, and then... no more dwarf. It was sad, yet beautiful. I only wish Romero would have put a spin on the zombie genre and allowed the dwarf to be part of the tallie's team because the few moments he's in the film are a treat to watch.

> Dwarf with flashy suit and cowboy hat.
> Tallie lifts up dwarf.
> Dwarf bellies up to the bar.
> Dwarf stashes gun in suit.
> Dwarf shoots at tallie's back.
> Dwarf in sights of tallie's rifle.
> Dwarf's head tries to escape tallie's gun through fence.
> Tallie shoots dwarf in head.
> "Someone shot the little fat man."

Leprechaun (1993)

> Written and Directed by Mark Jones
> Starring: Warwick Davis, Jennifer Aniston
> Featured dwarf: Warwick Davis
> "Try as they will and try as they might, who steals me gold
>   won't live through the night!"

Yes, my friends this is the movie that started it all. And I'm not talking about Jennifer Aniston's career either. I'm talking about one of the greatest dwarf franchises ever: the *Leprechaun* series! The plot revolves around a man who foolishly tries to steal the leprechaun dwarf's gold and pays dearly for it, although not before he's able to lock the dwarf in a crate and secure it with a four leaf clover. As we learn in this series, the four leaf clover is like kryptonite to evil leprechaun dwarves. And then, of course... ten years later the house is bought by a new family (clearly the realtor didn't give them full disclosure on the place before buying) with a pouty, materialistic, yet super-hot teenager (Jennifer Aniston) and, as we know from watching countless teenagers over the years in horror movies, it never takes too long before they do something stupid and unleash the evil that was locked away ten years ago. From there on out, Aniston and a crappy homemade painting squad consisting of a Fabio-looking teenager, a slow-minded fat teenager and a young boy serve as torture practice for the evil dwarf leprechaun.

The first *Leprechaun* (1993) takes sort of a kitchen sink approach. After all, this was the first starring dwarf role in the series and they needed to see what worked and what didn't. So, the dwarf leprechaun rhymes a bit, engages in a lot of sports that draw attention to his lack of height and make him look like a cute little doll as he's killing people. There are also chase scenes in fast motion, the intent of which escapes me. Maybe the director was a big fan of Benny Hill and wanted to do a dwarf version of it. "Chucky" is clearly more frightening than the leprechaun, but they both share a love of bad one-liners and the dwarf leprechaun's great makeup work certainly provides for an effective and cool looking franchise villain (which clearly worked because there are to date six *Leprechaun* movies out there).

Will we ever get the true dwarf-on-dwarf throw down we've all been dying to see: "Chucky vs. Leprechaun"? Only time will tell. I'll wait patiently in the meantime and hope for a part seven to hit home video soon because there's got to be something bringing Warwick Davis back to keep signing up for these movies. Is it the epic character, the money, or the chance to kill lots of normal-sized people in very creative ways?

> Dwarf dressed in funny little leprechaun outfit.
> Dwarf leprechaun gleefully plays with his gold.
> Dwarf leprechaun hides in suitcase and uses a little boy's voice to disguise himself.
> Dwarf leprechaun scares an old lady into falling down the stairs.
> Dwarf leprechaun puppeteers the old lady he just killed.
> Dwarf leprechaun scared by four leaf clover.
> Dwarf leprechaun waddles/runs away from gunfire.
> Curse inducing dwarf leprechaun.
> Bug-eating dwarf leprechaun.
> Dwarf leprechaun crawls under truck and pets Aniston's leg.
> Dwarf Leprechaun attacks dad's hand through tree hole.

Tricycle riding dwarf leprechaun.
Pogo stick hopping dwarf leprechaun.
Mini car-riding dwarf leprechaun.
Cop-taunting dwarf leprechaun.
Tree falling and attacking dwarf leprechaun.
Dwarf leprechaun crawls on stepladder to look for gold.
Dwarf leprechaun eats cheap Lucky Clover cereal.
Dwarf leprechaun primps himself in vanity mirror.
Dwarf leprechaun traps Fabio in a bear trap.
Dwarf leprechaun and Fabio teenager fight.
Engine-chomping dwarf leprechaun.
Dwarf leprechaun attacks through car window.
Dwarf leprechaun attacks truck with little car.
Mobile, severed dwarf leprechaun hand.
Dwarf leprechaun uses cop's voice.
Gold sniffing dwarf leprechaun.
Dwarf leprechaun jumps out of fridge.
Chimney dropping dwarf leprechaun.
Skateboarding, bodysurfing dwarf leprechaun.
Dwarf leprechaun hand pops through phone.
Shoe-polishing dwarf leprechaun.
Teleporting dwarf leprechaun.
Fast motion chasing dwarf leprechaun.
Rollerblading dwarf leprechaun.
Wheelchair-riding dwarf leprechaun.
Dwarf leprechaun chases Jennifer Aniston.

Leprechaun 2 (1994)

Written by Turi Meyer and Al Septien
Directed by Rodman Flender
Starring Warwick Davis

After out-acting Jennifer Aniston in the first *Leprechaun* (1993), Warwick Davis comes back for a sequel (Hollywood finally woke up and noticed the box office magic of dwarves). It starts in Ireland and then goes right to a perfect place for a mischievous, greedy, degenerate to have further adventures: Hollywood, California. At the beginning of the film, the Leprechaun gets cock blocked and even though it's by a slave of his whose daughter he was trying to bang we still feel a little sorry for him. Not because he's a dwarf not getting laid, but because he's cursed to wait one thousand years to do it again. Now that's what I call an extremely long dry spell!

This installment of the popular demonic leprechaun dwarf series centers around a kid who works with his drunken uncle, giving tours through Hollywood's dark side. The tours end up being extremely cheesy and the kid keeps pissing his girlfriend off. Then, just when he's about to get her back, the dwarf leprechaun abducts her. With plans to make her his bride, he takes her back to his home, which looks a lot like the Keebler elves' tree. Unlike those elves in the cartoons, the evil dwarf leprechaun lives in the cavernous regions underneath the tree. *Leprechaun 2* (1994) continues most of the same shenanigans as the first one: cheesy dwarf leprechaun rhyming, different types of kills and trickery, etc.

The one scene however, that really stands out in the movie and makes it worth watching just for that one scene alone, is when the drunken uncle challenges the dwarf leprechaun to a drinking contest in a bar on St. Paddy's Day. Several dwarves (including the brilliant Tony Cox) enter the bar just in time to see and cheer on their dwarf brethren. As a dwarf appreciator and audience member, we are treated to extremely drunken dwarfism and multiple dwarves cheering on one of their own. It was a truly inspired and beautiful moment.

>Slave-owning dwarf leprechaun.
>Dwarf leprechaun educates slave on history.
>Dwarf leprechaun tries to bone slave's daughter.
>Dwarf leprechaun steals bottle of whiskey from old drunk.
>Dwarf leprechaun spits out crappy blended Canadian whiskey.
>Dwarf leprechaun rips out old bum's gold tooth.
>Dwarf leprechaun rips Hollywood agent's gold ring off along with his finger.
>Dwarf leprechaun lures horny teenager with the illusion of scoring with a hot chick.
>Dwarf leprechaun imitates a hot chick's voice.
>Dwarf leprechaun hides under couch.
>Dwarf leprechaun hides under kitchen counter.
>Dwarf leprechaun throws ring collar on girl's neck.

Leprechaun 3 (1995)

>Written by David DuBos
>Directed by Brian Trenchard-Smith
>Starring John Gatins, John DeMita, Michael Callan
>Featured dwarf: Warwick Davis
>"I'm a leprechaun, me lad, and you're a bleeding thief. For trying to steal me gold, I'll be giving you some grief."

Leprechaun 3 (1995) takes place in Las Vegas, the perfect place for a movie about the greed and lust for gold. Anyone who's been there understands that, and when you throw a killer dwarf based on popular leprechaun folklore into the mix, you have all the elements in place for cinematic magic. We don't, of course, get that. Like the other *Leprechaun* films, none were Oscar contenders, but they're not meant to be either. They're meant to be enjoyable, cheesy entertainment. *Leprechaun 3* (1995) treats us to some entertaining moments and more clever kills as our favorite dwarf leprechaun takes on even more of a *Wishmaster* (1997) style role (aka giving people what they wish for, then making their dreams turn into devices of their own death). His character becomes even more grandiose than the previous two films, swilling whiskey and filled with swagger. This time around, the plot is about a young kid who passes through Vegas on the way to Hollywood and stops along the way to help out a large-breasted woman with car trouble. From there on out, he gets his hands on some leprechaun gold and battles for the fate of his own soul, as well as his life, against the stingy bastard leprechaun.

Leprechaun 3 (1995) added a few touches the previous two films haven't, including a few television commercials where the dwarf leprechaun plays a lawyer and a female psychic. He also dresses up in scrubs, which was pretty amusing. As with the other films in the series, Warwick Davis seems to be having a blast playing the villainous lead as he disposes of tallies left and right in increasingly diabolical ways. However, next to his Elvis impression, the biggest highlight of the film is where he uses his evil magic to increase a woman's lips, breasts and backside to the point of explosion, then uses an umbrella to cover himself from the aftermath. And, of course, the ending opens with him looking pretty damned dead but never leaving us with a second of a doubt that he'll be back for part four.

Look closely for Warwick out of make up playing the slot machines next to his real life wife. Also notable is that dwarf acting legend Ed Gale worked in the stunt department on this one.

Dwarf statue.
Dwarf leprechaun feet on table.
Ear-biting dwarf leprechaun.
Toe-biting dwarf leprechaun.
Dwarf leprechaun hides in small kettle.
Slow-motion jumping dwarf leprechaun.
Gambling dwarves.
Whiskey-drinking dwarf leprechaun.
Axe-wielding dwarf leprechaun.
Dwarf leprechaun does shitty Elvis impression.
Elvis style, hip-swinging dwarf leprechaun.
Dwarf leprechaun magically makes his green excrement appear in a cheesy magician's hand.
Dwarf leprechaun gambles on top of table.
Dwarf leprechaun room service.
Dwarf leprechaun falls out of window.
Dwarf leprechaun's head framed next to a roulette wheel.
Dwarf leprechaun infomercials.
Dwarf leprechaun impersonates plastic surgeon.
Telekinetic dwarf leprechaun.
Magician's assistant dwarf leprechaun.
Chainsaw-wielding dwarf leprechaun.
Barbecued dwarf leprechaun.
Flying dwarf leprechaun in flames.

Leprechaun 4: In Space (1997)

Written by Dennis A. Pratt
Directed by Brian Trenchard-Smith
Featured dwarf: Warwick Davis
"Your shrieks, my dear, provide a perfect accompaniment to this romantic evening."

The last time we saw our favorite diabolical leprechaun dwarf he was burned to a crisp via the great Fazio the Magician's flamethrower, and now we pick up with him in part four in space with no apparent explanation? I guess the producers just really wanted to have a part four in space since *Hellraiser 4* (1996) and *Critters 4* (1992) took place there as well. However, the movies just mentioned never had a dwarf in space!

Anyhow, back to the continuing adventures of our favorite diabolical leprechaun dwarf. In this installment, the dwarf yet again saves the movie by making it watchable. If it weren't for the dwarf, the bad writing and acting may still be enjoyable on a bad movie level but the dwarf is the one who really makes it fun to watch. With all his little disguises and shenanigans and clever ways he kills people, I just love that little leprechaun dwarf. It's no wonder the series has been such a successful franchise. In this installment, you get to see the leprechaun dwarf use a machine gun and a mini light saber. The mini green light saber was my personal favorite and it appears towards the beginning of the movie and is never used again. Must've cost too much, budget-effects wise. This film will go down in history for one of the most unique ways for a screen villain to die and come back. You'll have to see it for yourself but the dwarf leprechaun is reborn through a man's wang. Fortunately, the poor bastard dies soon after the leprechaun flies out of what was left of his manhood.

Also notable, this is also the closest the dwarf leprechaun has gotten to having a love interest in the movies thus far, although he does have the space princess kidnapped, and when she does express interest in him it's clearly for his money. So, basically the dwarf leprechaun has the same problem as guys on Earth. He does get to kiss the space princess but further sequels will have to reveal whether our favorite dwarf leprechaun gets any closer to actually scoring, and I'm sure that when I watch part five again the leprechaun dwarf will end up in the hood without any connection whatsoever to his being in space in this movie. I'd bet a pot of gold on that.

> Distinguished, tuxedo wearing, cigarette-with-filter-smoking leprechaun dwarf.
> Space princess-imprisoning dwarf leprechaun.
> Mini, green light saber-wielding dwarf leprechaun.
> Self sacrificing, grenade-jumping dwarf leprechaun.
> Severed dwarf leprechaun head.
> Dwarf leprechaun reborn through man's mutilated wang.
> Dwarf leprechaun does shitty John Wayne impersonation.
> Horny dwarf leprechaun trips and mounts hot space marine chick.
> Spacesuit-wearing dwarf leprechaun.
> Self mutilating dwarf.
> Multiple-exploding dwarf leprechaun.
> Crotch violence by dwarf leprechaun.
> Distinguished, tuxedo wearing, cigarette-with-filter-smoking

leprechaun dwarf.
Plate-throwing dwarf leprechaun.
Dwarf leprechaun kisses space princess.
Mocking dwarf leprechaun.
Detonator-holding dwarf leprechaun.
Hostage-taking dwarf leprechaun.
Dwarf leprechaun does shitty drill instructor impression.
Misogynist dwarf leprechaun.
Dwarf leprechaun turns space princess into a zit-covered hag.
Dwarf leprechaun undergoes growth spurt of Godzilla-like proportions.
Giant dwarf leprechaun checks out his newly enlarged crotch.
Dwarf leprechaun flies through space and explodes yet again.
Severed dwarf leprechaun hand flips the bird in space.

Leprechaun In The Hood (2000)

Written by Doug Hall, Jon Huffman
Directed by Rob Spera
Starring Ice-T, Coolio, Anthony Montgomery, Rashaan Nall
Featured dwarf: Warwick Davis
"Flee while you can, the future's not good, for no one is safe from a lep in the hood."

In this installment which is nowhere near connected to part four (imagine that), which took place in space, the brilliant idea of placing the diabolical dwarf leprechaun in the hood is finally committed to film. What follows is dwarf weed smoking, dwarf rhyming and ghetto inspired carnage. Oh yeah, and we're treated to a marvelous performance by Ice-T, as well. Ok, not really, but it's pretty enjoyable if you've had a couple of forties (especially the scene where Ice-T picks a bat out of his obviously-fake fro as if he were the live action version of Captain Caveman).

Leprechaun in the Hood revolves around the dwarf leprechaun's magical golden flute and how it gives every rapper that gets their hands on it the illusion of actually having talent. What follows next is the proverbial stuff that rap videos are made of: cash, fame and hoes a'plenty. But, fame, as they say, is fleeting, especially when the leprechaun dwarf is involved. No one's going to be able to enjoy the little guy's riches without a big personal cost. A rap band has a goal of delivering a positive message with their rhymes. They play the clubs with their positivity raps like multiple M.C. Hammers until meeting mogul Ice-T. He gives them a shot and decides to take them on, provided they change their music. His approach is a little different than theirs. He's all about the gangster rap, murder and hoes and embracing the less respectable side of the genre. The band gets on his bad side when they question his decision and they're back to square one. That is, until they discover the magic of the dwarf leprechaun's golden flute. Once that happens, things change and they change real quick. Fame, fortune and hoes step in for the hungry youngsters and before they know it they're compromising their morals, ethics and positive message for the sweet taste of their fifteen minutes of fame. Of course, things don't work out for these guys and the dwarf leprechaun makes them pay in one way or another for profiting from his wealth.

The true highlight of this film (although I suppose you'd have to see it for yourself before even thinking about calling it that) is dwarf rapping and dancing. This is something we've seen with other films starring dwarves, such as *Austin Powers: The Spy Who Shagged Me,* but it is indeed a first for the *Leprechaun* series, especially since he performs an entire song. Other cinematic treats include watching Warwick Davis get stoned on Ice-T's weed (I wonder if that happened in real life or not?) and the dwarf leprechaun being so high he doesn't even notice brothers dressed up like women trying to seduce him. Recommended only if you're stoned, drunk or are a completist (like I am) of the series.

> Dwarf leprechaun statue.
> Dwarf leprechaun smokes Ice-T's weed.
> Dwarf leprechaun's golden flute is the key to rapper's fame and fortune.
> Cross dressing tallie tries to seduce dwarf leprechaun.
> Dwarf leprechaun on fire.
> Dwarf leprechaun slaps skins with a brother.
> Dwarf leprechaun telekinesis.
> Sister spoon-feeds dwarf leprechaun like a baby.
> Stoned dwarf leprechaun passed out from clover-laced joint.
> Brothers dress like women for more attempted dwarf leprechaun seduction.
> Sunglass-wearing dwarf leprechaun.
> Rapping dwarf leprechaun.
> Dwarf leprechaun picked up by girls.

Leprechaun: Back 2 Tha Hood (2003)

Written and Directed by Steven Ayromlooi
Starring Tangi Miller, Laz Alonso, Page Kennedy, Sherrie Jackson
Featured dwarf: Warwick Davis
"What the fuck you want, you little lucky charm looking motherfucker?"

Grab your forties and blunts because… oh shit, the evil dwarf leprechaun comes back to tha' hood! In the beginning of the movie, which feels like it's a continuation of part five (even though that one didn't end with a priest fighting the dwarf), a priest banishes the evil little bastard to the pit from whence he came. Multiple hands drag the dwarf leprechaun under and there he stays until those darn troublemaking kids from the hood stumble across his gold and invoke his wrath. The kids in the hood include a couple of hot sisters and two brothers (one a stoner and one a narcissist who's only out for himself). The kids don't waste any time dividing the dwarf leprechaun's gold so they can start making their dreams come true.

A lot of black stereotypes are included here as the girls do nothing but buy a shit-ton of bling. The guys follow suit, except for the stoner, who spends the majority of his share on two stuffed garbage bags of weed as well as the finest bongs magic dwarf gold can buy. There's a few things different in this movie from the last dwarf leprechaun's adventure in the hood, such as a dwarf/tallie fight that seems right out of the movie *Barfly* (1987) (with the dwarf as Mickey Rourke's character) and a dwarf/fat female tallie massage, topped off with a close up of nasty dwarf toenails. Most notably though, part six includes an extended scene where our favorite dwarf leprechaun gets stoned off a bong, commits murder on a brother with the same weapon and then stumbles into the kitchen high as a kite, where he raids the fridge and then proceeds to get stuck in it, giggling like a schoolgirl throughout the entire thing.

The whole movie was basically a lot like part five, but without Ice-T and with a lot more weed references. Watching this film made me wonder, just how much weed does it take for a dwarf to get stoned? I know they can get drunk off of significantly less alcohol but I wonder how that works with weed. And do things change when it's a magical dwarf leprechaun? Do his magical powers and extreme resistance to death give him an extra tolerance boost? Unfortunately, this question may never be answered. That's why we've all got to do our part to badger the studios to make a part seven in the hood! Who's with me?!

> Dwarf leprechaun attacks priest.
> Jack the ripper lookalike dwarf leprechaun.
> Dwarf leprechaun banished by priest.
> Psychic has terrifying dwarf leprechaun flashbacks from part five.
> Dwarf leprechaun lurks in tree.
> Bong-smoking dwarf leprechaun.
> Wasted dwarf leprechaun falls to ground.
> Dwarf leprechaun uses bong as a murder weapon.
> High angle close-up of dwarf leprechaun's hands reaching for pickle jar.
> Dwarf leprechaun raids fridge.
> Dwarf leprechaun gets stuck in fridge.
> Dwarf leprechaun framed under large woman.
> Dwarf leprechaun massages large woman.
> Close up of nasty dwarf leprechaun toes.
> Dwarf leprechaun walks on large woman's back.
> Dwarf leprechaun flies at screen.
> Dwarf leprechaun bitch-slaps hood rat.
> Dwarf leprechaun lies in tiny bed.
> Dwarf leprechaun jumps down from tree.
> Dwarf leprechaun steals hood sister's gold tooth and wears it.
> Dwarf leprechaun/cop fight.
> Dwarf leprechaun can't reach pedals in cop car.
> Dwarf leprechaun feet jump out of cop car.
> Dwarf leprechaun/gang member size differential.
> Dwarf leprechaun flies back against garbage cans.
> Dwarf leprechaun fights gang member, *Barfly* style.
> Dwarf leprechaun hangs on to the underside of moving car, *Raiders of the Lost Ark* style.
> Slow motion dwarf leprechaun.
> Levitating dwarf leprechaun.
> Dwarf leprechaun hand busts through door.
> Dwarf leprechaun jumps on tallie's back.
> Dwarf leprechaun jumps down into elevator.
> Melting dwarf leprechaun skull.
> Cement-sinking dwarf leprechaun.

Life Blood (2009)

> Written and directed by Ron Carlson
> Starring Charles Napier
> Featured dwarf: Danny Woodburn
> "Not too good a shot, huh, little man?"

Danny Woodburn is a great dwarf actor who gets decent roles. This is not one of them. All I should have to say is that it involves lesbian vampires, bad cock jokes and Charles Napier as a goofy sheriff and you get the picture.

Woodburn pops up in a decently-sized supporting role as a deputy. He is sadly introduced in a scene involving a way-too-long gag of cock jokes on a TV, demoralizing his presence at all. Soon after he finds some dead bodies while on patrol and ends up directing traffic. When one foreigner drives up wanting to see dead bodies that are now gone, he gets into it with Woodburn, ridiculing his size.

Unfortunately, Woodburn meets his demise when he should have been the hero of the film. A true waste of talent, but Woodburn comes close to saving it.

> Dwarf cop.
> Stands behind chair that's almost as high.
> Dwarf laughing at dirty jokes.
> Dwarf singing while driving.
> Dwarf with flare.
> Dwarf directing traffic.
> Dwarf ridiculed by foreigner.
> Dwarf with gun.
> Referred to as "Little man."
> Referred to as "Little fella."
> Dwarf shot.

Life Stinks (1991)

> Written by Mel Brooks, Rudy DeLuca, Steve Haberman
> Directed by Mel Brooks
> Starring Mel Brooks, Lesley Ann Warren, Jeffrey Tambor, Stuart Pankin

Featured dwarf: Billy Barty

Mel Brooks makes a movie about the homeless and adds a dwarf. God bless him! After all, the homeless take many shapes and sizes. In *Life Stinks (1991)*, Mel Brooks goes from riches to rags and rubs elbows with the homeless. One of the members of Brook's homeless clique is legendary dwarf actor Billy Barty, legless and riding around in a shoddily put together homemade wheelchair. Toward the end of the film, when the homeless attack the rich and invade their food tent, Barty is seen under a table drinking from a tipped-over bottle of booze. This is a classic scene in what is otherwise easily one of Brooks' weakest movies. Even Barty couldn't save this one. Unfortunately there are only a few scenes with the legendary dwarf. I would have enjoyed the film a whole lot more had the dwarf stayed in the picture. The best scene occurs during the finale when Barty helps Brooks hijack a bulldozer by lying underneath it and making the driver think he had run over his legs.

Unfortunately, touches of bizarre humor like this are way too few and far between to recommend the movie for viewing. If you really feel compelled to watch, fast forward to Barty in the hysterical-looking homemade wheelchair and call it a day.

> Legless dwarf rolls with homeless attackers in shitty wheelchair.
> Dwarf takes over rich tallie's food tent.
> Dwarf drinks from tipped-over bottle.
> Legless dwarf pretends bulldozer has run over his legs.
> Dwarf plays a major part in helping to save the day.
> Wedding dwarf throws what looks like crackers instead of rice.
> Wedding dwarf waves goodbye and wipes a tear from his eye as he watches his tallie friend drive off after being hitched.

Little Cigars (1973)

> Written by Louis Garfinkle and Frank Ray Perilli
> Directed by Chris Christenberry
> Starring Angel Tompkins
> Featured dwarves: Jerry Maren, Billy Curtis, Felix Silla, Frank Delfino, Emory Souza

The dwarf gets the girl. This is the way it should be in every movie.

When a gangster's former mistress robs and hurts him and then heads to the middle of nowhere, she goes into hiding as a waitress. When a drunken tallie starts messing with her, she's rescued by a couple of circus dwarves! Thus begins the brilliantly conceived fun of *Little Cigars* (1973), when she decides to pay their circus show a visit and meet the rest of the little crew. As the sheet goes down on the act, two of the little people in the act hit the parking lot to rob the audience. When her gun goes missing, she goes looking for it and the little people. As it turns out, she gets an offer to join this team of thieves and is forced to take them up on it when the gangsters come after her. It doesn't take long for this tallie beauty to start causing problems among the troupe as they vie for her attention. Besides the little people fighting amongst each other, one dwarf gets in a big bar fight to get his lady back and even gets laid in the process.

The dwarves then set out on a thieving rampage as they rob an auto repair shop, a movie theater, a laundromat, and more. Highlights include the troupe being bashed on by their leader about how they're midgets, being mistaken for kids by the police, a police line-up of dwarves (including

Angelo Rossitto as an honorary sheriff!), dwarf/tallie relationship problems and multiple fight/robbery scenes.

This movie is a MUST see for any dwarf enthusiast. It's funny as hell with some great voiceover one-liners, a hot babe banging little people (the way it should be!), dwarves in great situations, and so much more. *Little Cigars (1973)* is a pure classic that you won't soon forget.

The cover to the book also stands as a testament to why it's not a good idea to piss dwarves off.

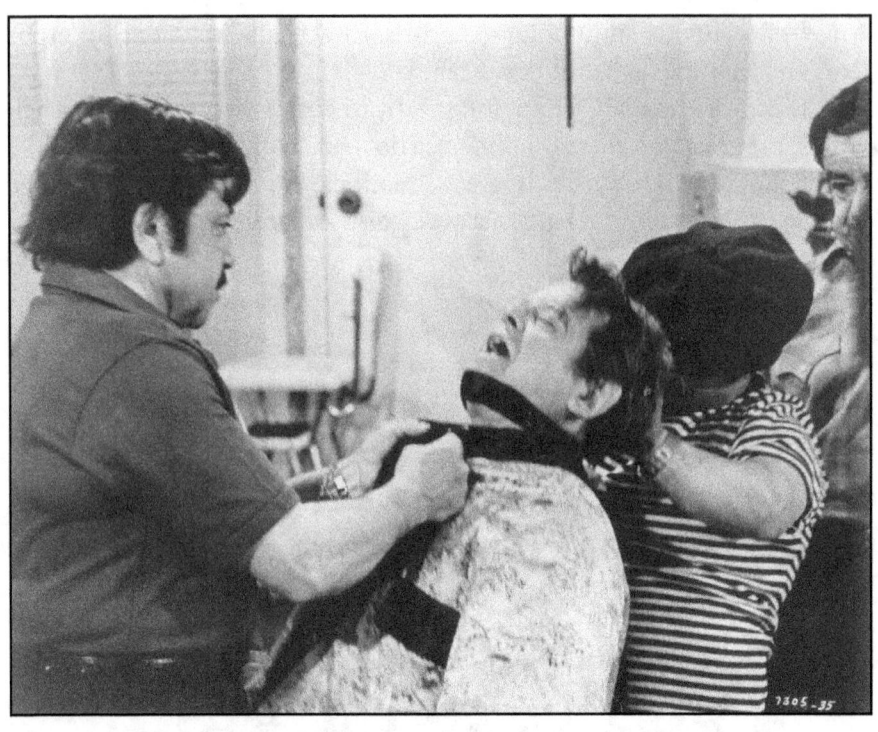

This movie hits the dwarfsploitation jackpot. It even gives us dwarf on dwarf violence. What more can you ask for?

"Hey, look at the shrimps."
"Must be a circus in town."
Dwarves in bar.
Dwarves beat up tallie.
Dwarves leap on barstools.
"Why that cigar's bigger than he is."
Dwarf with cigar.
Dwarves with top hats.
Dwarves dancing.
Dwarves collecting money.
Thieving dwarves.
"Where are those lousy midgets?"
Angry dwarf.
"Little man, you've got something that belongs to me."
Dwarf drinking.
"Drink up! Let's have an orgy!"
"Yeah, we could all fit in the same bed."

"You have nothing better to do than to get drunk with a bunch of squirts?"
"You know, every now and then a chick like you comes around here and thinks she's Snow White and wants to fool around with the little people."
"Well, well, well, if it isn't Mighty Mouse."
"Too bad we don't have the march of the toy soldiers for you."
"I'm not working for no dwarves."
"Don't ever call a midget a dwarf."
"What's the difference?"
"A broken heart."
Tallie picks up and carries little person off stage.
Dwarves fighting.
Dwarf driving.
"Why you little degenerate!"
"Is that the name of the game today, teasing midgets?"
Dwarves ogle over hottie tallie.
Dwarves doing laundry.
Dwarf thrown in tub of water.
Dwarves throwing water at each other.
"Hey look at the midget!"
"How's the weather down there shorty?"
Dwarf jumps on bar top to kick tallie.
Dwarf beaten up by tallie.
"You rub a midget's head, it's good luck."
Dwarf with shotgun.
"You get mixed up with midgets, there ain't no way you can do anything big."
'Things must be tough, Cleo, you sleeping with a dwarf."
"He's a midget."
"So, what's the difference?"
"A split lip."
"Don't shoot, they're kids!"
"You look nice enough, but getting a bunch of kids to break into a market—that's really lousy."
"On that robbery last night involving five juveniles and a girl? Change that to five midgets.
That's right, I said five midgets!"
Dwarves jump on top of each other.

Dwarf shot.
"If a chick can't satisfy a midget..."
"I'm your old lady and I dig your little ass."

Little Nicky (2000)

Written by Tim Herlihy, Adam Sandler, Steven Brill
Directed by Steven Brill
Starring Adam Sandler, Patricia Arquette, Harvey Keitel, Rhys Ifans, Rodney Dangerfield
Featured dwarves: Joseph S. Griffo, Cindy Sorenson

We know Adam Sandler is a dwarf appreciator from the dwarves he's put in his other films, such as *Happy Gilmore (1996)* and *Bedtime Stories (2008)*. We certainly appreciate his mutual admiration for the little thespians, but what we have a problem with is that the dwarves in his films are usually limited to cameos. Sandler has never even so much as given a dwarf a Steve Buscemi-sized role in one of his films (which, for those familiar with Sandler's movies is usually a side character role but often involves a very juicy part that is remembered long after watching the film (take Buscemi's character in *Billy Madison (1995)* for a great example of the above). Come on, Sandler. We know you're a good guy. Can't you just throw a dwarf a bone? Protest aside, let's talk about the one very short dwarfsploitation scene in *Little Nicky (2000)*.

For those of you who are unfamiliar with the plot, *Little Nicky (2000)* is about one of the devil's sons (played by Sandler) who speaks with an annoying speech impediment throughout the entire movie and has to stop his brothers who have escaped from Hell and are attempting to take over Earth. Unfortunately, dwarves don't show up until toward the end when Sandler has a magic battle with his Billy Idol-looking brother. The evil brother performs dark magic while Sandler performs happy magic, the climax of which involves two dwarves who instantly fall in love with one another and make out. It's not much, but we do get to see two dwarves make out and after all, a short dwarf scene is better than no dwarf scene at all. Plus, for those of you who are dwarf-curious, it's an extra-special treat.

Dark magic turns a baby into an evil dwarf.
Evil dwarf kicks tallie woman in shins, punches her stomach

and bites her arm.
Good magic turns tallie woman into dwarf.
Steamy, makeout session between two dwarves.
Evil tallie pushes happy dwarf couple out of the way to attack speech impaired tallie Sandler.

Little People (1982)

Directed by Jan Krawitz and Thomas Ott
Starring Karla Eastburg, Beth Loyless, Len Sawisch, Mark Trombino
Featured dwarf: Billy Barty
"For 200 years my people were sold as slaves."
"For a thousand years my people were given away as gifts."

If you've ever been curious about what it's like to be a little person, this is a documentary for you. It is a very simple film, not even including the context to tell you who's who, but the discussions that the little people interviewees bring up are fascinating. The best part for me was when the filmmakers went inside the little people's world; showing them at the grocery store or stories of romance or working out next to tallies or their worries behind having children. Seeing the interactions they had with tallies, such as when a dwarf is stared at while buying groceries, is heartbreaking while at the same time giving you even more respect for little people everywhere. I recommend this for everyone, not only so you can learn and understand little people more but so you can hear dwarves compare themselves to African-Americans.

Protests being picked up, patted on the head…trips to conventions, hospitals, movie acting.
Little people walk by tallies.
Dwarves helped on boat by tallies.
Dwarf tapping foot close up.
Dwarf dancing with tallie.
Dwarves party.
Dwarf smaller than schoolkids.
Dwarf has to crawl onto schoolbus.
"Midgets of America" convention footage shown.

Dwarf has to stand on ladder to get to table.
Dwarves using ladders to gamble.
Dwarf stared at when at grocery store.
Dwarf climbs onto freezer to get food.
Dwarf doing exercises.
Dwarves cooking.
Dwarf wedding.
Dwarf with cowboy hat dancing.
Dwarves compared to African Americans.
Dwarves playing baseball.

Living in Oblivion (1995)

Written and Directed by Tom DiCillo
Starring Steve Buscemi, Catherine Keener, Dermot Mulroney, James LeGros
Featured dwarf: Peter Dinklage
"The only place I've seen dreams with dwarves in them is in stupid movies like this!"

Living in Oblivion (1995) centers around Nick's (Steve Buscemi) struggle to finish an independent film as everything turns to chaos. This includes a scene where a dwarf appears in a dream sequence. The dwarf in question is Tito (the great Peter Dinklage), and his scene is one of the most classic moments in dwarf cinema history as he stands up for the rights of dwarf actors everywhere. He challenges the status quo as well as his employer by questioning why he is used in a dream sequence. The tension and dwarf anger build until Tito has a mental breakdown of epic proportions, questioning dwarf stereotypes in cinema and refusing to be exploited!

I can only imagine the number of drinks fellow dwarves have bought Dinklage after seeing him stand up to the man so heroically on the silver screen (although, he did reinforce the cinematic stereotype of an angry dwarf while doing so). The only thing I didn't like about this film was that I had to wait an hour to see a dwarf. Yes, be forewarned. You have to wait an entire hour before you get to see a dwarf. However, it's well worth the wait and will undoubtedly make Dinklage immortal in the eyes of dwarves for years to come.

Dwarf demands stool in bathroom.
Dwarf wears funny blue outfit.
Director tries to get a psychotic laugh out of dwarf.
Dream sequence dwarf.
Disrespected dwarf.
Smoke-covered dwarf.
Dwarf has mental breakdown.
Dwarf refuses to be a stereotype.
Arm crossed, protesting dwarf.

Lone Wolf McQuade (1983)

Written by B.J. Nelson
Directed by Steve Carver
Starring Chuck Norris, David Carradine, Barbara Carrera, Leon Isaac Kennedy, Robert Beltran
Featured dwarf: Daniel Frishman
"You made the deal, shorty."

One of the greatest Chuck Norris movies to date features a dwarf crime boss in an electric wheelchair. Sadly, this movie dropped the ball on all the possible scenarios they could have involved the main dwarf actor in. After all, why put a dwarf in a movie, have him be the lead bad guy and only feature him in a few scenes? And why didn't the filmmakers ever think of getting that dwarf out of the wheelchair so he could go one on one with Chuck Norris? What if Chuck kicked David Carradine's ass and then had to face off against the big boss: kung fu dwarf? Or what if Chuck's love interest was having sex with the dwarf instead of Carradine and the two had to duke to out for her affection? Or what if Chuck walked in on his love interest getting boned by the dwarf? The possibilities are endless.

It truly saddens me when I think of all the wasted dwarf potential in this film. Good thing it's a great movie. However, unless you want to wait a while to see a dwarf laugh maniacally at Chuck Norris, I'd skip this one. It's for dwarf completists only, but an awesome movie nonetheless.

Dwarf spies on Chuck Norris with big binoculars.
Dwarf laughs maniacally.

Dwarf stands up in electric wheelchair while it's moving (in what one can only assume is a failed attempt to make himself look taller and more intimidating).

Looney Tunes: Back in Action (2003)

Written by Larry Doyle
Directed by Joe Dante
Starring: Brendan Fraser, Jenna Elfman, Steve Martin
Featured dwarves: Arturo Gil, Kevin Thompson, Gabriel Pimental, Martin Klebba, Steve Babiar

Joe Dante helms this flick with very little dwarf action. When Brendan Fraser's secret agent father tells him he needs help and to find "Daisy Tails," Fraser heads to Vegas and finds her on stage at Yosemite Sam's casino. When she takes off her large dress in order to dance around in something slinky, out pop several mini versions of Yosemite Sam. They dance around, shoot guns off and get twirled around by scantily-clad background dancers. The downside is that we never get to hear them talk or, well, do anything else yet it's an all-star dwarf cast.

To make it worse, there's a scene later in the film where Fraser is trying to fly to France. Standing next to him is another dwarf actor who is talking to a scantily-clad woman. The dwarf looks over at Fraser and then continues his conversation—a complete waste of a perfectly good dwarf actor.

While Mr. Dante obviously knows little people add great value to a film, I wish he would have let them say a line or two. It's a waste of great talent.

> Mini Yosemites come out from under dress.
> Mini Yosemites shooting guns.
> Mini Yosemites dancing.
> Mini Yosemites picked up and twirled by dancing girls.
> Dwarves in masks.
> Dwarf flirts with tallie woman in background.

Loose Shoes (1980)

> Written by Ian Praiser, Varley Smith, Ira Miller, Royce D. Applegate
> Directed by Ira MIller
> Starring Royce D. Applegate, Lewis Arquette, Tom Baker, Dorothy van, Dan Barrows, J.J. Barry
> Featured dwarf: Billy Curtis
> "When I see injustice perpetrated… when I see such a total lack of regard for even these silly, insignificant little twerps… well, I go fucking crazy!"

Loose Shoes (1980) is a movie comprised of a bunch of fake movie trailers, most which are shitty, one or two classic, and a couple decent. The one with the dwarf features the great Billy Curtis as a munchkin and is a parody of the *Billy Jack* movies starring Tom Laughlin. For those unfamiliar with *Billy Jack*, the character was a man who preached peace while kicking ass and was very much, in my view at least, the predecessor to the legendary Steven Seagal, especially in films such as *On Deadly Ground (1994)* and *The Patriot (2000)*.

In the *Loose Shoes (1980)* fake trailer called *Billy Jerk Goes to Oz*, a tallie actor (well-cast as the Laughlin-esque role of Billy Jerk) winds up on the yellow brick road and meets a skipping dwarf played by the great Billy Curtis who is dressed to the nines in a suit and sporting a handlebar mustache. It's hard to hate even a shitty movie when it features a dwarf with a handlebar mustache. The munchkin dwarf enlists Jerk's help to save Oz and the tallie douche-bag accompanies the little guy on his journey, which is basically just a few skips to the Scarecrow. After the munchkin dwarf makes a joke about the Scarecrow being well hung, he and Jerk allow him to tag along. Things go well until the Scarecrow calls the munchkin dwarf 'shorty' and Billy Jerk goes ballistic, spouting off a long tirade about the injustice of disrespecting dwarves while at the same time blatantly insulting the munchkin dwarf right in front of his face.

While the skit did have merit in making fun of the pretentiousness of *Billy Jack (1971)*, it is not anywhere near as funny as it thinks it is and seems more like a cheap excuse to make fun of dwarves.

> Munchkin dwarf skips down yellow brick road.
> Skipping dwarf.

Suit-wearing dwarf.
Dwarf lifts up Scarecrow and says, "He's well hung, isn't he?"
"Shorty?" Did I hear you just call that midget shorty?"
"Thanks, mister. You just saved us from the wicked bitch of the north by southwest"
"This witch was a real bitch."

Wizard of Oz (1939) alumnus Karl Slovak.

Lost Reality 2: More of the Worst (2005)

Produced by Scott Kalvert, The Jay and Tony Show
Created by The Jay and Tony Show, Scott Kalvert, Mark Hankey
Featured dwarf: Chuy Bravo
"We're not midgets, we're little people! We have the heart of lions!"

Now, here is a movie that not only is dwarfsploitaiton, it celebrates and boasts it. The idea behind *Lost Reality 2* (2005) is that it's basically a bunch of reality shows that were shot and never made it to TV. There's some really harsh and insulting material here (especially to dwarves), and, to make matters worse, the tallie hosts insult the dwarves before and after the segments. Now, I know reality TV is designed to dehumanize people, but this movie crosses the dwarf decency boundary and if I were one of the dwarves involved in this production, I'd be extremely pissed after watching this film.

There are two dwarf related pieces in the film: *Midget Wars* and *Money*. *Midget Wars* is basically a dwarf vs. tallie version of *American Gladiators*, which is unusually cruel because they don't even mix the teams up. They don't even have the team be half dwarf, half tallie on either side. The cruel bastards who made this movie apparently had one goal and one goal only: to maximize the suffering of dwarves and package it in a form of popular entertainment. And what happens next is we're forced to witness one form of dwarfsploitation after another as the tallies kick the living hell out of the dwarves via dodgeball, jousting, basketball, etc. The end result is pretty brutal. In fact, it's downright near a dwarf massacre.

The next installment of dwarfsploitation is *Money*, which features a dwarf who goes by the name of Chuy Bravo. He wears a bizarre Aladdin-esque hat, open vest, and silky trousers, and is the sidekick to a host who kind of looks like Marcy's first husband Steve on *Married With Children*. The host and dwarf duo approach people on the street and try to find out just exactly what they'll do for money. What follows is vomit inducing as the host has people on the street do foul things like lick the sweaty body of his dwarf sidekick. The coup de grace, though, is the moment where a stoner-looking kid eats what appears to be an uncooked hot dog out the back of the dwarf's ass, and for an extra hundred bucks flosses with the dwarf's pubic hair. Sure enough, the kid allows the dwarf to reach into his pants and take a pick out of his own personal veritable forest.

This is one of the nastiest things I've ever seen, but what makes it really hilarious is that the dwarf is smiling throughout the entire thing. The tallies may have used the Aladdin-looking dwarf for their own personal sick joke but it is clearly the dwarf who gets the last laugh in this movie. Recommended only for the extremely twisted dwarf-curious.

> Dwarf version of *American Gladiators*.
> Dwarves vs tallies.
> Dwarf dodgeball.
> Tallies pummel dwarves.
> Dwarf/tallie joust.
> Trash talking dwarf gets knocked off pedestal by tallie.
> Dwarf basketball.
> Dwarf/tallie football.
> Tackled dwarf.
> Tallie announcers ridicule dwarves, call them midgets.
> Dwarf in Aladdin style outfit.
> Dwarf sticks out tongue.
> Cigar-smoking dwarf.
> Dwarf licked like cat.
> Tallie gives shirtless dwarf piggyback ride.
> Dwarf with hot dog in ass.
> Stoner eats hot dog out of dwarf's ass.
> Stoner flosses with dwarf's pubic hair.

The Love Guru (2008)

> Written by Mike Myers, Graham Gordy
> Directed by Marco Schnabel
> Starring Mike Myers, Jessica Alba
> Featured dwarf: Verne Troyer
> "I would invite you, but I know you have your meeting with the Lollipop Guild."

Years after *Austin Powers in Goldmember* (2002), Myers makes *The Love Guru* (2008), and is still clearly dwarf obsessed, but this time the comedy doesn't work nearly as well as it did with the films in the *Austin Powers* franchise. Myers tries way too hard to be funny and I don't think he quite realized that humor about a guru isn't really all that funny to, say well, pretty much everyone watching but him. In *The Love Guru* (2008), Myers plays Guru Pika, a successful man who gets hired to fix a hockey player's personal problems and turn the team around. Unlike the Austin Powers movies which are mostly funny, *The Love Guru* (2008) is not funny at all except for the dwarf scenes.

If it weren't for Verne Troyer, I wouldn't have made it past twenty minutes of this movie. He excels in his performance, taking the angry dwarf stereotype to the next level and then past that in his portrayal of a hockey coach so angry the only thing missing is steam bursting out his little ears. Everything designed around the dwarf is great; from his mini office the tallies can barely fit in, to his mini dry erase board during his speeches. Troyer gives us plenty of physical humor here as well; from getting smacked in the face with a hockey puck and flying across the ice, to getting an ice bucket tossed over his head; which covers his entire body as he struggles to move inside it like something out of a cartoon.

Troyer's dwarf/tallie interaction with Myers is good as well, like it is in the *Powers* movies, but I could never in good conscience recommend watching this movie unless you're a dwarf cinema completist. Even then, I'd highly suggest fast-forwarding past every single scene that doesn't include Troyer. He is literally the only watchable part of this movie.

> Frustrated dwarf coach with Tom Landry-looking hat.
> Dwarf in mini chair.
> Dwarf sits uncomfortably cross legged on cushion and falls off.
> High angle on dwarf.
> Pep-talking dwarf.
> Dwarf drilled in face by hockey puck.
> Myers holds up dwarf, pretending he's an Oscar trophy.
> Office supply-throwing dwarf.
> Dwarf office cramps tallies.
> Myers holds up dwarf fork.
> Dwarf throws papers off desk.
> Tallie bashes head through dwarf ceiling.
> Dwarf thows chair through window.
> Dwarf gives angry speech around a mini dry-erase board.
> Dwarf punches Myers in crotch.
> Belching dwarf.

Farting dwarf.
Dwarf stands on player's bench to watch game.
Players toss ice bucket over dwarf's head and body.
Dwarf turned on by Jessica Alba's rant.
Dwarf fakes a heart attack.
Dwarf flies across ice.
Hookah- smoking dwarf.
Dwarf sings "The Joker."

Madigan (1968)

Written by Abraham Polonsky and Henri Simoun
Directed by Don Siegel
Starring Henry Fonda
Featured dwarf: Michael Dunn

You know those detective movies where they always have that informant they go to who does their job for them? That's basically what dwarf acting legend Michael Dunn does here as he's underused yet again, this time as a scared bookie. It's obvious to me that this is the most memorable part of the film. As usual, Dunn stands out. In just two scenes, he's what I went away remembering about the film. If I had produced this film, Dunn would have been *Madigan* (1968).

Dwarf referred to as midget.
Dwarf stands next to tallie.
Dwarf at luncheonette.
Dwarf offers egg cream.
Dwarf with bodyguard.

Mad Max Beyond Thunderdome (1985)

Written by Terry Hayes and George Miller
Directed by George Ogilvie and George Miller
Starring Mel Gibson and Tina Turner
Featured dwarf: Angelo Rossitto
"Who runs Bartertown?"

When someone steals from Mad Max, he goes looking for them and ends up in Bartertown. Amongst a variety of odd characters is The Master, played by dwarf legend Angelo Rossitto, who sits atop a 'special person' to make up Master Blaster. The Master is cocky and mistakenly tries to convince Tina Turner that he runs Bartertown, leading her to try and get Mad Max to take out the Blaster in a fight in Thunderdome.

Angelo and the whole Master Blaster character are definitely one of the most interesting and memorable moments of the worst of the Mad Max series.

> Bossy dwarf.
> Dwarf who can't speak properly.
> Dwarf points at tallie.
> Dwarf picked up.
> Dwarf knocked over.
> Dwarf sits in tallie's lap.
> Dwarf clapping.
> Dwarf brought up on rope.

The Man with the Golden Gun (1974)

> Written by Richard Maibaum and Tom Mankiewicz
> Directed by Guy Hamilton
> Starring Roger Moore, Christopher Lee, Britt Ekland, Maud Adams, Herve Villechaize.
> Featured dwarf: Herve Villechaize.
> "I've never killed a midget before, but there can always be a first time."

In *The Man with the Golden Gun* (1974), our favorite dwarf from Fantasy Island (Herve Villechaize) shows up not as the friendly sidekick to Ricardo Montalban, but instead as a diabolical, manipulating toadie to the evil and even more diabolical Christopher Lee. The film brilliantly opens with a dwarfsploitation sight gag of Villechaize carrying a drink tray in front of his face, which is completely hidden from view. Soon after, it's revealed that a man has come onto the island with the intention of taking Christopher Lee's golden gun.

The dwarf gives false hope to those that pursue a cat and mouse game with Lee that he will help them. Before they know it, they've fallen into his sly dwarf trap and are soon after dead at the hands of Christopher Lee before even laying so much as a hand on his infamous golden gun. But then again, none of those aspiring gun owners were James Bond. When he enters the picture, (played with silky smooth style by Roger Moore)

He may look adorable but Villechaize is beyond dangerous in
The Man With the Golden Gun (1974).

both the dwarf and Christopher Lee are given a run for their money.

All of a sudden, Lee's and the dwarf's traps aren't foolproof. Bond is impervious to death at the hands of diabolical villains, even dwarves. This is definitely a very different Bond film. It's much more isolated as a good half of the film takes place on the villain's evil island fortress. It certainly stands out as being different from many of the other Bond films that seem to merge together with similar plot lines.

To hell with a golden gun. Villechaize has a double barrel.

Dwarfsploitation highlights include a spinning, rising dwarf chair, a scene where Villechaize dons a creepy island mask and bashes Bond over the head with a pitchfork, dwarf organization of a duel between James Bond and Christopher Lee and the coup de grace: dwarf spying on Bond about to have sex, jumping from the boat's ceiling and attacking Bond with wine bottles. And the scene where Bond puts the troublesome little guy into a suitcase? Priceless.

> Dwarf carries a tray of drinks, which cover his face.
> Dwarf opens champagne.
> Butler dwarf.
> Disembodied dwarf voice.
> Clapping dwarf.
> Killer dwarf.
> Dwarf in funny hat.
> Dwarf inspects dead body.
> Christopher Lee-sidekick dwarf.
> Statue acting, mask-wearing dwarf.
> Dwarf attacks Bond with oversized pitchfork.
> Binocular-spying dwarf.
> Bond shoots out dwarf's champagne glass.
> Dwarf does cattle call for lunch.
> Cooking dwarf.
> Dwarf announces rules for Bond/Lee duel.
> Dwarf on levitating seat.
> Hysterically laughing dwarf.
> Control room-operating dwarf.
> Dwarf spies on Bond as he's about to bang a girl on the boat.
> Wine-throwing dwarf.
> Bond puts dwarf in suitcase.
> Bond sticks dwarf in cage near ship's sails.

Masters of the Universe (1987)

> Written by David Odell
> Directed by Gary Goddard
> Starring Dolph Lundgren, Frank Langella, Meg Foster
> Featured dwarf: Billy Barty

"I don't like adventure."

For those of you who remember the cartoon, this version takes place on Earth and isn't exactly the most faithful adaptation to the series, however it does at least try. No Orko, though. And for those of you who suffer from severe cases of 80's nostalgia, you'll relate to this. I watched the cartoon again after recently reviewing the movie for the dwarf book and forgot how shitty it was. So, from that point of view, the movie wasn't half bad. It does concentrate way too much on the human plot and less on actual characters from the cartoon. That was my biggest protest. Well, that, and that it's shitty in several parts.

Yet, dwarfsploitation wise, the filmmakers did give the dwarf more than ample screen time. He's basically in the entire thing, tagging along with He-Man and his band of warriors as a token sidekick toadie. The great thing is the dwarf in question not only has an awesomely funky red beard, he's also played by powerhouse dwarf actor Billy Barty, God rest his amazing soul. Perhaps the best thing about this movie is the fact that Barty's character of Gwildor is the most important character in the film, next to He-Man. The entire plot revolves around him. And that's a rare thing in the world of dwarf cinema.

In *Masters of the Universe* (1987) our dwarf hero invents a cosmic key that can open a doorway to anywhere, which of course gets the attention of the evil Skeletor, in awesomely freakish makeup and played with relish by the great Frank Langella. Dwarfsploitation is introduced early on in the film after He-Man saves the netted dwarf from his enemies, then enters his home before the plot is revealed. He-Man and his tallie companions are forced to bend over just to make it inside the dwarf's hobbit-style residence. The dwarfsploitation continues as He-Man and the others crack a few jokes at the dwarf's expense, yet protect him from the clutches of the evil tallies throughout the remainder of the film. The dwarf gets into all kinds of dwarfsploitative moments that reinforce the dwarf cinema stereotypes we've talked about throughout the book, such as comic relief dwarf (dwarf trying to communicate with a cow, among other things), hungry dwarf (stealing a tallie's bucket of ribs and chowing down), clumsy dwarf (getting stuck in a muddy creek and flailing around on his back like some kind of a helpless turtle dwarf), materialistic dwarf (dwarf instantly is fascinated by a classic car and feels he must have it) and he does start out as the stereotypical cowardly dwarf, yet stands on his own by refusing to serve Skeletor toward the end.

The main reason to watch this movie, though, is simply to see Billy Barty in that bizarre gnome makeup, pointy ears and red beard. It's f'ing hilarious. The scene where he's wearing a Hawaiian shirt and oversized sunglasses reminds me of an episode of *Alf*.

He-Man rescues netted dwarf.
Red-bearded ginger dwarf.
Keymaster dwarf.
Dwarf has most important role next to He-man.
Locksmith and inventor dwarf.
Tallies crouch to enter dwarf home.
Paranoid, multiple lock-using dwarf.
Dwarf makes a cosmic key that can open a doorway to anywhere.
Cane-using dwarf.
Dimension-hopping dwarf.
Dwarf stuck in muddy creek.
Dwarf sprays water out of his gill slits.
Dwarf tries to communicate with cow.
Dwarf steals food from tallies.
Dwarf drives classic car.
Technological dwarf.
Dwarf dressed in Hawaiian gear.
"What are you looking at Shorty?"
Key-typing dwarf.
Gun-shooting dwarf.
Dwarf breaks up fight.
Dwarf refuses to serve evil master.
Tallie teaches dwarf how to play keyboard.
Victory-yelling dwarf.
Tallie-hugging dwarf.
Time-manipulating dwarf.

Meet the Spartans (2008)

Written and directed by Jason Friedberg and Aaron Seltzer
Starring Kevin Sorbo and Carmen Electra
Featured dwarf: Martin Klebba

Dwarf enthusiasts Friedberg and Seltzer are back to try and spoof a ton of movies. As they are spoofing *300* (2006), they introduce an early enemy—a penguin with happy feet, spoofing *Happy Feet* (2006). It's vulgar to say the least as the penguin gets upset with the tallie and takes him on, sticking his testicles in the face of the tallie and even letting some feces loose. This wouldn't be notable if the penguin were not played by *Pirates of the Caribbean* star Martin Klebba, who deserves so much more. It's short and not worth watching unless you are a Klebba completeist.

Dwarf penguin balls in tallie face.
Dwarf penguin craps on tallie,
Dwarf penguin fights tallie.
Dwarf penguin dancing.

Memories of Me (1988)

Written by Billy Crystal and Eric Roth
Directed by Henry Winkler
Starring Billy Crystal, Alan King
Featured dwarf: Phil Fondacaro

This schmaltzy movie is about a doctor (Billy Crystal) who has a heart attack and decides to look up his father (Alan King). King's character happens to make his living being a movie extra. He introduces his son to all the cliché characters, ranging from the fat guy to the little person, played by Phil Fondacaro. While the movie doesn't point out the fact Phil is a little person it does bunch him up with King's other weirdo friends. It's notable that Phil is also one of the best little people actors out there but he isn't given much to do here. While he gets to speak, it could have been more and that's what I watched this movie for was more Phil action. However, this movie is pretty lame so it was probably best in the end.

Cliché dwarf character.
Dancing dwarf.
Drinking dwarf.

Me, Myself & Irene (2000)

> Written by Peter Farrelly, Mike Cerrone, Bobby Farrelly
> Directed by Bobby Farrelly, Peter Farrelly
> Starring Jim Carrey, Renée Zellweger, Anthony Anderson, Chris Cooper, Michael Bowman, Richard Jenkins, Robert Forster
> Featured Dwarf: Tony Cox
> "I'm gonna' give you a lesson in low center of gravity."

The great Tony Cox shines as an alpha-male dwarf limo driver who instantly gets in a heated argument with Jim Carrey for wanting to pay by check. Although Carrey remains passive, the dwarf becomes increasingly more aggressive until he whips out a pair of nunchucks and beats the crap out of Carrey's legs. What makes matters worse is the dwarf has just driven Carrey and his new wife back from their honeymoon, but before Carrey can take his wife through the threshold, the dwarf has already made an instant connection with her.

It turns out they're both members of Mensa. Before too long, Carrey's wife is pregnant with the dwarf's baby, which turns out to be triplets (unfortunately none are dwarves). The dwarf plays the deadbeat dad role and doesn't claim to be the father even though all three babies are black and Carrey is pasty white. Before too long, Carrey's wife walks out of the house with a picture of Tony Cox on her T-shirt, jumps in the dwarf's car and engages in a vulgar tongue dancing display with the little sexual dynamo right in front of her poor tallie husband. The dwarf drives off stealing Carrey's wife and leaving him a lonely single father.

So, in a nutshell, *Me, Myself & Irene* (2000) gives us the portrait of a philandering, womanizing, deadbeat dwarf dad who's a member of Mensa. Leave it to the Farrelly brothers to gives us elements of dwarfsploitation we never knew existed.

> Dwarf limo driver doesn't accept checks.
> Dwarf uses nunchucks on Jim Carrey's legs.
> Mensa tallie falls in love with Mensa dwarf.
> Tallie tongue dances with dwarf.
> Tallie has picture of dwarf lover on her T-shirt.
> Jim Carrey's wife has dwarf's babies.

Men in Black (1997)

>Written by Ed Solomon
>Directed by Barry Sonnenfeld
>Starring Tommy Lee Jones, Will Smith, Linda Fiorentino, Vincent D'Onofrio, Rip Torn
>Featured dwarves: Verne Troyer, Debbie Lee Carrington

With all the opportunities *Men in Black* (1997) had to put dwarves in this movie, they really dropped the ball on this one. After all, it's a sci-fi extravaganza and pretty much a given that dwarves and sci-fi go together like peanut butter and chocolate, especially because they often choose to cover the face of dwarves in sci-fi movies and realistically they could save money and just recycle the same dwarf over and over again. In the case of *Men in Black* (1997) there's a slight redeeming factor with two very brief cameos by famous dwarves. This is definitely not the movie to see if you're a dwarf enthusiast and are expecting to be treated to various dwarves serving as cinematic treats. However, if you're a trivia buff, this one's worth a look. Unfortunately, a look is about all you get. Literally, if you blink, you may miss it. In fact, it's almost a hidden dwarf scene.

The dwarves in question are played by Verne Troyer and Debbie Lee Carrington. They are in alien suits and Debbie Carrington plays the alien father while Troyer plays the son. Now, if I were in a Q and A with the filmmakers after a screening, I would ask them why they used dwarves when the rest of the effects were primarily CGI, and more importantly, why there weren't more dwarves in a sci-fi movie where there was clearly unlimited potential for multiple dwarves?

Dwarves in alien suits.

Mesa of Lost Women (1953)

>Written by Orville H. Hamilton and Herbert Tevos
>Directed by Ron Ormond and Herbert Tevos
>Starring Jackie Coogan
>Featured dwarves: Angelo Rossitto and John George

A mad scientist has created a group of "spider-women," which basically consists of women with long fingernails, and as with any movie with a mad scientist, he has to have some dwarf assistants. While John George gets some okay screen time leading a researcher around, the rest of the movie he and dwarf legend Angelo Rossitto get not much more than close-ups of their faces and the occasional wide shot as they take on the tallies. This movie is a great example of dwarfsploitation—they're give nothing much to do but the film keeps cutting to them as the filmmakers realize their movie sucks horribly. While the movie is a waste of time, you do get to see two legendary dwarf actors in action.

> Dwarf on the rocks.
> Dwarf through hole.
> Dwarf opens door.
> Dwarf checks out tallie.
> Dwarf handed hat but does nothing.
> Dwarf looking from behind trees.
> Dwarf running.

Midgets Vs. Mascots (2009)

> Written by Kevin Andounian
> Directed by Ron Carlson
> Starring Jason Mewes, Paul Rae, Ron Jeremy, Scottie Pippen
> Featured dwarves: Jordan Prentice, Gary Coleman
> "Hey, aren't you Gary Coleman?"
> "Unfortunately, yes."

In *Midgets Vs. Mascots* (2009), a famous porn star by the name of Big Red Bush makes the two types of people he sympathizes with the most (midgets and mascots) compete for his massive fortune. This is a very exploitative dwarf film that opens right away with dwarves causing all kinds of chaos, running from police and even getting picked up by one of them as if they're about to be tossed. No elements of dwarfsploitation are left out of this mockumentary about the ultimate competition between dwarves vs. tallies in mascot outfits. There's dwarves in furry outfits, dwarves in porn, dwarves in wheelchairs, pot smoking dwarves, vomiting dwarves, the list goes on. The sheer ambition of dwarfsploitation seems endless here. It's almost as if the filmmakers got together, got as liquored up as possible and thought up every conceivable way possible to exploit dwarves. Most likely right before they passed out, they came up with a list and did their damnedest to commit every element on that list to film. And I'll be damned if they didn't do it too!

Now, you may say 'here's a movie that pretty much finds every possible way to exploit dwarves,' and from a curiosity/guilty pleasure standpoint there's something to be said for that, but is it is a good movie? The answer is yes and no. No, it's not a great movie, but yes it's certainly worth watching, and yes it's entertaining all the way through and laugh-out-loud funny in several spots. If anything else, check it out just for the fact the filmmakers actually got on film the bizarre antics they had planned. Hell, they even had Gary Coleman play a major role! There's an extremely funny moment during his introduction where the other dwarves refer to him as the Shaquille O'Neal of little people. He also has a scene where's he's performing oral sex on a woman while she's on the toilet. During the act she breaks wind in his face. Like the scene just described, this is often an extremely un-p.c. movie. I don't think I've heard so many dwarf insults in a movie since *Under the Rainbow* (1981). To give you an example of some of the nasty swipes tallies take at dwarves in the movie, I've comprised a list of quotes here.

> "I have no problem using a midget as a toboggan to get from point A to point B. Especially with these gas prices, right?"
> "They're barely real people."
> "Truth be told, I fucked a dwarf once… it died."
> "You're like, the Shaquille O'Neal of little people." (to Gary Coleman)
> "I can tell you that they don't even smell right."
> "Question, why would I respect the little people?"
> "These guys are worse than cockroaches, man. They're worse than Mexicans."
> "Stand tall. Go grab a Flinstones vitamin or something."
> "Now I'm trying to get the life insurance just so I can stick them in a pillowcase."
> "Gary Coleman touch girl between legs with mouth. Midget win!"
> "Hey, I got to call you back. I'm about to fuck Gary Coleman."
> "They say midgets can lift one hundred times their body weight."

"My fucking team can't even reach the fucking doorbells! They're supposed to sell ladders?!"
"Who smooshed you?"
"Cheer to midgets!"
"Shut up, Willow!"

Yeah, I know, it's pretty brutal, isn't it? I was wondering how this movie actually got made, especially considering the title includes the word midget and that's a hot button in the dwarf community right now. The answer is, the movie does do the standard Hollywood apology for its vulgar, anti-pc humor by punishing the bad guys, teaching lessons about tolerance and even going so far as replacing the title *Midgets vs. Mascots* (2009) with *Little People vs. Mascots*. This of course doesn't happen until the very end of the movie, after all the jokes at the dwarves' expense have already occurred. Looks like someone got to have their cake and eat it too.

Montage of dwarves causing chaos.
Dwarf lifted up by cop.
Dwarf in cowboy outfit.
Dwarf in furry outfit.
Dwarf gives oral to tallie woman in Dorothy outfit.
Dwarf statue.
Dwarf rides in pimped out wheelchair.
Dwarf smokes oversized bong.
Dwarf images on porno movie box covers.
Dwarf has arm around naked tallie woman.
Dwarf rides on tandem bike with Asian tallie sidekick.
Gay dwarf fondles tallie man in bunny outfit.
Gary Coleman confronted by fellow dwarves.
Gary Coleman gets mistaken for Webster.
Dwarves and mascots in obstacle course with fight song from
    The Karate Kid (1984) playing in the background.
Dwarf steals tallie's wallet.
Gay dwarf ogles neud male statue.
Drunken dwarf lusts after tallie widow.
Armageddon (1998)-style slow motion shot of dwarves walking
    beside each other while entering rodeo.
Dwarves chase pig.
Dwarves have great difficulty getting on mechanical bull.

Gator mascot farts in Gary Coleman's general direction.
Coleman bashes tallie gator mascot's head into toilet.
Dwarves vomit milk.
Dwarf projectile-scats herself through the pants.
Tallie girl farts on Coleman as he gives her oral.
Tallie taunts Coleman with watermelon.
"What are you gonna' do? Punch me in the knee?"
Dwarves make porn called *Small Time Cocks*.
Dwarf disrobes.
Two dwarves make out.
Dwarves sell ladders to a fellow dwarf.
Shirtless dwarf practices karate in front of mirror.
Gay dwarf dances between tallies.
Dwarf punched by tallie.
Dwarf donkey kicked by tallie.
Dwarf does snow angel on baseball field.
Dwarf Elvises.
Dwarves jump for tetherball.
Tallie drools on dwarf.
Dwarf/tallie UFC-style fight.
Naked dwarves fight each other.
Losing dwarf gives pep talk.
"We will win this for the little people!"
Dwarf karaoke complete with dwarf backup singers.
Dwarf pole vaults to *The Bionic Man* sound FX.
Basketball playing dwarves.
Dwarves attack Scottie Pippen.
Dwarf falls in love with Asian tallie.

The Minis (2008)

Written and Directed by Valerio Zanoli
Starring Dennis Rodman
Featured dwarves: Joe Gnolfo, Gabriel Pimentel, Bradley Leise, and Dana Woods

This film is a work of dwarfsploitation genius. Just the idea of a team of dwarf basketball players and super tallie Dennis Rodman together had me hooked but this movie goes above and beyond.

It's a very family-friendly, schmaltzy movie that takes standard story plots and twists them to work for dwarves. The stories mostly revolve around two dwarf characters. The first is Roger, a dwarf with a tallie son that is embarrassed about his father and the fact that he did not get into college under the basketball scholarship that he wanted. So, to put his son through college, Roger needs money. Little does he know that he really doesn't want to play basketball but instead wants to go to clown college in France. Next, we have Chevy. Chevy is a lonely dwarf. He has the hots for a beautiful blonde who has an obsession with cows but she can't remember his name and treats him like a child while loving a tallie wannabe basketball player. To get her, he thinks he needs to play basketball and be a star.

To solve both their problems, they discover that a basketball tournament with a reward of $50,000 is happening in Venice Beach. Of course, they only have a few weeks to put together a team and train. Luckily for them, Dennis Rodman is out of money-making ideas and teams up with his agent to create The Minis. This leads to yet another plot about The Minis' newfound fame when they were used to being looked down upon. With Rodman's help, they go from a bunch of haphazard players to pretty darn good players.

The movie is endlessly entertaining and I must have laughed out loud a dozen times which rarely happens. This is an absolute must-purchase.

Not only is the film entertaining, but it also teaches a lot of important lessons including:
- Dwarves can love tallies.
- Respect thy dwarf.
- Its hard being a dwarf's kid.
- Its hard being a dwarf.
- Punk kids do not like dwarves.
- Hot women are only after money.
- Money is not that important (unless you want a hottie tallie girlfriend).
- You are as tall as you want to be.
- You achieve your dreams no matter how big or small you are.
- If you believe in yourself, nothing is impossible.
- It's dwarves, not midgets.
- Dwarves can play basketball too.

- Dwarves aim for the crotch first.
- Dwarves can dance with tallies.
- Dwarves can dunk if thrown.
- Dwarves can drive big cars.
- Dwarves can become tallies by standing on each other... and so on.

Dwarves play basketball next to playground with kid noises in background.
Dwarf sits on basketball.
Dwarves dream of being taller.
"Is the circus back in town?"
"Look, midgets playing basketball."
"Dwarves, not midgets."
"You think just because we are dwarves that we can't play?"
Dwarf tries to get a stuck basketball down from hoop.
Dwarf laughs.
Dwarf patted on head by hottie.
Sad dwarf.
Dwarf jumping down.
"He doesn't look up to me."
"Dude, you have to bring a ladder for him to do that."
Dwarf climbs up chair to sit at table, but he ends up falling off.
Dwarf hit in crotch by ball.
Dwarf not tall enough for pass.
Dwarf in trash can.
Depressed dwarf.
"You might be little but I'm going to make you big!"
Dwarves work out at Muscle Beach.
Dwarves modeling.
"My father's bigger than you will ever be!"
Dwarf lifted onto chair.
Dwarves dancing with tallies.
"If you want to make people laugh, become a dwarf. Look at me, I'm tiny!"
Dwarves asked to be spokespeople for diaper company.
"At least there's one midget who knows how to play ball."
Dwarves referred to as Smurfs.
Hugging dwarves.

Rodman kneels down to talk to dwarves.
Dwarves pile hug Rodman.
Dwarf dribbles under tallie's legs.
Rodman throws dwarf to dunk.
Slow motion shot of dwarf team walking towards camera
"Tonight I feel like the tallest man in the world."
Dwarves in love montage.
Dwarf eats raw eggs.
Dwarves on trampoline.
Dwarf hanging from tree.
Dwarf flexing, then water is dumped on him.
Dwarf driving Hummer.
Dwarves depants tallie.
Dwarf commits crotch violence to get ball.
Dwarves glow and stand on top of each other to form a tallie.
"When I grow up, I wanna be a dwarf."
Romantic running dwarf.

Monkeybone (2001)

Written by Sam Hamm
Directed by Henry Selick
Starring Brendan Fraser, Bridget Fonda, Chris Kattan, Rose McGowan, Whoopi Goldberg
Featured Dwarf: Arturo Gill

This movie could have been great and certainly started out that way. There are certainly some very impressive visuals and interesting concepts, but with each minute that passes, it gets shittier and shittier. It's about a cartoonist (played by tallie Brendan Fraser) who goes into a coma and battles the Monkeybone character he created in order to rejoin the real world and his hot tallie girlfriend (played by Bridget Fonda). After the film's descent into shittiness, the great dwarf actor Arturo Gill fortunately-shows up to breathe some life into the film. He's a prison guard made up to look like a giant rat. His scenes are humorous but short, and not enough to recommend the movie. Basically, this one's a pass unless you're really high and/or have a fetish for dwarves that look like Mickey Mouse on acid.

Dwarf rat prison guard.
Yelling dwarf rat guard.
Dwarf rat guard blows whistle.
Dwarf rat guard calls for visitor.
Dwarf rat guard cockblocks Fraser and Rose McGowan.
McGowan pins down dwarf rat guard so Fraser can escape.

Monster High (1989)

Written by Roy Langsdon and John Platt
Directed by Rudiger Poe
Featured dwarf: Phil Fondacaro

How *Monster High* (1989) is not considered the worst movie of all time is beyond me. It sounded ok—aliens start doomsday at a high school. Unfortunately for them, the mediocre guy takes them on and wins. The movie is filled with stupid characters and situations. In one such case, a character decides to dry his shoes, called Stinksuckers, in the microwave. Notably, the shoes also come with a warning not to have them near radiation. When the character puts the shoes back on, he explodes and the shoes grow into a creature that is played by dwarf legend Phil Fondacaro. Stinksucker chases the hero around a little but suddenly becomes an unimportant background character, appearing later as a cheerleader for the alien team in a strange, clichéd high school basketball game.

In most films, the creature outfits are fitted for the actors. In this beauty, Phil's "Stinksucker" outfit is nothing more than a monster outfit that looks unfinished and can be slipped on anyone, exposing the wearer's feet and legs. It's just another silly aspect to a horrible movie that wastes its best actor.

Dwarf in bad costume.
Dwarf in bathroom.
Dwarf cheerleader.
Dwarf with no lines.

Moulin Rouge (2001)

> Written by Baz Luhrmann, Graig Pearce
> Directed by Baz Luhrmann
> Starring Nicole Kidman, Ewan McGregor, John Leguizamo, Jim Broadbent, Richard Roxburgh
> Featured dwarf: Kiruna Stamell
> "Never fall in love with a woman who sells herself. It always ends bad."

This is a tough one to get through unless you're a fan of musicals. It certainly isn't one worth watching if you're a dwarf enthusiast because there's not nearly enough of the dwarf to see in this film. I'm not saying it's a bad movie, I'm just saying its not my thing. Now, a musical about an entire dance hall/bordello of dwarves, I could definitely be down with without feeling the urge to hit the fast-forward button. Although, they did try and pull off an all dwarf musical before in *The Terror of Tinytown* (1938), that didn't necessarily go over so well. But, there were clearly less-talented individuals in charge of the music in that film, so who know what heights dwarves could reach given the proper production.

The dwarf in *Moulin Rouge* (2001) is simply used to add atmosphere to the circus sideshow-esque backdrop of this movie. Unfortunately, all Luhrmann really uses her for is a few sparse cutaways of dancing and reactions. However, I will say that for the dwarf-curious it's worth a look just to see this sexy dwarf actress in her burlesque outfit. Other than that, on the dwarf level I was very unsatisfied and confused that the far more annoying tallies in the film took all the roles in the film that actually had characters. And the dwarf, as usual got stuck with not nearly enough cinematic table scraps to make a meal out of. Disappointing, Mr. Luhrman. Very disappointing. Recommended only for those who desire a lap dance from a sexy dwarf in saloon style seduction gear.

> Hot female dwarf in burlesque outfit.
> Dwarf pokes head out from under table.
> Dwarf in bellydancer outfit sings *Rythym of the Night*.
> Bird's eye view of dwarf dancer.
> Dwarf dancer gets freaked out by gun.

Munchies (1987)

>Written by Lance Smith
>Directed by Tina Hirsch
>Starring Harvey Korman, Charlie Stratton, Nadine Van der Velde, and Alix Elias
>Featured dwarves: Michael Lee Gogin, Larry Nicholas, Kevin Thompson
>"C'mon, snap it up short stops, okay?"

This movie is a blatant rip off of *Gremlins* (1984), where, at the beginning, a dorky kid and his father (famous comedy tallie Harvey Korman) find a cute and cuddly creature and, all of a sudden, the creature gets incredibly dangerous. It's a cheap imitation of a much better movie. Needless to say, this movie's not very good and if you're looking for dwarves it's certainly not worth your time, as you have to sit through a whole lot of this movie to get even just a little bit of dwarf in return. I have no idea why they even had dwarves in this movie in the first place. It's almost as if the director or producer knew a couple of dwarves and just wanted to throw them a bone or maybe the dwarves appeared in the movie as a favor to the filmmakers because all that happens in this movie dwarfwise is the munchies attack the dwarves while they're working at a burger joint, with the dwarves running away like scared little girls, arms flailing all over the place. It's a really sad misuse of dwarves and is such a short sequence it doesn't even do anything to enhance the movie.

Definitely skip it and watch the far superior *Gremlins* (1984) instead. And even though that film doesn't have any dwarves that I know of, at least they didn't waste the talents of a good dwarf, or in *Munchies'* case, three of them.

>Three dwarves work at fast food burger joint with an a-hole boss.
>Dwarves run away from the burger joint, arms flailing and scared out of their minds.

My Bloody Valentine (2009)

Starring Jensen Ackles, Jamie King, Kerr Smith, Tom Atkins
Featured dwarf: Selene Luna

In this remake, a killer is on the loose and on a rampage. Unfortunately in his path is the owner of a hotel, played by Selene Luna. Selene is first seen out looking for her dog and that's how we see her next as well. Unfortunately the second time is when the killer is chasing after a fully nude woman. When Selene enters looking for her dog, she goes for the closet thinking she hears the dog. Sadly, she is wrong and it's the killer who slams the pick axe into the bottom of her head and lifts her up, knocking out some lights in the ceiling.

It's unfortunate that her screen time is so short but still a worthy addition to a solid horror film.

Dwarf with dog.
Dwarf held up by pick axe.
Dead dwarf.

My Son, My Son, What Have Ye Done (2009)

Written by Herbert Golder and Werner Herzog
Directed by Werner Herzog
Starring Michael Shannon, Brad Dourif
Featured dwarf: Gabriel Pimentel

Herzog brings his unique style to a tale of a lunatic son (Michael Shannon) who has killed his mother with a sword he was using as a prop in a play. While the movie is great at showing how crazy most actors are, it's a little low on the dwarf quota. In ONE bizarre scene, Shannon's uncle (played brilliantly by Brad Dourif) is talking about how he had an insanely large rooster that was going to be in a commercial with a small but fully grown pony with a dwarf on it. The dwarf on the pony would still be smaller than the rooster, which apparently was the great joke of this commercial that the uncle has no idea what it was for. Standing on a VERY large stump behind them is a nicely dressed dwarf. He gets to say nothing and looks more like Mini-Me than we needed. At the conclusion of the scene, all three just stare at the camera until the song is over.

This one scene is bizarre and will probably be hailed by many as artsy. The dwarf is there for no real purpose and doesn't even fit into the scene directly.

> Dwarf extra.
> No lines for dwarf.
> Dwarf on large stump.
> Dwarf dressed up.
> Dwarf looking like Mini-Me.
> Dwarf discussion.

The New Guy (2002)

> Written by David Kendall
> Directed by Ed Decter
> Starring DJ Qualls, Eliza Dushku, Zooey Deschanel, Lyle Lovett, Eddie Griffin
> "Who's that little dude?"

The New Guy (2002) is your typical, by-the-numbers coming of age story about a scrawny tallie dork that is the butt all the evil tallies' jokes, no matter what school he goes to. That is, until the day he goes to prison and gets schooled by Eddie Griffin about the ways of being street. When he gets out of the slammer, he goes to a new school and reinvents himself as a completely different, undorky tallie. Part of his being the cool new guy as well as the fact anyone would believe this toad would rise to heroic feats is his likeability factor, which includes defending a tuba playing dwarf.

During an earlier scene in the film, an evil jock tallie puts gum in the dwarf's tuba, picks him up, jams him in a garbage can and kicks him down the stairs. When the new guy stands against the evil jock tallie, spits gum on the dwarf nerd's hair, tosses him in a trash can and kicks him down a hill. When tallie Qualls fights the evil jock, he gains the instant admiration of the tuba-playing dwarf.

The tuba dwarf's scenes are pure black and white pick-on-a-dwarf scenes and aren't nearly extensive enough. However, the fact that cinema rarely if ever gives us tuba-playing dwarves and the fact the tuba dwarf is granted revenge on his tallie oppressor, adds to the movie and allows it to be in the "rent if you're bored and have a spare dollar" category.

> Tuba-playing dwarf.
> Jock tallie spits gum on tuba dwarf's hair.
> Tuba dwarf celebrates first winning football game.
> Tuba dwarf tossed in trash can and kicked down a hill.
> Tuba dwarf plays bagpipes in *Braveheart* outfit.
> Tuba dwarf sits on tallie's shoulders.
> Dwarf tossing.
> Tuba dwarf beats tallie with trash can.
> Tuba dwarf unleashes duct tape on tallie.

Nice Dreams (1981)

> Written by Tommy Chong and Cheech Marin
> Directed by Tommy Chong (as Thomas Chong)
> Starring Cheech Marin, Tommy Chong, Sandra Bernhard,
>   Michael Winslow, Paul Reubens
> Featured dwarf: Tony Cox (as Joe Anthony Cox)

When Cheech and Chong get surrounded by nut cases, it's an all star cast including comedians Sandra Bernhard (from TV's *Roseanne*), Michael Winslow (Larvelle Jones from *Police Academy (1984)*) and Paul "Pee Wee Herman" Reubens. Of course, a bunch of nut cases would not be complete without a couple of dwarves running around. There is one dwarf extra who is randomly swinging on an out-of-place swing who is also later being carried around. Then we get a weird scene where Cheech appears to be tripping and he's front and center as Winslow does his imitation of Jimi Hendrix. Standing on each side of Winslow are two dwarves in karate outfits, which is notable for one of them being a very, very young Tony Cox. The dwarves are randomly and nonsensically placed, thus being there only for exploitation purposes. The movie itself is for Cheech and Chong enthusiasts only.

> Swinging dwarf.
> Dwarf being held.
> Dwarves in karate outfits.
> Dwarf extras.

Night of the Creeps (1986)

Written and Directed by Fred Dekker
Starring Elizabeth Alda, Tom Atkins, Todd Bryant, Elizabeth Cox, Tex Donaldson
Featured dwarves: Kevin Thompson, Joseph S. Griffo, Daniel Frishman

Night of the Creeps (1986) doesn't waste any time introducing dwarves as it opens on a spaceship where two dwarves in alien suits chase another dwarf in an alien suit while holding guns half the size of their bodies. The dwarf being pursued successfully outruns the other alien dwarves and makes it into an escape hatch only to be destroyed before escaping, but not before his experiment makes it out of the ship and floats into space out of the reach of the alien pursuers. The alien pursuers are played by notable dwarf actors Kevin Thompson and Joseph S. Griffo while Daniel Frishman plays the alien zombie they pursue. Frishman of course is the excellent dwarf actor from the classic dwarfsploitation film *Lone Wolf McQuade* (1983).

The dwarf scene serves as the basis for the rest of the movie but unfortunately there are no flashbacks to alien dwarves and they don't even land on planet earth where the rest of the movie takes place. *Night of the Creeps* (1986) is a fantastic cult movie for tallies but from a dwarf enthusiast's point of view I can't recommend it unless you have a fetish for dwarves in weird alien suits.

Dwarves in alien suits.
Dwarves running with guns.
Subtitled dwarf aliens.

Night Patrol (1984)

Written by Jackie Kong, Murray Langston, William A. Levey (as Bill Levey), and Bill Osco
Directed by Jackie Kong
Starring Linda Blair, Pat Morita, Andrew "Dice" Clay
Featured dwarf: Billy Barty

This super crazy and goofy comedy is a vehicle for the Unknown Comic, playing a motorcycle cop named Melvin (perhaps inspired by the superior *Toxic Avenger* (1984)) who has screwed up so many times that he's relegated to the night patrol. Apparently with too much time on his hands, he decides to moonlight as a stand-up comic with a bag over his head and ends up being successful. Things go wrong when someone starts imitating the Unknown Comic and goes on a robbing spree.

Determined to wipe out crime is Captain Lewis, played by the ultra-talented Billy Barty, feisty as ever as the constantly flatulent, small ball of rage. The best moments are definitely delivered by Barty's angry captain, eager to wipe out crime but is constantly getting information wrong ("Who called me a liar?!") and can't seem to stop farting. The highlight is definitely a scene in which Barty pulls a gun on an innocent tallie, who in turn punches him and sends him flying.

The movie is completely insane and something you'll definitely talk about for years to come, but take it in knowing that it's complete trash.

> Dwarf stands on top of desk to be eye level with tallie.
> Dwarf farts uncontrollably.
> Angry dwarf peaks through window.
> Dwarf with hot chicks in car.
> Maniacally laughing dwarf.
> Dwarf in cowboy hat.
> Dwarf lead by cheek.
> Dwarf lifted up.
> Screaming dwarf.
> Dwarf sees one of many girlfriends.
> Dwarf presses into girl's breasts.
> Dwarf threatens tallie with gun.
> Dwarf flies after being punched.

No Way to Treat a Lady (1968)

Written by John Gay
Directed by Jack Smight
Starring George Segal, Rod Steiger
Featured dwarf: Michael Dunn

George Segal plays a detective on the trail of a serial killer played by Rod Steiger. As serial killer mania hits, an impostor claiming to be the serial killer comes to turn himself in. The only problem for this imposter, Mr. Kupperman, is that he is a dwarf. Playing Mr. Kupperman is dwarf acting legend Michael Dunn, giving a scene-stealing riot of a performance with some of the greatest dwarf exchanges in film history.

The shame is that this is only one scene—it's hilarious and an absolute must see for any dwarf enthusiast.

> Dwarf is the size of sitting tallie.
> "I'm very sensitive on certain subjects."
> "You're a midget."
> "Lots of people are midgets."
> "He was taller than you."
> "See how I fooled them. I'm a master of disguise."
> "You're a bigot! You're prejudiced against midgets!"
> "You'd believe me in a minute if I wasn't a midget!"
> "Would you like your sister to marry a midget?!"
> Angry dwarf.
> Dwarf throws chalk at tallie.

O Brother, Where Art Thou? (2000)

> Written by Joel and Ethan Coen
> Directed by Joel Coen
> Starring George Clooney, Charles Durning, John Goodman and Holly Hunter
> Featured dwarf: Ed Gale
> "Homer stokes, servant of the little man. Ain't that right little fella?"
> "He ain't lyin."

When a group of convicts escape and go in search of a treasure, they run across a bevy of oddball characters in this story based upon Homer's *Odyssey*. In one subplot, there's a tight race for governor. There's newcomer Homer Stokes, who uses a little person (the always great Ed Gale) as his sidekick during the campaign trail, with the running motto of "serving the little man." Gale mostly imitates Stokes, such as when Stokes holds up a broom during the speech, we see Gale doing the same. Running for re-election is 'Pappy McDaniel' (played by Charles Durning), but he's unable to get his election going and seems to be losing to Stokes. At one point Durning is talking to his inept campaign team and they start discussing getting their own "midget" for the campaign but even smaller. The movie itself is fun and Ed is only an added bonus to an already good movie. Really, it's worth watching just for Ed as a KKK member but they could've given him more lines.

> Dwarf as campaign tool.
> Sweeping dwarf.
> Dwarf copies movements of tallie.
> Dwarf referred to as a midget.
> Dwarf klansman.

Penelope (2006)

> Written by Leslie Caveny
> Directed by Mark Palansky
> Starring Christina Ricci, James McAvoy, Catherine O'Hara,
>   Reese Witherspoon, Peter Dinklage
> Featured dwarf: Peter Dinklage

This is a movie about a girl named Penelope (played by Christina Ricci) who's cursed to have the nose of a pig. Her family is rich but once potential suitors get a look at her they jump right out the window and never return. That is, until a dwarf tabloid reporter (Peter Dinklage) with a bunch of nerdy technical equipment in his van pays tallie James McAvoy to woo Penelope until he can get the perfect shot of her with her pig nose and get rich. Unfortunately, even a dwarf couldn't save this movie, and when the dwarf in question is Peter Dinklage (who is for my money the best dwarf actor working today), you know there's a problem.

This problem could have been fixed by simply making Dinklage the main character instead of bland tallie Fabio McAvoy. Damnit, dwarves deserve to be the main love interest! Enough of these limited screen-time side character roles they keep getting! But of course the filmmakers wouldn't give the lead to the dwarf, which is why the movie failed. It didn't help that the whole thing was so damn boring, either. I was excited when I saw the dwarf on the DVD menu screen, amused at the beginning when I saw the pig nose, stayed amused when multiple suitors keep jumping out the window at the sight of it, got happy when Dinklage appeared wearing that private eye hat and eyepatch, then almost feel asleep for the rest of the movie. Even the dwarf in the rowboat couldn't bring me back to life.

> Dwarf in menu screen of DVD.
> Eyepatch-wearing dwarf.
> Detective hat-wearing dwarf.
> Tech-savvy dwarf.
> Periscope-looking dwarf.
> Nosy hot dog-eating dwarf.
> Dwarf talks on creepy red phone.
> Typing dwarf.
> Dwarf with a conscience.
> Dwarf in boat.
> Rowing dwarf.
> Photographer dwarf.

Penitentiary 2 (1982)

> Written and directed by Jamaa Fanaka
> Starring Mr. T, Leon Isaac Kennedy and Glynn Thurman
> Featured dwarf: Tony Cox (as Joe Anthony Cox)

The sequel to Jamaa Fanaka's *Penetentiary* (1979) finds Leon Isaac Kennedy forced to go back to boxing in the prison system. Since the fights tend to be lame, Jamaa did the smartest thing possible—he threw a dwarf prisoner that needed to get laid into the mix. Just randomly during fights, the movie would shift to some great comic relief, first of Tony gambling and making money. He would then go looking for poontang by crawling under the ring and lifting it so he could talk to the women watching the match. He would make the women an offer and then they'd want more. It's not until the end of the movie that Tony finally gets what he wants. As the end credits come up, the entire group is in the ring congratulating the winner. In front of the group flies Tony with his woman in hand. His excited face is hilarious as he points to the woman, letting us know he FINALLY got laid.

While the movie is rather lame, Tony is awesome as the horny side character. Worth a fast-forward.

Notably, part 3 also features a dwarf so Mr. Fanaka must have agreed that Tony definitely spiced this one up.

> Dwarf prisoner.
> Dwarf gambling.
> Horny dwarf.
> Dwarf propositions tallies.
> Dwarf gets laid.
> Dwarf excited.

Phenomena (1985)

> Written by Franco Ferrini and Dario Argento
> Directed by Dario Argento
> Starring Jennifer Connelly, Donald Pleasence and Tanga
> Featured dwarf: Davide Marotta

The daughter of a famous movie star starts at a boarding school where she has some trouble with sleepwalking. As it turns out, someone is on a killing spree which comes out while she's sleepwalking. As luck would have it, she befriends an entomologist and together they discover that she has an uncanny ability to communicate with insects, which is the only protection she has from the mad people around her. In the climactic scene, what appears to be a mutated child (but is really dwarf stuntman Davide Marotta) attacks her until he's swarmed by flies.

The movie is definitely not worth watching just for the dwarf actor but it is worth watching for the chimpanzee.

> Dwarf glove doesn't fit young girl.
> Dwarf with mutated face.
> Dwarf with spear.
> Dead dwarf.

Pierrot Le Fou (1965)

>Written and directed by Jean Luc Godard
>Starring Anna Karina and Jean-Paul Belmondo
>Featured dwarf: Jimmy Karoubi

Pierrot and Marianne are on the run. In one scene, while on a boat, there is a dwarf running alongside the dock yelling at them. She gets nervous as they pull up and he's next to a car. She ends up going off with him but soon discovers it's dangerous. He wants to know where the money is and guns come into play in a weird arthouse exchange, where he's pointing the gun at the screen and she has scissors. We come back to him and he's been killed with the scissors, "A glorious death for a little man."

A classic Godard film that gets a little extra punch thanks to a great dwarf actor.

>Dwarf running with large phone.
>Woman is scared of dwarf.
>Dwarf with large guns.
>Dwarf points gun at screen.
>Dead dwarf.
>Dwarf corpse lifted up and laid upside down on chair.

Pinata: Survival Island (2002)

>Written and directed by David and Scott Hillenbrand
>Starring Nicholas Brendon and Jaime Pressly
>Featured dwarf: Ed Gale
>"Let's open you up there, big guy."

Also known as *Demon Island (2002)*, this one has a group of college kids who go to an island for a scavenger hunt/party during Cinco De Mayo. When they conveniently split up in pairs, one group finds the cursed piñata floating in the water. When they start beating on it and then turn their backs, it comes to life and begins slaughtering these silly teens.

It's a standard horror movie setup, with all the clichés intact (hot teenagers doing stupid things and being attacked by a killer as they become separated, etc.). Playing the killer piñata is none other than dwarf legend Ed Gale—perhaps cast because he also played "Chucky" in the *Child's Play* series. While most movies would not credit the dwarf actor playing the killer (look to see where his credit is in the *Child's Play* series), this one gives Ed billing in the opening credits and deservedly so. Unfortunately, it happens that the movie is by no means a classic.

The movie typically falls into the horrible movie category. It's not *Monster High* (1989) bad, but it's by no means good. I think it's a passable horror film made better by the weird piñata character that may have been just too strange a killer for horror enthusiasts to accept. The only downside of the piñata for me is that when they use CGI to add to our little killer, it's laughable, and nothing ages quicker than CGI. The upside is when it's just the regular old piñata running around and destroying the dumb youth.

This movie is recommended just on the basis of the notoriety of the great Ed Gale, but be prepared for some cheese and tons of bad CGI.

>   Dwarf Piñata kills tallies.
>   Close up of dwarf piñata legs.
>   Angry dwarf piñata.
>   Dwarf piñata flies across screen.
>   Dwarf piñata growls.
>   Dwarf piñata kills tallies with shovel.
>   Dwarf piñata commits crotch violence.
>   Dwarf piñata jumps from tree.
>   Close up of dwarf piñata legs hitting ground.
>   Dwarf piñata Predator-vision.
>   Dwarf piñata swinging.

The Pink Panther Strikes Again (1976)

>   Written by Frank Waldman and Blake Edwards
>   Directed by Blake Edwards
>   Starring Peter Sellers
>   Featured dwarf: Deep Roy

Among the bunch of assassins trying to kill Inspector Clouseau is Tim Burton's dwarf of choice, Deep Roy, in a silly costume that reminded me of Robin Hood. In the short amount of screen time he gets, a man at a table picks Roy up and treats him like a child. When Clouseau steps in to help, Roy is shot accidentally by another assassin. Not worth the viewing just for Deep Roy.

> Dwarf in costume.
> Dwarf assassin.
> Dwarf trips man woman.
> Dwarf lifted up by tallie.
> Dead dwarf.

Pirates of the Caribbean: Curse of the Black Pearl (2003)

> Written by Ted Elliott, Terry Rossio, Stuart Beattie, and
>   Jay Wolpert
> Directed by Gore Verbinski
> Starring Johnny Depp, Keira Knightley
> Featured dwarf: Martin Klebba

When they need to get a group of pirates together, they end up with a group of misfits. And we all know that a group of misfits is not complete without the inclusion of a dwarf. In the introduction of our misfits, they are lined up being introduced to Captain Jack Sparrow (Johnny Depp). One by one introduced are tallies and then the camera dips down as we are introduced to Martin Klebba. The highlight is unfortunately this and a classic cut to Johnny Depp looking down at Klebba weirdly, an image I still can't get out of my head, days later. Unlike the sequels, where Klebba gets a lot more action, he unfortunately doesn't get much to do here.

> Camera scrolls tallies and goes down to dwarf.
> Sparrow looks down at Klebba weirdly.
> Dwarf loading cannon.
> Dwarf covering ears.

Pirates of the Caribbean 2: Dead Man's Chest (2006)

Written by Ted Elliott, Terry Rossio
Directed by Gore Verbinski
Starring Johnny Depp, Keira Knightley, Bill Nighy and Orlando Bloom
Featured dwarf: Martin Klebba

Captain Jack Sparrow (and pretty well everyone from the first one) returns in the second of the *Pirates* series to fight off Davy Jones, a slothy mutant (played by Bill Nighy). Sparrow owes Jones his soul but is looking for the key to the Dead Man's Chest. All this leads to various adventures with the crew of his ship, which once again includes "Marty" as played by Martin Klebba—I'm guessing they couldn't think of anything original? While Martin is great, he is only given one line at a time it seems and his screen time mostly consists of cut-to's and inserts, thus making it look like he's only there because he's a dwarf. The only good parts come when Martin is involved in an action scene. For instance, when the crew is in a ball made of bones, all the tallie's feet hit the ground but not Marty's, even though he keeps moving his legs as if he can. That almost makes this movie worth watching—almost.

Angry dwarf.
Dwarf sitting on objects to be same height as tallies.
Dwarf picking up after zombie monkey.
Shirtless dwarf running.
Caged dwarf.
Screaming dwarf.
Dwarf legs don't reach ground.
Swimming dwarf.
Running dwarf.
Dwarf with gun.
Dwarf licking finger.
Scared dwarf.
Dwarf on ropes.
Dwarf bosses others while doing nothing.
Dwarf sits on boat top.

Pirates of the Caribbean 3: At World's End (2007)

    Written by Ted Elliott and Terry Rossio
    Directed by Gore Verbinski
    Starring Johnny Depp, Keira Knightley, Chow Yun-Fat
    Featured Dwarf: Martin Klebba

In the third installment of the *Pirates* series, the dwarf pirate "Marty" continues to follow around Jack Sparrow and company. The movie is mindless fun and Martin is again in it for what seems like no reason other than the fact he's a dwarf. There are some great visuals, including a large war scene where Marty is standing high above on the ship, blowing away bad guy after bad guy. This one also includes the infamous scene where Martin fires a large gun and flies backwards. The film also includes another pirate dwarf during the scene with the Nine Pirate Lords of the Brethren Court. This dwarf also gets very little screen time and seems to only be there because he's unique. The movie itself is overlong and very boring at times but is enough fun with the addition of "Marty" that it almost makes it worth watching.

    Dwarf walking standing up while tallies have to crawl.
    Dwarf sits on top of fatty and hits him with a shovel.
    Dwarf lighting bombs.
    Dwarf uses big gun and gets blown backwards.
    Running dwarf.
    Another dwarf pirate extra.
    Marty stands alone firing gun.

Planet Patrol (1999)

    Written by Benjamin Carr
    Directed by Russ Mazzolla
    Starring Alison Lohman
    Featured dwarf: Jon Simanton
    "Shut up, you little space flea!"

This movie stinks really, really bad. I'm not even sure if one could find any enjoyment in this one while drunk. When Lord Doom, a Skeletor-type baddie, puts his dwarf sidekick Chamberlain in charge, everything goes wrong. They try Godzilla-like monsters, giant robots, and every other piece of junk in the Full Moon catalog of stock footage but fail miserably because they are stopped by a group of teens who dress up in tighter versions of the Star Trek outfits. The dwarf is played here by Jon Simanton, who must have been given a 1:1 filming ratio because he stumbles through his lines on a constant basis. His outfit looks ridiculous, with him being covered in white with silly sunglasses/goggles over his eyes. While he could have easily stolen the show, we are instead left to find the entertainment in the bewildering number of times a crotch or hand "accidentally grazes" Lohman's dark places.

> Dwarf in stupid outfit.
> Dwarf on mini screen.
> Dwarf talking in microphone.
> Surprised dwarf.
> Dwarf sent to ice room with rubber duckie as punishment.
> Dwarf runs away.
> Dwarf in mini prison.

Pocketful of Miracles (1961)

> Directed by Frank Capra
> Starring Glenn Ford, Peter Falk, Bette Davis
> Featured dwarf: Angelo Rossitto
> "All you little people in there, you start workin.'"

Annie (Bettie Davis) is a broke bum who goes around selling magic apples, promising little people inside that make them special. When her daughter has the chance to marry someone with money and come out for a visit, she doesn't want them to know she's broke. With some help, they transform her into someone amazing that her daughter can be proud of.

No broke bum is complete without a group of misfit bum friends. And no group of misfits seems to be complete without the use of a dwarf, played this time by the wonderful yet often underused Angelo Rossitto. Although short in stature, Angelo sticks out in a crowd and is just wonderful.

> Dwarf is part of a group of misfits.
> Camera goes down to film dwarf with money.

Poltergeist (1982)

Written by Steven Spielberg, Michael Grais, Mark Victor
Directed by Tobe Hooper
Starring Craig T. Nelson, JoBeth Williams, Beatrice Straight, and Dominique Dunne
Featured dwarf: Zelda Rubinstein
"What side of the rainbow are you operating on today?"

Whereas *E.T.* was a movie filled with warmth that was very heartfelt and left me with a good feeling as a child, *Poltergeist* (1982) scared the living crap out of me. However, not unlike *E.T.* (1982), the dwarf in this film appears as a friend to the tallies in their time of need via supernatural salvation. Like *The Exorcist* (1973), various methods of help outside the supernatural are exhausted first.

Then, Craig T. Nelson and company finally come to their senses and hire the psychic services of Tangina, played with equal amounts of maternal conviction and creepiness by dwarf actor Zelda Rubinstein, who looks a lot like a miniature female version of Jim Jones here with her oversized glasses. Now personally, if it were me, I would have hired the dwarf first before exploring the other options. Well, before that, I would have never actually bought land on cursed burial ground in the first place but, if I did, the first thing I'd be doing afterward is thumbing through the phone book and looking to find the services of the first renowned dwarf psychic/exorcist I could. And, as we can see here, nothing was effective until the clueless tallies finally pulled their heads out of their asses, discovered their brains and consulted psychic dwarf services.

The interesting thing about *Poltergeist* (1982) (other than the fact it's a great movie) is that it's also audio dwarfsploitation as well as visual. Now indeed, the typical dwarfsploitation shots are used to draw attention to Rubinstein's lack of height as well as lots of extreme close up shots on the strange looking dwarf as she reacts to all the weirdness around her. However, even more attention is drawn to the incredibly distinct dwarf's voice. It's as if you could hear a pin drop whenever the dwarf speaks and all the attention is suddenly focused to her. The dwarf is clearly the most fascinating character in the film and must have kept hack psychics who attempted to cash in on her fame employed for years. Kudos to the unusual forms of dwarfsploitation used here by Spielberg and Hooper's dwarf loveathon of a family horror movie.

Large-glasses-wearing dwarf.
Psychic dwarf.
Dwarf kisses kneeling tallie
Extended dwarf exposition.
Dwarf makes tallies crazy.
Extreme dwarf close up.
Tennis ball-holding dwarf.
Dwarf throws tennis ball into the other side.

Poltergeist 2 (1986)

Written by Michael Grais, Mark Victor
Directed by Brian Gibson
Starring JoBeth Williams, Craig T. Nelson, Heather O'Rourke, and Oliver Robins
Featured dwarf: Zelda Rubinstein
"There's a presence."

Fortunately we don't have to wait too long in *Poltergeist 2* (1986) to get our dwarf fix. After a brief intro (that frankly feels unrelated to the first *Poltergeist* (1982), we're treated to the reappearance of the highly knowledgeable dwarf psychic Tangina. When she first shows up, it's in a large hole left from the house in the first *Poltergeist* (1982) movie. This of course is dwarfsploitation in and of itself, since it clearly makes the dwarf look even smaller in comparison to the massive opening she stands next to.

In this installment of the trilogy, Tangina's shown instantly in a buddy/buddy position with a Native American. The dwarf is clearly smart for doing this because, as the movies have taught us, Native Americans always have the upper hand when it comes to fighting the supernatural, and of course, most of the other tallie characters in the movie are at odds with the dwarf. Folks, come on now. When are you going to learn? The plot of *Poltergeist 2* (1986) revolves around a creepy looking tallie ghost who resembles Angus Scrimm from the *Phantasm* (1979) series. And once again, the dwarf has to come to the rescue of the tallie family as they continue to deny the presence of the supernatural. The dwarf senses they're in trouble after the hauntings continue and bails the tallie's asses out of the fire by taking them into the core site and leading the charge, attempting to silence the ghosts, once and for all.

This is one brave dwarf, trudging through decaying corpses and skeletons while confronting unearthly danger head on. She needed to be the star of her own *Ghost Hunters* style TV show because she's much more charismatic that anyone's who's in the number of reality shows on TV now about the paranormal. There are a few good scenes in *Poltergeist 2* (1986) but it's not nearly the classic part 1 is and the movie definitely could have used more dwarf, instead of having her absent for a great deal of the movie and then having most her screen time spent toward the very end of the movie as fearless, hero dwarf.

> Dwarf framed next to large hole in ground.
> Dwarf senses tallie family in danger.
> Lantern holding dwarf.
> Dwarf frightened in cave.
> "There's something terrible. Too much power."

Poltergeist 3 (1988)

> Written by Gary Sherman, Brian Taggert
> Directed by Gary Sherman
> Starring Heather O'Rourke, Tom Skerritt, Nancy Allen
> Featured dwarf: Zelda Rubinstein
> "I'm one of your brother in law's weirdo psychics."

Poltergeist 3 (1988) is definitely the weakest installment of the series and most likely the one that buried the franchise (that is, until the remake of part 1 rolls around). It does, however, make the smart decision of increasing the screen time for psychic dwarf Tangina (played by the awesome Zelda Rubinstein), who's been present throughout the series. This is most definitely a step up from part 2 which was seriously lacking in dwarf screen time. In *Poltergeist 3* (1988), the albino tallie girl moves in with her aunt, her husband and daughter to distance herself from the traumatic events of the previous two films. While she lucks out and ends up with a rich family, she's unfortunately given therapy by a tallie who somehow brings the poltergeists back just because he gets her thinking about them again. Thinly veiled plot, anyone? The ignorant therapist of course, doesn't listen to all-knowing power-dwarf psychic Tangina and that's when all hell breaks loose. This is the third time now these tallies haven't listened to the dwarf! What in God's name is wrong with these people?

The dwarf's introduction is this film is pretty awesome as it reminded me of a mini, female version of Jim Jones with the oversized glasses as she drinks tea with an old broad and senses something's wrong with the child. The tallie parents of the albino would have been a lot better off if they would have just hired Tangina as their nanny. That way they could have avoided all this unnecessary setup reintroducing the dwarf, and she could have been present constantly! Unfortunately, Hollywood doesn't think this way and we're only treated to the dwarf in sporadic doses throughout the trilogy.

Rubinstein is definitely the highlight of this movie and it saddened me when she stepped into the light because I knew I'd never see her again. She will live in our hearts and minds, as well as the cinema forever though. R.I.P., Zelda Rubinstein. You were truly one of the greats.

> Dwarf tries to telepathically communicate with albino child after she crawls up the mirror.
> Dwarf on plane.
> Dwarf talks on oversized phone.
> Dwarf sports powerful amulet with Native American powers.
> Dwarf stares at sealed off room menacingly.
> High angle dwarf close up.
> Dwarf holds tallie back and schools them on "the other side."
> Dwarf faces off against tallie colleague.
> Tallie parents choose dwarf over quack hypnotist.
> Dwarf framed walking in front of tallies.
> Creepy dwarf watches as tallies kiss.
> Dwarf explains the power of her amulet to skeptical tallie.
> Dwarf always framed in front of tallies as she leads the charge against the ghosts.
> Doors open to show dwarf in front of tallies.
> Dwarf gives long monologue while walking in front of tallies.
> Tallies foolishly avoid advice of dwarf.
> Drowning dwarf.
> Self-sacrificing dwarf.
> Dwarf saves tallie family.
> Dwarf goes into the light.

Postal (2007)

Written by Uwe Boll and Bryan C. Knight
Directed by Uwe Boll
Starring Dave Foley, Zack Ward and Uwe Boll
Featured dwarf: Verne Troyer

Imagine if John Waters meshed with a Troma movie and a touch of Uwe Boll and you get *Postal*, the movie based on the video game. An unlucky slacker has had such a bad day that he ends up teaming up with his Uncle Dave (played by *Kids in the Hall* alum Dave Foley) to steal a load of Krotchy dolls. The voice of the Krotchy dolls is none other than huge international superstar Verne Troyer. In the midst of everything they get mixed up with terrorists, including Osama Bin Laden himself. Troyer ends up getting kidnapped by the slacker (who becomes known as "The Postal Dude") and Uncle Dave's group when it's revealed that in uncle Dave's bible it talks about how a little celebrity would be ass-raped by a thousand monkeys. Yep, we're even treated to a little bit of the raping. The movie is tasteless and, at times, hilarious. Like a *South Park* movie, no one gets left out of the insult flinging—foreigners, cops, fat people, etc. so it's only a given that they go after little people as well. Troyer spends most of his screen time being angry, gets insulted plenty and there are lots of size differential shots to boot.

> Dwarf is the size of a suitcase.
> Dwarf pushing oversized suitcase.
> Pissed off dwarf.
> Dwarf picked up and put on ground.
> Dwarf walking between two sides of tallies.
> Dwarf placed on seat.
> Greedy dwarf.
> Dwarf tossed.
> Dwarf and kid fight.
> Dwarf ball punching.
> Dwarf put in suitcase.
> Dwarf uses dildo as light.
> Dwarf smoking pot in suitcase.
> Dwarf carried by big breasted woman.
> Dwarf flipping off Uncle Dave.
> Angry dwarf tries to fight.

Woman holds dwarf and makes baby faces at him.
Dwarf kicking ass.
Dwarf getting raped by a thousand monkeys.

Pulp Fiction (1994)

Written and Directed by Quentin Tarantino
Starring John Travolta, Bruce Willis, Uma Thurman
Featured dwarf: Michael Gilden

While researching dwarf movies I came across a guy making the comment, "Show me a classic movie and I'll show you a dwarf." Well, *Pulp Fiction* (1994) is another case proving that this guy is dead on. In Quentin Tarantino's masterpiece *Pulp Fiction* (1994), you can see a dwarf a little over 30 minutes into the film during the scene at "Jack Rabbit Slim's." Unfortunately the dwarf mostly gets to stand and walk around (and very, very briefly, at that) but he does get to bellow out some dialogue, although it's with his back turned to the camera.

Dwarf in bellhop uniform.
Dwarf looking at list.
Dwarf hidden behind Uma Thurman's body.
Dwarf opens door to table.

Putney Swope (1969)

Written and Directed by Robert Downey Sr.
Starring Arnold Johnson, Laura Greene
Featured dwarves: Pepi and Ruth Hermine

Putney Swope (1969) is a classic in my book. It's smart, original and manages to entertain me despite its limitations. The story is simple and on the surface; the head of an advertising company dies and when there's the vote to replace him, everyone votes for the guy they think no one else will vote for—Putney Swope, an older black man who speaks his mind. Swope ends up turning the place into a place that's more like the Black Panthers doing advertising.

About 1/3 of the way in, Pepi Hermine (*Even Dwarves Started Small* (1970)) shows up as the President of the United States, who is pressuring Swope and the ad agency into helping out a pot smoking friend of his. Later, the President is very upset that Swope won't advertise war toys, cigarettes and alcohol, calling it "discrimination." The scenes of Pepi laughing hysterically and talking to Swope about shooting up are beyond hilarious. It just wouldn't work the same without Hermine.

The movie becomes all the more interesting when you look at the comparisons of African Americans to little people (see the documentary *Little People* (1982), for instance). Not only is a black man given power at an ad agency but a dwarf is given power of the entire country. The downside of the film is that they both choose to use their power negatively. I, for one, believe it is time our country elects a little person to office—the world would be a better place for it. This film is a must see.

> High-pitched-voice dwarf.
> Dwarf as President of the United States.
> Dwarf wearing silly hat.
> Dwarf cleaned with small brush.
> Close up of dwarf feet not touching the ground.
> Dwarf playing piano.
> Dwarf crawls under table.
> Dwarves hang with pot smoker.
> Dwarves laugh hysterically.
> Dwarf wife slaps her husband.
> Dwarves have threesome with tallie.

Raiders of the Sun (1992)

> Written by Frederick Bailey, Thomas McKelvey Cleaver
> Directed by Cirio H. Santiago
> Starring Richard Norton, William Steis, Henry Strzalkowski, Nick Nicholson, Rick Dean
> Featured dwarf: Ray Bacho

The great Richard Norton is indeed great in this movie but the dwarves are the real stars. In this post-apocalypse action flick, Norton saves several headband-wearing warrior dwarves from being burned alive by a bunch of dwarf-hating, gasoline-pouring baddies. Norton gets injured in the process and the dwarves use teamwork to carry him to safety in a stretcher. Norton recovers from his injuries and teams up with the dwarves to take down more post-apocalyptic thugs. Since this movie was made well after *Return of the Jedi* (1983), we can only assume the writers and director were clearly fans of the Ewoks and wanted to pay homage to those classic little warriors who so bravely took down the Empire. If this wasn't the intention, it's a bizarre coincidence because everything from the dwarf warriors' garb to "yub, yub" style mutterings are reminiscent of Lucas' kiddified vision of lovable, cuddly bad-asses. Every time the warrior dwarves are on screen in *Raiders of the Sun* (1992), the film picks up significantly, and when Norton and the warrior dwarves rush into battle together it's magical.

The problem is, the dwarves aren't on screen nearly long enough. They show up thirty-five minutes into the movie and are occasionally cut back to. There are simply far too many main characters that aren't dwarves in the movie. So, the truly brilliant scenes, such as one where the dwarves overpower their enemy by outflanking, back jumping and axe attacking are unfortunately few and far between.

>Gasoline poured on dwarves.
>Coffee-drinking dwarves.
>Driving dwarf.
>Multiple dwarf warriors carry Richard Norton out on a stretcher.
>Mine-working dwarves.
>Rock-moving/rescue dwarves.
>Dwarf warrior limbos out of truck.
>Axe-wielding, running dwarves.
>Dwarf back attack.
>Dwarves use teamwork to kill their attackers. Several dwarves flank and attack one man.
>Celebrating, axe-raising dwarves.
>Dwarves hail Richard Norton.

Ratman (1988)

Written by Dardano Sacchetti (as David Parker Jr.)
Directed by Giuliano Carnimeo (as Anthony Ascot)

Starring David Warbeck, Janet Agren, Anna Silivia Grullon
Featured dwarf: Nelson de la Rosa

What happens when a monkey is injected with rat sperm? You get Ratman! Within the first few minutes of the film, Ratman escapes and goes on a killing rampage, beginning with supermodels and those around them.

While it sounds like something created in B-movie heaven, the movie unfortunately falls flat when Nelson de la Rosa (*Island of Dr. Moreau* (1996) and at one time the smallest man alive) is not on screen as the title character. When he's on screen, it's wonderful to watch him scamper after and attack his victims. When he's off screen the movie is a total bore. What should have been a classic becomes a movie you only show clips to your friends.

The ending leaves a lot to be desired. We see a bag carted around that's alluded to having Ratman being in it, as it's loaded on a plane. *Flight of the Ratman* is something I'd like to see—200 victims in an enclosed area.

> Dwarf in cage.
> Dwarf taunted by tallies.
> Small dwarf paws rip into woman.
> Dwarf leaps from up high.
> Dwarf gnaws on woman.
> Woman's hand on dwarf's back.
> Dwarf eyes close up while being a peeping tom.
> Dwarf crawling.
> Dwarf makes noises.
> Dwarf under sheet.
> Dwarf claws out tallie's eyes.

Ray (2004)

Story by Taylor Hackford and James L. White
Screenplay by James L. White
Directed by Taylor Hackford
Starring Jamie Foxx
Featured dwarf: Warwick Davis

In the story of musician Ray Charles (Jamie Foxx in his Academy Award winning performance), Ray is at the Rocking Chair when we see the emcee for the evening is played by dwarf actor Warwick Davis. The few members of the crowd paying attention give Warwick weird looks, trying to establish how lame the acts of the evening have been. When Ray gets the chance to perform, he's a little nervous. A couple of seats down is Warwick, smoking pot. He kindly offers Ray some to "calm his nerves." We get Warwick making a few more announcements and then a nice scene where he gets Ray the record company info despite others backstabbing him. Other than a brief scene where the circus and midgets are mentioned, it's a part that could have been played by anyone and worked. However, I think Warwick brings something special to an ordinary role and that's what makes it so great.

Emcee dwarf.
Pot-smoking dwarf.

The Red Dwarf (1998)

Written and directed by Yvan Le Moine
Starring Jean-Yves Thual, Anita Ekberg, Dyna Gauzy, and
    Michel Peyrelon
Featured dwarf Jean-Yves Thual
"Dwarves are always joking."

The Red Dwarf (1998) is a pretentious, yet very well done French movie that drew me in because it had a subplot revolving circus dwarves as well as a dwarf seducing an overweight senior citizen tallie, and not only that, but the dwarf gets emotionally attached to the granny love interest in question to the point of tears. Another thing I really liked about this movie was the fact that it featured a Clark Kent-looking dwarf. I'm serious. This dwarf was basically the French dwarf version of Christopher Reeve. And with those glasses he wore... it was amazing! I defy anyone to say this dwarf isn't the mini version of Christopher Reeve. In fact, if Christopher Reeve were still alive today, they could reboot the "Superman" franchise with tallie Superman and dwarf sidekick Superman. Just thinking about how awesome that would be makes my head spin from the possibilities.

Even though this is more or less an art film, there are several dwarfsploitation elements included here, most notably a horny dwarf. This dwarf was so incredibly horny while trying to bang the senior citizen, who knows what he would have done had there actually been a hot, young girl around. Not only that, but he appears fully nude in this film several times, plays with a train set with the glee of a child, drinks his face off, cross dresses, commits murder, is part of the circus, and even goes so far as to piss his employers off and take a fresh, steaming crap on their desk after getting fired. Now that's what I call going out in style, not to mention taking dwarfsploitation to new heights. Even B-Movies rarely hit this many exploitative marks. I suddenly have a new found respect for the French.

French dwarf.
Dwarf can't reach mailbox.
Suit-wearing dwarf.
Dwarf plays in train set.
Girl refers to dwarf as a goblin.
Girl gets barrel for dwarf to jump on.
Dwarf writer.
Mini Christopher Reeve-looking dwarf.
Dwarf drenched by rain.
Drinking dwarf.
Dwarf looks at old woman's cleavage.
Nude dwarf plays in old rich lady's tub.
Fully frontal nude dwarf.
Close up shots of exposed dwarf ass.
Dwarf seduces old woman.
Robe wearing dwarf.
Artistically shot dwarf/tallie sex.
Dwarf carries large package.
Dwarf on stilts.
Dwarf wears angel wings.
Dwarf goes into a fit of rage when rejected by old tallie woman.
Dwarf with hair in curlers.
Cross-dressing dwarf.
Dwarf strangles old woman.
Dwarf does push ups.
Out of control, laughing dwarf.

Dwarf signs document with his blood.
Dwarf makes duck noises.
Dwarf scats on his employer's desk.
Fired dwarf works at the circus.
Dwarf clown hangs from circus wire.
Martin Short-looking dwarf.
Dwarf attacks tallie and beats him up.
Dwarf pulls sword on tallie.
Dwarf stands on head.
Dwarf tries to ban tallies once a week from circus.

Rescue Dawn (2006)

Written and Directed by Werner Herzog
Starring Christian Bale, Steve Zahn
Featured dwarf: Kriangsak Ming-olo

U.S. Navy pilot Dieter Dengler is shot down and captured, becoming a prisoner of war. In the camp, he and the other P.O.W.s are not treated well except by a dwarf named Jumbo. Apparently, Jumbo is very friendly and loves to smile at the prisoners and does what he can for them, like sneaking them extra food. When the prisoners are escaping and blowing away the bad guys, they let only Jumbo go free. Written and directed by dwarf enthusiast Werner Herzog (*Even Dwarves Started Small* (1970)), *Rescue Dawn* (2006) is a very serious prisoner of war movie that strangely has a dwarf thrown in a small part like several other Herzog films.

Herzog seems to love dwarves as much as we do.
Dwarf called "Jumbo."
Dwarf with gun smiling.
Dwarf tricked, laughs when Bale grabs nail.
Confused dwarf.
Weaving dwarf.
Waving dwarf.
Dwarf eating.
Shocked dwarf.

Return of the Jedi (1983)

Written by Lawrence Kasdan, George Lucas
Directed by Richard Marquand
Starring Mark Hamill, Harrison Ford, Carrie Fischer, Billy Dee Williams, Anthony Daniels.
Featured dwarves: Warwick Davis, Tony Cox, Phil Fondacaro, Debbie Lee Carrington
"You're a jittery little thing, aren't you?"

Jedi is famous for being the movie that was responsible for changing the tone of the *Star Wars* series, making it more light hearted and kid friendly (which is very evident by the time parts 1-3 rolled around) with all the robots with annoying voices and endless amounts of toys, not to mention the universally hated Jar-Jar Binks. Dwarves had a great deal to do with this, since they were the ones inside the Ewok outfits. Many famous dwarves don teddy bear garb for dwarf lover Lucas' puppetfest, including the likes of such big names as Warwick Davis, Debbie Lee Carrington, Tony Cox and Phil Fondacaro (all of whom have already been established as favorites of this book by now).

I guess you could look at *Jedi* in two different ways. One is that the teddy bear phase really f'ed up the rest of the series and two is that *Jedi* really kicked off the careers of several now very famous dwarves. After all, if *Jedi* weren't around, then maybe we wouldn't have *Willow* (1988). And if we didn't have *Willow* (1988), maybe we wouldn't ever have the six *Leprechaun* movies that have been covered in this book, let alone the two TV Ewok spin off movies, *The Ewok Adventure* (1984) and *The Battle for Endor* (1985). Depending on your opinion of those movies, this could be either a very good or a very bad thing. It's a hard call since it really is the beginning of the pendulum swing for the tone of the series. It's certainly something to contemplate.

Moving on, let's take a look at the dwarfsploitative elements of this movie. First, there's R2-D2 in his usual comic relief role. He doesn't fix the hyperdrive as he does in *Empire*, yet he does spend a bit of time being exploited as a serving droid dwarf during his stay at Jabba's palace. Speaking of which, I wonder exactly just how many dwarves would fit inside Jabba the Hutt. Anyway, moving on again, most of the real dwarsploitation occurs on Endor when the formerly mentioned Ewoks come into play. The dwarves here are kind of a mix between Native Americans and

Rambo. They make booby traps and work as a team to defeat the evil Imperial tallies. How a bunch of teddy bears could take down the Empire is about as believable as Chucky being able to kill as many people as he does (couldn't you just throw him against a wall or punt him?) but that's all beside the point.

The dwarf Ewoks are loveable, kindhearted creatures, yet clearly stereotyped by being completely archaic-thinking simpletons. They do after all worship C-3PO. They're also made to do a lot of idiot dancing and all kinds of other silliness, but hey, they sold an assload of toys which is really what movies are all about, right?

> R2-D2 droid dwarf gives Jabba powerful Jedi message that seals his fate as a slave.
> Jawa dwarf behind Boba Fett.
> Drink-serving R2-D2 droid dwarf.
> Dwarf Wicket feet.
> Dwarf Wicket pokes Leia with stick.
> Leia temps dwarf Wicket with people food.
> Dwarf Wicket scared by Leia's helmet.
> "You're a jittery little thing, aren't you?"
> Dwarf Wicket slips under tree.
> Dwarf Wicket holds Leia's hand.
> Dwarf Ewoks point sticks at heroes.
> Dwarf Ewoks worship 3PO.
> Dwarf Ewoks carry heroes in stretcher.
> Dwarf Ewok sounds horn.
> Dwarf Ewoks plan on cooking Han Solo.
> Dwarf Ewoks frightened by levitating C-3PO.
> R2-D2 shocks Ewok dwarves.
> R2-D2 bonds with Wicket dwarf.
> Smoking dwarf Ewok.
> Dwarf Ewoks fascinated by C-3PO's story.
> Dwarf Wicket clings to Solo's knee during story.
> Dwarf Ewok hugs Solo and Chewie.
> Dwarf Ewok steals speeder from the Empire.
> Dwarf Ewok swings on vine.
> Dwarf Ewoks jump on storm troopers
> Swinging dwarf Ewok attack.
> Rock-dropping, hanglider dwarf Ewok.

Rock-slinging dwarf Ewok.
Catapault-using dwarf Ewoks.
Short circuiting R2-D2 dwarf.
Dwarf Ewok massaacre.
Dwarf Ewok mourns dead friend.
Dwarf Ewoks take over AT-AT.
Dwarf Ewoks set boobytraps for speeders.
Cheering, victorious dwarf Ewoks.
Horn-blowing, celebrating dwarf Ewoks.
Dancing dwarf Ewoks.
Somersaulting dwarf Ewoks.
Wicket dwarf tries to dance with R2-D2.
Wicket dwarf hugs R2-D2.

Rockula (1990)

Written by Luca Bercovici, Jerery Levy, Chris Ver Wiel
Directed by Luca Bercovici
Starring Dean Cameron, Toni Basil, Thomas Dolby, Tawny Fere, Susan Tyrrell, Bo Diddley
Featured dwarves: Tony Cox, Tamara De Traux
"That was my mother you just boned!"

Rockula (1990) features Dean Cameron, star of several great 80's movies like *Summer School* (1987) and *Ski School* (1990). Sadly, this isn't one of them. He plays the title character of Rockula, who's been a virgin for 400 years due to the fact he's cursed to live the same brutal event over and over again where his fiance is murdered by a pirate who hits her over the head with a hambone before killing her. This event occurs like some kind of an evil Groundhog Day before poor Rockula ever gets a chance to score. I know, it sounds like something made by someone who's on crack (and perhaps the filmmakers were when they made this). All I can say is that *Rockula* (1990) was made at the tail end of the 80's, a time that was ripe with cinematic experimentation. The movie is a really terrible one. The music's bad, everything's bad, but it's one of those movies you just keep watching because you A: can't believe someone actually made it, B: there's something compelling you to see just how bad the celluloid train wreck is going to get and C: there are dwarves in the movie.

During an early scene where Rockula is interacting with his mom, one of our all-time favorite dwarf actors (Tony Cox) is revealed on the other side of the bathtub Rockula's mom is in. Cox's character is cleverly named Big Al and he is immersed in bubbles (except for his face) as he tries to make small talk with the disturbed and uncomfortable Rockula. A few dwarves show up as extras in a club to tide us over until Rockula finally reveals to his love interest, Mona, that he is a bona fide vampire. She of course doesn't believe him, and feels instead he's merely too far into his on stage persona to know the difference.

What happens next is the point in the movie that completely won me over to its charm, despite all its formerly-mentioned bad movie qualities. Rockula changes into a vampire to give Mona proof he's not lying… a dwarf vampire! And not just any dwarf vampire, either: one played by Tamara De Treaux, who according to IMDB, was the world's smallest actress during the time the film was made. Unfortunately, she passed in 1990 due to respiratory and heart problems. Treaux was also famous for helping portray E.T. and gave us in *Rockula (1990)* easily the most unique version of a film vampire I've ever seen.

> Dwarf in tub with Rockula's mom.
> Rockula appears as a dwarf version of himself in a funny mirror.
> Dwarf cheers on singer.
> Fat dwarf praises Rockula after show.
> Rockula transforms into a dwarf vampire to convince love interest he's the real thing.
> Rockula transforms into dwarf vampire to battle evil pirate nemesis.

Saboteur (1942)

> Written by Joan Harrison, Dorothy Parker, and Peter Viertel
> Directed by Alfred Hitchcock
> Starring: Robert Cummings
> Featured dwarf: Billy Curtis

Barry Kane is on the run in Alfred Hitchcock's thriller and ends up jumping on with some circus performers. Circus performers are not complete without the inclusion of a dwarf, this time played by Billy Curtis.

Curtis, as "Major," doesn't like the two on the run and wants them off, coming off like a little asshole as the rest of the circus troupe helps them out.

A short role is not enough to make this a worthy look but if you're checking out Hitchcock you might as well check out the performance of Billy Curtis.

> Dwarf part of circus freaks—fat lady, Siamese twins, bearded lady.
> Dwarf with mustache and cigar.
> Angry dwarf.
> Dwarf referred to as "cold hearted."
> Dwarf referred to as "little stinker.
> Tallie grabs dwarf by face.

Salome's Last Dance (1988)

> Screenplay by Ken Russell
> Play by Oscar Wilde
> Directed by Ken Russell
> Starring Glenda Jackson, Stratford Johns, Nickolas Grace, and Douglas Hodge
> Featured dwarves: Mike Edmonds, Willie Coppen, Anthony Georghiou

When Oscar Wilde walks into a brothel in 1892, they find the prostitutes putting on the play *Salome* by Oscar Wilde. Among the members of the cast are three dwarves playing Hasidic Jews. It's a strange enough film to begin with and maybe they were trying to make a statement by casting dwarves, but it's not really notable for dwarves unless seeing this sight is what you dream of.

> Dwarves as Hasidic Jews.
> Dwarves drinking.

Santa Buddies (2009)

>Written by Robert Vince and Anna McRoberts
>Directed by Robert Vince
>Starring Christopher Lloyd, George Wendt
>Featured dwarves: Danny Woodburn, Mikey Post

This straight-to-video Disney film relies on the cuteness of a bunch of dogs, but the real highlight is the few dwarf actors they employed. The story is sort of simple—Puppy Paws just wants to be a regular dog so he goes in search of regular dogs. In his search he ends up finding the reason behind Christmas and lifting Christmas Spirit so that Christmas can actually happen.

As is the case with most Christmas movies, there are elf characters played by dwarves. The talented Danny Woodburn leads the way, seeming like his main direction was, "Smile, something cute is happening…again." The downside to the elves is that ¾ of them seem to be played by children, leaving me feeling cheated. Come on Disney, it's not like you don't have the money to fork over for a few more dwarf actors.

The movie is a cutesy kid movie that might entertain a five year old but not the dwarf enthusiast who wants to see more dwarves.

>Dwarf singing.
>Dwarf elf.
>Dwarf rings large bell.
>Dwarf running.
>Dwarf mechanics.
>Dwarf waving.
>Dwarf with oversized toolbox.

Santa Claus Conquers the Martians (1964)

>Written by Glenville Mareth
>Directed by Nicholas Webster
>Starring Pia Zadora, John Call
>Featured dwarf: Ivor Bodin

Santa Claus Conquers the Martians (1964) is considered by many to be one of the worst films around, and rightfully so. It's ridiculously bad.

However, it tries to be Santa movie completist by including two dwarves as Santa's helpers. A couple of things are notable about this. First, the two that are featured are played by dwarves, but all the other helpers seem to be kids. Next, they make the dwarves wear ridiculously fake-looking beards. When the aliens "attack" Santa's workshop, one dwarf grabs a bat and the other tries hiding behind Santa. We're even treated to a ridiculous alien robot picking up one of the dwarves.

Cinema would not be the same without movies like these. It's what makes us appreciate the good ones when we find them, so we can be entertained by how horrendous the movie is. This one might have been a little better if Santa's helpers had dropped in with some machine guns to save Santa. Just a thought.

> Dwarves working like slaves.
> Dwarves with fake beards.
> Dwarf laughing.
> Dwarf blocks robot.
> Dwarf with bat.
> Dwarf picked up by robot.
> Dwarf hides behind Santa.
> Dwarves frozen.

Satan's Whip (2006)

> Written and Directed by Jason Maran
> Starring Dennis Albanese, Pete Barker, Bob Connelly, Sarah Huling, Kimm R. Schwert
> Featured dwarf: Kimm R. Schwert

In this coming of age horror movie about a rookie priest who wants to be part of a secret order that fights evil, the priest is on a mission to find a missing priest and discovers a dwarf with crappy aging makeup in the process. The dwarf role is clearly for a woman in her sixties but is played by a dwarf who looks to be in her thirties. The dwarf is hardly in the movie (which is the filmmaker's main mistake) and doesn't speak (which may not be a mistake). It appears as if she's only there to add some random creepiness, which involves nothing more than opening the door to the priest's room and staring at him. However, if you stay with the movie until the end you will be treated to a scene where the dwarf takes a bite out of a newly-born tallie baby, then goes back to staring at the priest through the door.

The dwarf adds some flavor to an otherwise slow, yet sometimes interesting movie but doesn't save it by any means. However, to credit the filmmakers, I have never seen a movie where a dwarf actually eats a human baby. They certainly earn points in the dwarfsploitation originality department.

>Dwarf stares through door.
>Dwarf eats tallie baby.

Scared to Death (1947)

>Written by Walter Abbott
>Directed by Christy Cabanne
>Starring Bela Lugosi
>Featured dwarf: Angelo Rossitto

We start off with a corpse and after some bad dialogue it transitions into the dead man's story. Every now and then it even goes back to the corpse (which is obviously lifeless and nothing is happening there), and then back to the flashback. In the flashback we meet Bela Lugosi. I guess they didn't think he would be strange and scary enough, so they threw in a dwarf who instantly gets angry and starts stomping on the tallies.

Unfortunately, "Indigo" (played by Angelo Rossitto) is underused, mostly relegated to listening in on the tallie's conversations because he can get around without being seen. It's a shame to watch the legendary Angelo Rossitto get wasted.

>Dwarf with large bag.
>Dwarf looks tallie up and down.
>Dwarf stomps tallie's foot.
>Dwarf holds tallie's hand.
>Dwarf lifted onto chair by tallie.
>Angry dwarf.
>Dwarf spying from stairs.
>Dwarf holds tallie's pant legs.
>Dwarf crawls on floor.
>Dwarf hides behind couch standing up.

Dwarf running.
Dwarf excited and clapping.

Seizure (1974)

Written by Edward Mann and Oliver Stone
Directed by Oliver Stone
Starring Troy Donahue, Mary Woronov
Featured dwarf: Herve Villechaize
"I'll give you anything, just break that midget's leg!"

A simple story of a writer who has nightmares about a couple of characters, including dwarf legend Herve Villechaize, that come to life. The movie hasn't held up very well considering it's an Oliver Stone movie with cult figures (that would normally lead to a nice restoration), but it surprisingly held my interest. For a while I was worried Herve would get to do nothing but look creepy, but he gets an incredible fight scene where he takes on a room full of tallies that makes the whole movie worth watching. It's reminiscent of the Austin Powers vs. Mini Me fights.

It's notable that Herve is also credited for "stills."

Draws picture of dwarf.
Dwarf looking through window creepily.
Dwarf running in a dream.
Dwarf with tooth necklace.
Dwarf hands close up.
Dwarf breaks through window.
Dwarf in tights.
Dwarf fights/chokes tallies.
Dwarf kicks out old guy's cane.
Dwarf beats up cripple.
Dwarf with torch.
Tallie kicks dwarf.
Dwarf slapped by tallie.
Dwarf mechanic.
Referred to as "Funny little man."
Held up by tall black man.
Dwarf chokes tallie.

Shaolin vs. Evil Dead (2004)

>Written by Ho Yiu-Wang
>Directed by Douglas Kung
>Starring Gordon Liu

When I saw the title of this for the first time I was excited beyond belief. The idea of combining a kung fu movie with zombies could only bring magic to the screen. Throw in Gordon Liu, of *Kill Bill* (2003) and *The 36th Chamber of Shaolin* (1978), as the star and it's got magic written all over it. The movie does start as I wanted, looking like a wild, unforgettable ride. Part of the fun is a weird dwarf zombie who shows up to wreak havoc and get thrown around by Liu and company. Unfortunately, the dwarf leaves the scene too soon. Perhaps it's connected that the movie dies at about the same point this dwarf zombie loses screen time? The movie is a total mess all the way through and even ends abruptly, like they ran out of money. However, it did spawn a sequel. If you watch this one, turn it off mid-way through—it doesn't get better.

>Dwarf zombie.
>Dwarf zombie gets ass kicked.
>Dwarf zombie's chest is stood on.
>Dwarf zombie gives speech to other zombies.
>Hiding dwarf zombie.
>Begging dwarf zombie.
>Dwarf zombie follows group.

She's All That (1999)

>Written by R. Lee Fleming Jr.
>Directed by Robert Iscove
>Starring Freddie Prinze Jr., Rachael Leigh Cook, and Matthew Lillard
>Featured dwarves: Debbie Lee Carrington, Clay Rivers
>"I want to be like Mike."

Not only is this cut-and-paste teeny bopper romantic comedy cheesy and unbearably hard to watch, it's also a strange choice of a film for dwarves to show up in, since it is a teeny bopper romantic comedy and not a sci-fi or horror film. I do, however, applaud the filmmakers for realizing the value of dwarves enough to cross them over in a different genre of film. It's just too bad it wasn't a good one, and as expected, there's no new breaking of dwarf cinema ground. The dwarves are exploited here just as they are in so many other dwarfsploitation films. They're used for comedy and to add weirdness to the scene.

She's All That (1999) is the same movie we've seen a million times over, where a jock tallie makes a bet with another jock tallie to make a pretty/ugly girl (Rachael Leigh Cook? Ugly? Are you fucking kidding me?) popular and then dump her. But in the process he becomes attached to her and… there's no point in finishing. You've all seen it a million times before.

Dwarves enter the scene in the early courting stages of the jock tallie (Freddy Prize Jr.) and the pretty ugly female tallie (Rachael Leigh Cook). The jock tallie goes to see the pretty/ugly tallie's performance experiment piece, which involves a bohemian tallie prancing around in his underwear and two dwarves who look like miniature versions of the Blue Man Group, complete with painted faces. One of the dwarves proclaims, "My soul is an island. My car is a Ford." The other dwarf states, "I want to be like Mike." The dwarves and the tallies hug while echoing the words, "Be silent, be still." And, as the only weird part in the movie is over, the dwarves are no longer needed and don't show up in the film again.

I did connect with this moment in the film because I had a performance class in college but we were never blessed enough to have dwarves in our class. Only in the movies (which of course almost always waste great dwarf potential).

Dwarves in blue outfits with blue makeup.
Dwarves hug tallies.

Sherlock Holmes (2009)

Screen story by Lionel Wigram and Michael Robert Johnson
Screenplay by Michael Robert Johnson, Anthony Peckham,
   Simon Kinberg
Directed by Guy Ritchie

Starring Robert Downey Jr., Jude Law, Rachel McAdams

When Lord Blackwood needs someone to assist him in doing massive tricks (for instance, like making it appear that he has come back from the dead), he calls on a little person. What's odd about this one is that he's referred to as 4'10 (technically a little person) but there's never a shot that made me think "Oh, that's a little person." Instead of visual exploitation, they have constant verbal exploitation, constantly bantering about whether he's a dwarf or midget while also calling him a ginger (when kids were beaten for being red heads, a.k.a. gingers, this term was accredited to *South Park*).

There is also one brief scene where Downey is in disguise, chasing after Rachel McAdams. One of the areas he runs through appears to have a circus/carnival going on and this would not be complete without a dwarf, who is seen slightly blurred out in the background.

Two dwarves without lines
Dwarf extra.
Dwarf referred to as "Ginger dwarf."
Dwarf referred to as "Ginger midget."
Dwarf referred to as "Midget."
Dwarf scientist.
Dwarf involved in occult acts.

Ship of Fools (1965)

Written by Abby Mann
Directed by Stanley Kramer
Starring Lee Marvin, George Segal
Featured dwarf: Michael Dunn
 "I think that you are a sawed-off intellectual."

Narrated and co-starring the excellent Michael Dunn in his Oscar-nominated performance, this movie is a strange little gem that is definitely worth a look. The title says a lot, and it's just that—a ship of fools. Several oddball characters converge on a ship and it would not be complete without a dwarf. It's the type of film where Dunn should have been able to just be a "regular" character but instead is constantly reminding

The sharp dressed dwarf is baffled that the tallie actually thinks he has some artistic talent.

the audience that he is a dwarf. My personal favorite scene in the film is when Dunn and the great Lee Marvin are having a drunken intellectual conversation—it's just wonderful to watch, as is the film.

"There's a dwarf, this high!"
"I have a minority of my own."
Dwarf with cane.
Smoking dwarf.
Dwarf refers to self as "fool"
Dwarf climbs up to see over.
Saluting dwarf.
Dwarf looked down upon.
Dwarf in pajamas.
Dwarf knocked over by children.
Angry dwarf.
Dwarf with hat on.
Dwarf drinking.
Scared dwarf.
"Bottoms up shorty."

Dwarf sings along.
Dwarf narrator.

Sideshow (2000)

Written by Benjamin Carr
Directed by Fred Olen Ray
Starring Jamie Martz, Jessica Keenan, Peter Spellos
Featured dwarf: Phil Fondacaro

Dr. Abbot Graves (the always great Phil Fondacaro) is leading a group of freaks in finding new subjects to turn into fellow freaks. When some youngsters go on a double date with a crippled brother in tow, they go to the wrong place for a little fun. Phil is picked up and ridiculed by one of the tallies before completely setting his plan in motion to turn the group in this light horror film from B-movie legend Fred Olen Ray and Full Moon. Phil gives a very campy performance in a role that was large enough that he should have gotten top billing. The movie is okay and Phil is not given a whole lot to do even though he has a lot of lines. If it weren't for Phil, I would tell anyone to skip it but if you have some free time this one might be worth checking out to see some freaks going on the attack. The movie had a lot more potential than the end product.

Dwarf in top hat.
Killer dwarf.
Angry dwarf.
Tallie runs into dwarf.
Dwarf referred to as "little fella."
Dwarf picked up by Fabio tallie.
Dwarf sulking.
Dwarf gives evil smirk.
Dwarf pitching freaks.
Dwarf laughs maniacally.
Cigar-smoking dwarf.
Dwarf referred to as "little mistake of nature."
Painting dwarf.
Extreme dwarf close-up.

The Sinful Dwarf (1973)

> Story by William Mayo
> Screenplay by Harlan Asquith
> Directed by Vidal Raski
> Starring Torben Bille

A sleazy tale of a mother and her dwarf son, who drug up young hot women and store them in the attic to serve as whores. Olaf the dwarf is played beautifully by Torben Bille. His face is in a constant Jack Nicholson from *The Shining* (1980) state and his voice is amazing, constantly sounding like he's drunk. Olaf uses a cane in the movie and hobbles around, taking way too long to get from one place to another but that does not stop the filmmakers from sticking with him and not cutting. This movie is about as disturbing as movies come, with the mother/son antics being one that walks the line of doable and disgusting. The "rape" scene conducted by Olaf is a pure exploitation classic moment. This film definitely falls into classic exploitation just because of how they exploit the dwarf in title and box cover—there's no mention of momma or a family. A definite must-see in dwarf cinema.

> Dwarf hobbling.
> Perverted dwarf.
> Dwarf playing with toys.
> Dwarf maniacally laughing.
> Dwarf feet shots.
> Dwarf shadows.
> Angry dwarf.
> Dwarf jumping from high places.

Sixteen Candles (1984)

> Written and directed by John Hughes
> Starring Molly Ringwald, Justin Henry, John Cusack, Anthony Michael Hall, Paul Dooley
> Featured dwarf: Zelda Rubinstein
> "Oh, I need a drink."

Before the great John Hughes passed on he left us with several outstanding movies that will most assuredly be talked about and referenced for years to come. One of his most well known films, *Sixteen Candles* (1984), is even more memorable due to Hughes' casting of a dwarf as the church organist. Near the end of the film, Molly Ringwald's family walks up to the church for her sister's wedding. They first run into Zelda Rubinstein (a.k.a. the church organist). She asks if everything's alright and why they took so long. Right around the time Ringwald's sister tells her she was late due to the fact she took four muscle relaxers, Rubinstein steps down from the stairs she's on and reveals her true dwarfish height in comparison to the rest of the wedding party tallies.

More dwarf treats in the film include Rubinstein playing the organ and singing *Here Comes the Bride* during the wedding ceremony and standing amongst the crowd of church tallies after the ceremony. But by far the best dwarf highlight in the film occurs when Ringwald walks back into the church after the ceremony to retrieve her sister's veil. She has a brief exchange with Rubinstein where she explains that her sister's out of it. Rubinstein agrees by responding in the creepy *Poltergeist (1982)* voice, "Just a little bit." After Ringwald leaves to go back to the wedding party, the dwarf mutters to herself, "Oh, I need a drink." It's a very funny comic moment that perfectly compliments one of the quintessential 80's teen movies.

Dwarf/tallie size differential.
Dwarf organist.
Singing dwarf.
Dwarf badly needs a drink.

Skinned Deep (2004)

Written and directed by Gabriel Bartalos
Starring Jay Dugre, Kurt Carley, Karoline Brandt
Featured dwarf: Warwick Davis

A family goes on a road trip and gets attacked by a crazy-ass backwoods family. Don't be thrown by the incredibly generic description of the plot, however. Unlike *The Texas Chainsaw Massacre (1974)* and countless other imitators, this family includes a man with a large brain (very similar to the *Liquid Television* cartoon *The Head*) and a straitjacket-wearing, plate-throwing dwarf brilliantly named Plates (the great Warwick Davis)!

I have no idea what the filmmakers were smoking when they decided to make the dwarf character unique by giving him the ability to throw plates. Even when Davis spews out a hilariously drawn out, bad monologue about the significance of plates, it makes absolutely no sense at all. When Davis isn't throwing plates at people, he's meticulously cleaning them, which was oddly really funny to watch, but that's not all. Plates is also really skilled at throwing plates at people from moving vehicles and burying plates in dirt. This of course comes in handy later on in the film, when Plates finds himself empty handed in a fight to the death with a crazed senior citizen. Good thing he buried those plates!

Skinned Deep (2004) features a lot of poor acting, out-of-sync dubbing, and a cheap, '70s drive-in style look, but it's worth it just to see a dwarf in a straitjacket throwing plates, right? If it wasn't such an incredibly ridiculous concept, I couldn't in good conscience recommend this movie, but because *Skinned Deep* (2004) has some pretty bizarre moments, some good gore, and they were actually committed enough to this cracked-out idea to put it on film, I'd say go ahead and check it out. After all, it's not every day you get to see a movie featuring a plate throwing dwarf named Plates. In fact, I think it's safe to say this is the only time. What the hell were they thinking?

- Psychologically damaged dwarf.
- Tired looking dwarf.
- Lipstick-wearing dwarf.
- Confused dwarf.
- Grey hair-dyed dwarf.
- Dwarf excited as violence is about to happen.
- Dwarf jumps off stools and throws plates.
- Dwarf feet chasing kids through fog.
- Double plate-unsheathing dwarf.
- Dwarf laughs as little boy is killed in front of him.
- Obsessive plate-cleaning dwarf.
- Plate-sharpening dwarf.
- Dress-carrying dwarf.
- Dwarf wraps hands with athletic tape.
- Double plate-wielding dwarf.
- Dwarf throws plates at a moving truck from a moving truck.
- Plate holster-wearing dwarf.
- Dwarf jumps down from truck.

Dwarf gives epic monologue about plates.
Dwarf taunts man with plate.
Dwarf vs. crazy old man.
Old man/dwarf chase through cactus field.
Dwarf digs up buried plates in cactus field.
Crazy old man beats the hell out of dwarf with his own plate.
Crazy old man rips dwarf's head off, drinks its blood and kicks it over the freeway.
Dwarf's flying, severed head continues to speak.

Slaughter Party (2005)

Written by Fred Rosenberg Jr.
Directed by Buck Jones Jr.
Starring Ron Jeremy, Adam Glasser, Felissa Rose, and Lloyd Kaufman
Featured dwarf: Mighty Mike Murga
"Now with the killer midget running loose I've got to look under my shins."

A homicidal dwarf chases hot girls in bikinis through the desert with a knife. Dwarfsploitation cements itself as a reputable genre once and for all.

Slaughter Party (2005) has perhaps the best concept for a dwarfsploitation movie ever. A crazed, bloodthirsty dwarf chases a bunch of mostly hot girls around the desert, knife in hand. It's so simple, it's brilliant! What more do college kiddies and fat guys without girlfriends need to entertain themselves on a Friday or Saturday night? *Slaughter Party* (2005) is best enjoyed when combined with mind altering substances. If viewed sober, a few flaws may make themselves a little more known to the audience, but that's besides the point. This film really hits the nail on the dwarfsploitation head. If the budget was higher the filmmakers would have been given the ability to allow their dwarfsploitation ambitions to reach unprecedented heights.

The plot is about a crazy bastard (played by tallie Ford Austin) who hangs out by the desert and attacks anyone that goes there, except for the dwarf that stumbles across his path. The crazy bastard has other things in mind for the dwarf. The little guy's friends he slaughters, but the dwarf, he corn holes! That's right, folks. The dwarf gets corn holed! The only other movie featuring dwarf cornholing from what I've seen during my research on this book is *Postal* (2007), where the great Verne Troyer is violated by an insane number of chimps. As it turns out in *Slaughter Party* (2005), the crazy bastard's true intentions aren't revealed until the end of the movie. Until that point, we're treated to dwarfsploitation aplenty as the tallie's cornhole violation of the dwarf somehow turns him into a mad, crazed micro killer of scantily clad young girls.

Highlights include tallie/dwarf body-part feeding, dwarf running knife in hand after tallie girls in bikinis while their garbonzas bounce every which way but loose, dwarf Jack Nicholson and Chucky impressions and bra-over-the-head-wearing dwarf. A true classic in the genre of dwarfsploitation.

> Silent-movie music plays to dwarf intro.
> Dwarf hidden by truck.
> Dwarf whining.
> Dwarf waddles after tallie companions.
> Dwarf wobbling.
> Dwarf insulted for whacking off to episodes of *Lizzie McGuire*.
> Tallies taunt frightened dwarf.
> Hanging dwarf.
> Chained dwarf.
> Mad scientist gives dwarf a goodbye kiss.
> Dwarf squeals like a little girl as his tallie friends are slain before his eyes.
> Dwarf fed the body parts of his freshly slaughtered tallie friends.
> Depantsed dwarf.
> Dwarf cornholed by tallie.
> Internet dating dwarf.
> Knife-wielding dwarf.
> Dwarf does Nicholson impression from *The Shining* (1980).
> Dwarf pleasures himself into victim's knife wound.
> Smoking dwarf.
> Dwarf with bra on head spies on tallie girl about to shower.
> Dwarf rummages through drawers looking for a killing weapon.
> Dwarf knocks table to the ground and crawls after tallie victim.
> Tallie victim attacks dwarf with mini shovel.
> Dwarf hides in back of tallie kid's car.

Dwarf tries to strangle tallie girl.
Dwarf runs after tallie girl and wrestles with her.
Dwarf limps up to tallie girls.
Bloody-headed dwarf.
Tallie girl carries wounded dwarf off.
Dwarf attacks and tries to strangle tallie girl who carries him to safety.
Dwarf pulls out knife and screams like Chucky.
Dwarf chases after tallie girl with knife.
Dwarf chases tallie girl into cave.
Dwarf stabs sleeping tallie girl and runs off.
Dwarf stabs tallie girl in back.
Mad dwarf exits cave swinging knife.
Dwarf runs behind awesome jiggling-boobed tallie girl.
Dwarf strangles tallie girl with great boobs.
Bloody-faced dwarf.
Dwarf stabs tallie girl with screw.
Dwarf crawls out of barrel after tallie girl.
Dwarf fondles tallie girl's boobs.
Tallie girl swings stick at dwarf.
Tallie girl hits dwarf with fake rock.
Dwarf thought dead, comes back and strangles tallie girl, who in turn strangles dwarf.
Gentlemanly dwarf lines:
"Hey bitch!"
"Stupid dyke!"
"I'm gonna' eat your tit."

Smoking Aces 2 (2010)

Written by Olatunde Osunsanmi, Olumide Odebunmi, Tom Abrams
Directed by P.J. Pesce
Starring Tom Berenger, Clayne Crawford, Tommy Flanagan, Maury Sterling, Ernie Hudson, Michael Parks, Vinnie Jones
Featured dwarves: Matt Phillips, James Ram Jattan

This bad sequel to a great movie wastes a good cast of dwarves as well as tallies. The filmmakers try to throw in some dwarves to spice things up, but they use them for such a short amount of time they might as well have not even appeared in the movie at all. The dwarves in *Smoking Aces 2* (2010) are basically the equivalent of a cinematic punch line. Circus dwarves are spotted by tallies and quickly designated as cannon fodder. One of the tallies gets the idea to use a circus dwarf as a combination between a bomb and human cannonball as they literaly strap a bomb to a dwarf and launch him from a cannon into the window where rival tallie gunmen are positioned. When the dwarf lands the bomb detonates.

I must say that even though this movie is basically just a series of shootouts framed around a dull, straight-to-video center, I've got to give it points for its creative use of dwarfsploitation, even though it seems the filmmakers clearly had dwarficidal intentions toward the poor little guys. Too bad they couldn't have given the dwarves a bigger role or had them turn the cannon on the tallies. Well, maybe in the next sequel. On second thought…

Circus dwarves.
Human dwarf bomb.
Human dwarf bomb literally used as cannon fodder.

Snow White: Cannon Movie Tales (1987)

Written and directed by Michael Berz
Starring Diana Rigg, Sarah Patterson
Featured dwarves: Billy Barty, Mike Edmonds, Ricardo Gil,
 Arturo Gil, Malcolm Dixon, Gary Friedkin, Tony Cooper

The classic tale of *Snow White* and *the Seven Dwarves* (1937) is revisioned in this musical version. It begins with the prince riding and singing through the forest until he comes upon Snow White in a very cheap clear coffin. Luckily, the movie is instantly saved by the arrival of the seven dwarves. The dwarves are lead by dwarf hero Billy Barty, with a large red beard and funny nose. All the dwarves are dressed very, very poorly as Barty begins telling him the tale of Snow White from the point of her birth.

The movie feels like it skids to a halt for the next twenty minutes, as the seven dwarves are absent. When they finally show up again, it feels like the film is again filled with life. Barty naming off all the dwarves to get an answer has me instantly hooked for any scene they are in. When the dwarves discover the door open, it causes the dwarves to get scared and make funny observations around the dinner table. When they discover a young Snow White, their guesses as to what it is range from an elephant to a donkey, despite her small stature. With the young girl in bed, one dwarf has to find somewhere to sleep. We end up following him hysterically jumping from bed to bed with no luck—he's thrown and kicked off of every one. As if that wasn't enough, the seven dwarves do a confusing song and "dance" number explaining their names that is hilarious and catchy despite not making much sense. The movie is worth this bit alone but if that wasn't enough it's followed soon after by yet another song outside their hut. It's so wonderful to watch, it's a guaranteed dwarfgasm. However, when the dwarves aren't on screen this movie becomes quite the bore. You would think the producers would have realized this and rewritten even a classic story to keep it at the top level it's at for so long.

Also notable is the difference made by the dwarves not being animated. This experience was a far better one because of the live dwarves and the talented actors, led by Barty, that were involved.

> Dwarf narration.
> Scared dwarves.
> Shaking dwarf.
> Comical music playing when dwarves arrive.
> Dazed dwarf.
> Singing and dancing dwarves.
> Dwarves digging while singing.
> Dwarves with log.
> Dwarf jumping.

Something Wicked This Way Comes (1983)

> Written by Ray Bradbury
> Directed by Jack Clayton
> Starring Jason Robards, Jonathan Pryce, Diane Ladd, and Royal Dano
> Featured dwarves: Phil Fondacaro, Jerry Maren
> "Sorry boy, too young. Come back in ten years."

Tasty lollipop or deadly weapon in the hands of Jerry Maren?

Dwarves courtesy of Ray Bradbury about a town invaded by an evil carnival sideshow that kind of reminds me of *Needful Things* (1993) with dwarves. In this creepy film made by Disney, none of the dwarves play anything more than side roles as is usual with dwarfsploitation, of course, and in true dwarfsploitation style, the dwarves are cast as frightening figures. One appears in a clown outfit and a spiked red Mohawk, and another in a clown outfit clasping cymbals the entire time he's walking in a parade sequence. If the director was intending the scene to be creepy, he certainly acheived that result, and it comes off even more creepy than usual because it's a kid's movie. Indeed, as a kid, this movie did scare the hell out of me but I can honestly say the dwarves were not the reason for this…the spiders were. I don't even remember the dwarves in this movie from when I was a kid and I first saw it. Now, that is a terrible sign. Unmemorable dwarfsploitation is dwarfsploitation of the worst kind.

Cruel dwarfsploitation is also shown in this film in the form of two dwarves who take great delight in tormenting two tallie kids who try to sneak into a strip club. Or, I guess in this movie it would be the carnival equivalent of a strip club, aka a strip tent. One of the dwarves tells the kids they're too young to watch such a thing and forces them out of the tent. The dwarf near him acts as security to make sure the kids leave, and all before the poor kids even get a chance to see boobs of any kind. Even harem-style dancing girls not showing bare flesh have enough see-through clothing to be enticing. It's an injustice to deprive young men of that experience.

In conclusion, the dwarves in this movie are not only used as scary clowns meant to frighten children, they're also use to cock block horny young kids and keep them from seeing boobs and delaying the date they enter puberty. Shame on you, Ray Bradbury. You're a brilliant author but we never thought you'd stoop to dwarfsploitation so low as this.

> Dwarf with cane, hat and beard stands outside erotic dancer booth. Kids have to move away to reveal him.
> Cock-blocking dwarves.
> Laughing dwarf smacks peephole and stops boys from spying.
> Dwarf with clown mohawk plays mini tuba.
> Dwarf claps cymbals.
> Close up on evil dwarf with cymbals.
> Film keeps cutting back to clown dwarves next to Jonathan Pryce in parade sequence.
> Random shots of extra dwarves in parade.
> Tallie framed over back of dwarf head.
> Music man-looking dwarf.
> Cane-walking dwarf.
> Laughing dwarf.
> Dwarf attempts to pick up tallie corpse.

Spaceballs (1987)

Written by Mel Brooks, Thomas Meehan, Ronny Graham
Directed by Mel Brooks
Starring Mel Brooks, John Candy, Rick Moranis, Bill Pullman, Daphne Zuniga, Dick Van Patten
Featured dwarves: Tim Russ, Ed Gale, Antonio Hoyos, Felix Silla, Arturo Gil, Tony Cox, John Kennedy Hayden
"Did I miss something? When did we get to Disneyland?"

This is one of Mel Brooks' last truly great movies to date. The humor here is pitch perfect and Brooks makes good use of dwarves as well. In *Spaceballs* (1987), Bill Pullman plays the character modeled after Han Solo, accompanied by John Candy in the perfect toadie role as a half man/half dog named Barf. They're on a sellout mission to save a Princess played with diva-ish delight by Daphne Zuniga. During a scene where the heroes are passed out in the desert, they are found by a bunch of famous dwarves in Jawa outfits. Strangely enough, the Jawa dwarves communicate by only using the word "dink," almost as if they're some sort of live action dwarf version of *The Smurfs*. Wait a minute... a live action version of *The Smurfs* starring dwarves! That would be awesome, wouldn't it? Sorry, back to *Spaceballs*. After saying the word "dink" (and only dink) several more times, the dwarves take the tallies to the fortress of "Yogurt," which is Mel Brooks doing a parody of Yoda. As in *Tiptoes* (2003), Brooks is a tallie playing a dwarf, as the Yogurt character he walks around on his knees, shamelessly impersonating a dwarf much as Oldman did in the previously mentioned movie. He shows the tallie heroes *Spaceballs* (1987): The Movie merchandising. Then he tells them about the Force, which he calls "The Schwartz," and provides additional help in the battle against Dark Helmet (played by honorary dwarf Rick Moranis).

Spaceballs (1987) is a very funny movie and deserves a recommendation for the dwarf completist, but Brooks should have stepped back and humbly allowed a real dwarf to play the Yogurt character. What is it with these tallie actors stealing roles that rightfully belong to dwarves all the time?

Dwarves find tallie heroes passed out in desert.
Dwarves are dressed in Jawa robes and only say the word "dink."
Dwarves attempt to revive John Candy by pouring water in his mouth.

Dwarves curiously point at Candy's tail.

Dwarves take tallies to underground fortress of Yogurt the fake tallie dwarf.

Dwarves open door to show tallies *Spaceballs* (1987) movie merchandising.

Dwarves give Pullman a thumbs-up and wish him luck before he flies off.

Spaced Invaders (1990)

Written by Patrick Read Johnson and Scott Lawrence Alexander
Directed by Patrick Read Johnson
Featured dwarves: Tony Cox, Debbie Lee Carrington, Kevin Thompson
"I suppose they're little people?"

You would think a movie with Tony Cox, Debbie Lee Carrington and Kevin Thompson, to name just a few, would be a classic piece of dwarf cinema. Unfortunately, the opportunity the filmmakers had is severely and foolishly ruined. To start, they are running around in alien costumes. Sure, I can excuse this since it is called "Spaced Invaders" and the whole plot is about aliens landing in a small American town. Excusing that, you expect to see dwarves running around in alien costumes but it's not that easy. For starters, the only little person voice used in the end is Kevin Thompson—the rest belong to some tallies with high pitched or just annoying voices. And if that wasn't bad enough, the aliens are oddly staged. A lot of the time they are standing and not moving. It's noticeable that this only happens when the aliens are on screen; everyone else is shot and staged normally. The movie itself really isn't that good and is rather annoying so I don't think I could suggest this to anyone at all. Maybe if they had used dwarf voices instead it wouldn't have been as annoying and off putting in general. Did I mention how annoying their voices were? In fact, this whole movie is a cinematic crime for its misuse of dwarf legends. May this film be shown in film schools across the country as an example of what not to do. Note: the director did a much better job with the excellent fat kid tale *Angus*, which is definitely worthy of a viewing despite the lack of little people actors.

Dwarves in alien costumes.
High pitched voiced alien dwarves.
Alien dwarves mistaken for kids.
Maniacal laughing dwarf aliens.

Star Slammer (1987)

> Story by Miriam L. Preissel, Fred Olen Ray, Michael Sonye
> Screenplay by Michael Sonye
> Directed by Fred Olen Ray
> Starring Sandy Brooke, Ross Hagen, John Carradine, Johnny Legend

B-movie legend Fred Olen Ray brings us *Star Slammer* (1987), aka *Prison Ship* (1987), a women-in-prison-in-space film that gathers a huge pile of exploitation clichés and throws them into one bad film. Starting the film off on the right foot is our hero, "Taura," surrounded by dwarves. Apparently the dwarves are dumb (according to a brief dialogue between "Taura" and a random old guy in the forest, played by Johnny Legend), and just make weird, unintelligible noises the whole time. While it's fun watching them wandering around in silly costumes, and making funny noises, they can't get too much screen time or it'd be a classic film. Instead, the bad guys arrive and start blasting away our dwarf friends. One dwarf even poses for a fight with baddie Ross Hagen, like badly choreographed kung fu is about to begin. Unfortunately, Hagen just puts his hand on the head of the dwarf and zaps him dead. "Taura" is taken away to prison, just like we as viewers are. The potential was great here but the end result is just lame.

> Dwarves in silly costumes.
> Dwarves making weird noises.
> Dwarves eating.
> Dwarves killed.

Star Trek (2009)

>Written by Roberto Orci, Alex Kurtzman
>Directed by J.J. Abrams
>Starring Chris Pine, Zachary Quinto, Leonard Nimoy, Eric Bana, Bruce Greenwood, Karl Urban
>Featured dwarf: Deep Roy

This movie was far better than I ever thought it would be and almost everyone I've talked to about it agrees. I'm not a Trekkie by any means, but I've seen all the movies and I was not disappointed. However, this was a sci-fi movie and should have included parts for more dwarves. Throughout the years, *Star Trek* has always done a good job of including a variety of different races, but is a dwarf ever going to join the crew? I want to see this happen by the time a sequel rolls around. There's got to be room in there somewhere between Sulu and Chekov. It's not like the dwarf would take up much space.

Now, since this is an origin story I will forgive the filmmakers for not including a dwarf in the entire movie - this time. But if it keeps happening, I may just have to boycott the series, regardless of how good they turn out. Unfortunately, a dwarf doesn't show up until damn near the end of the movie. Fortunately, the movie is so damn good, it keeps you fully involved until the entrance of the dwarf. Famous dwarf actor Deep Roy plays Scotty's sidekick. He's in full alien garb and in true sci-fi fashion we never see his face. He follows Scotty around so much he almost comes off as a stalker dwarf. Why, I have no idea. Scotty constantly scolds the dwarf and bosses him around. That dwarf should have done what Mini-Me did in *Austin Powers in Goldmember* (2002) when he wasn't being respected. He should defect to the other side. I'm just crossing my fingers and hoping the filmmakers respect him enough to give Roy a larger role in the sequel.

>Goggle-wearing dwarf.
>Dwarf scolded by Scotty after he says he's starved.
>Dwarf follows Scotty around.
>Abandoned dwarf.
>Sad dwarf.

Star Wars (1977)

Written and Directed by George Lucas
Starring Mark Hamill, Harrison Ford, Carrie Fisher, Peter Cushing, Alec Guinness
Featured dwarf: Kenny Baker

I may be wrong but I consider *Star Wars* to be the cinematic origin of George Lucas' obsession with dwarves. I can just imagine Lucas hiring convention dwarf favorite Kenny Baker as R2-D2 and loving his work. From that moment on, Lucas' head must have been spinning with the possibilities of dwarves in future films and I'll be damned if he didn't follow through on his obsession. Otherwise we would have never been blessed with the Ewoks in *Return of the Jedi* (1983), the two Ewok movies that followed, *Howard the Duck* (1986) (a highly misunderstood classic), and *Willow* (1988), among many others. It brings a smile to my face as I happily imagine those cinematic dwarf dreams in their early stages. I'm also a firm believer in the theory that one of the reasons *Star Wars* (1977) remains the classic it is today is because it instantly starts off with dwarf action as R2-D2 and C-3PO flee from the flying lasers of the Imperial army to hop on board an escape pod.

Dwarf actor Kenny Baker has an excellent role as R2-D2 in this film because his character is continuously connected to the plot and achieves great things, including but not limited to carrying Princess Leia's vital message, saving his tallie friends from being crushed by the garbage compactor, and locking down the stabilizer during the film's final battle scene. The dwarf and his tallie companion C-3PO also provide much of the film's comic relief as they constantly bicker like an old married couple.

More dwarves appear as Jawas (which was actually a mix of dwarves and children). Unfortunately, the Jawas faces are never revealed, keeping true to one of the basic elements of dwarfsploitation, which is to keep the dwarf actor covered up as much as possible. We find this recurs most consistently in the Sci-Fi genre. Perhaps the most unusual dwarfsploitation scene occurs when the bartender at the Mos Eisley Cantina refuses to serve R2-D2 and C-3PO. Droid discrimination or perhaps an analogy to the plight little people deal with every day while struggling to live in a tallie world? It certainly provokes a great deal of thought.

My favorite dwarfsploitation scene in the film occurs when R2-D2 stands next to a female droid dwarf during the Rebellion's briefing of the

Empire's battle plans. Lights blink, droid heads turn and chemistry sparks fly, which leaves us to ponder another deep thought: did droid dwarfs in the *Star Wars* universe mate?

> Dwarf actor completely concealed in droid dwarf suit.
> Droid dwarf and C-3PO on ship.
> Droid dwarf outruns lasers.
> Droid dwarf and C-3PO escape in pod.
> Droid dwarf argues with C-3PO and spins head around.
> Jawa blasts droid dwarf.
> Droid dwarf falls over head first.
> Droid dwarf gets sucked into Jawa vehicle.
> Droid dwarf spins head while conversing with 3PO.
> Droid dwarf sold into slavery.
> Protesting droid dwarf.
> Droid dwarf hides in cave as Luke is attacked by Jawas.
> Droid dwarf plays vital message, "Help me Obi-Wan Kenobi." You're my only hope."
> Drinking dwarf in Mos Eisley cantina.
> Droid dwarf discrimination.
> Droid dwarf incites Wookiee's anger during a chess game.
> Droid dwarf gives more important info about Princess Leia.
> Dwarf dwarf saves everyone from getting crushed by the disposal.
> Dwarf waddling when trying to move back and forth.
> R2-D2 stands next to what appears to be a female droid after hearing a briefing about the empire's battle plans and sparks appear to be flying.
> Droid dwarf rides as Luke's toadie in the Y-wing ship.
> R2-D2 locks down stabilizer during end fight.

The Station Agent (2003)

> Written and Directed by Thomas McCarthy
> Starring Patricia Clarkson, Bobby Cannavale, and Paul Benjamin
> Featured dwarf: Peter Dinklage
> "Here I am! Take a look!"

The Station Agent is (2003) in my opinion the *Citizen Kane* (1941) of misunderstood dwarf movies. For once, we finally, finally get an entire movie about a dwarf, and not only that, the lead actor is actually a real dwarf. Not like Gary Oldman, who played the lead dwarf in a movie filled with real dwarves. Oh no, that's not gonna stand out at all! *See the rant on the film *Tiptoes* (2003) for more information. I found myself getting excited while watching this movie. This was a straight up drama about a dwarf. I was finally going to learn about the plight of the little person. I, as a non-dwarf, was going to get insight and privileged information. I was going to learn how dwarves really think and feel. I was going to discover things that even my dwarf friends haven't told me. The experience of watching this movie was going to be an absolute revelation. I didn't exactly get that. The film doesn't give many answers. What it does, instead, is paint a sympathetic portrait of a dwarf as a multi-dimensional human being.

The dwarf in question, Peter Dinklage (the finest dwarf actor today) is incredibly bitter. His train hobby makes him happy but humans clearly don't. Then, when apparently his only true friend dies, he inherits a train depot in rural New Jersey. There are only a few people around him; an obnoxious yet likable coffee vendor (Bobby Cannavale) and a well-to-do artist (Patricia Clarkson). He clearly tries to avoid contact with any human being in his path (especially after a bunch of rat bastard kids laugh at him as he walks by). It doesn't help that Clarkson nearly runs him over… twice. And, even though it was an accident both times, it was enough to keep the dwarf jaded and isolated from society.

After rejecting several gestures of friendship by the painfully lonely but well-intentioned Bobby Cannavale, the dwarf slowly warms up to the film's non-dwarves and even starts to build relationships with them, but not, before having an angry dwarf tirade in a bar and going off on several occasions telling people to leave him alone.

Now, I can understand his dismissal of the non dwarf males and bratty kids but he's treated like a sex symbol in this movie by the non-dwarf females! Not only does Patricia Clarkson blatantly throw herself at him, an extremely hot Michelle Williams (all liquored up and ready) does everything but mount the dwarf in his own place and he still turns the both of them down. Was he so jaded against society he can't get a little tallie action of the side? I'm not a dwarf so it's hard to tell, but when you prefer chasing trains to having sex, you know you've got a problem, dwarf or not.

The real question about the *The Station Agent* (2003) is, is it dwarfsploitation or not? It contains many of the dwarf stereotypes so many of the Hollywood movies cater to. It's not beneath several sight gags and it's share of dwarf insults: "Are you a midget?" "What grade are you in?" However, it is a classy drama, filled with character and solid acting and the dwarf, for once is not a two-dimensional character, yet, it is a movie about an angry dwarf, and let's face it: the plot is pretty generic and wouldn't have nearly as much of a hook without a dwarf as the lead. So, is it dwarfsploitation? Yes. But it's classy dwarfsploitation. Perhaps we need to invent a separate category for movies like this.

Dwarf sulks past mocking kids taller than him.
Girl doesn't see dwarf when he walks in grocery store.
Dwarf's head framed next to a cash register.
Dwarf broods while watching train footage.
Lone, smoking dwarf.
Dwarf carries large suitcase.
Shirtless dwarf.
Dwarf walks next to tall trees.
Attempted automobile dwarf-slaughter.
Dwarf shuns tallie's friendship.
Lonely dwarf walks across train tracks.
Dwarf scares little girl.
Dwarf passed out in tub.
Dwarf's head framed next to doorknob.
Dwarf frightens girl in library.
Non-dwarf women sexually attracted to dwarf.
Dwarf smiles when he sees two kids taller than him.
Dwarf can't figure out how to use camera.
Pot-smoking dwarf.
Dwarf abandons little girl.
Dwarf puts feet on paint bucket.
Dwarf drinks beer from a little glass.
Dwarf pushed around by greasy redneck.
Stalker dwarf.
Dwarf stares at big house.
Dwarf does shots.
Dwarf tantrum in bar.
Horny dwarf.

Suit-wearing dwarf.
Teacher dwarf laughed at by students.

Tales From the Crypt Presents: Bordello of Blood (1996)

>Story by Bob Gale and Robert Zemeckis
>Screenplay by A.L. Katz and Gilbert Adler
>Directed by Gilbert Adler
>Featuring Phil Fondacaro
>"What can I say, boys, I know how to turn a woman on."

Have you ever wondered what Indiana Jones would have been like had a dwarf played the role? *Bordello of Blood* (1996) gives you the chance of making dreams come true as treasure hunter Phil Fondacaro, in Indiana Jones drag, is in search of "Lilith," the mother of all vampires. You get a few clichés with Fondacaro laughing maniacally and the size differential of him on a very large horse. What you don't get, as is often the case, is a dwarf actor with enough screen time. He's in the opening of the film and it definitely sets the tone for the rest of the movie, but I would have traded more screen time for Phil in exchange for the nudity. There, I said it. I prefer dwarves to breasts.

>Dwarf falling.
>Dwarf on horse.
>Lowering dwarf by rope.
>Dwarf laughing maniacally.
>Dwarf size differential.
>Dwarf Indiana Jones.

The Telling (2009)

>Written by Joe Lessard
>Directed by Jeff Burr
>Starring Bridget Marquardt, Holly Madison and Christina Rosenberg (as Lola LaBelle)
>Featured dwarf: Ed Gale

In this awful micro-feeling anthology, there are three sorority wannabes (so it seems) who are forced to tell scary stories to get in to the sorority. The second story is about a washed-up actress who is willing to accept anything to put her career back on track. When she goes to the spooky old house (which, as usual, offers the heroine no clues to what happens next) she steps right in despite the fact that a little person answers the door (after spooky house, that's usually the second sign that bad shit is going to go down in there). The little person, "Footcandle," is played by none other than Ed Gale. What makes his part fascinating is that he has no lines. The movie stars *Playboy* playmates and is filled with piles of bad-acting carcasses but they choose to give zero lines to the best actor (no question about it) in the movie. This is not only awful filmmaking but just damned poor judgment. The movie is undoubtedly horrible and each segment is just a horribly cheap knock off of something better but Ed is great in the limited screen time he is given as the mysterious sidekick/assistant/waiter/projectionist/lighting guy.

Notably the film also features *Slaughter Party* (2005) co-star Christina Rosenberg (credited as Lola LeBelle), the actress who was slaughtered by a screw in the head in that film by Mighty Mike Murga.

> Dwarf answers spooky old house's door.
> Camera goes from where a tallie would be to the dwarf.
> Camera shifts from dwarf to tallie.
> Dwarf waiter responds to bell.
> Non-speaking dwarf.
> Dwarf obsessed with light and shadows.
> Dwarf projectionist.
> Dwarf injects our heroine.

The Terror of Tiny Town (1938)

> Written by Fred Myton
> Directed by Sam Newfield
> Featured dwarves: John Bambury, Little Billy, Billy Curtis, Yvonne Moray, Billy Platt

The Terror of Tiny Town (1938) is (to my knowledge) the first and only all-dwarf musical Western. There are striking occurrences of the word midget in the film, obvious signs of the far less p.c. times when it was made. As a movie, *The Terror of Tiny Town* (1938) doesn't have a lot going for it. There are far too many musical numbers and the dwarves are absolutely terrible singers. They would have been better off going all the way with it and tweaking their voices in post to make a Chipmunk-esque soundtrack. The acting is wretched, the list goes on. But the fact that the cast is entirely comprised of dwarves who ride around on Shetland ponies makes up for all its shortcomings (no pun intended). Anyone whose curiosity isn't piqued by the concept of an all-dwarf musical Western can't possibly have a soul.

Producer Jed Buell wastes no time by announcing at the very beginning credits, "Featuring Jed Buell's Midgets" (as if he owned them. Sounds more like slavesploitation to me.).

> Arguably the worst singing dwarves in history.
> Dwarf Blacksmith.
> Dwarf pops out of a barrell.
> Dwarf ropes a baby cow.
> Chef dwarf shows up in another scene as an outlaw dwarf.
> Hot dwarf prostitute.
> No barstools. Platforms are added instead to allow the dwarves' heads to be seen over the top of the bar.
> Multiple Shetland pony dwarf chases.
> Dwarf chef crawls into cupboard.
> Dwarf uses giant pinchers to reach something on the wall.
> Old dwarf strangely resembles the landlady in *Kingpin* (1996).
> Two dwarves play the same cello.
> Dwarf bartender chugs a giant beer in one take. (I would so love to go drinking with that guy!)
> Eyepatch-wearing dwarf.
> Dwarf heads appear under a door.
> More dwarves crawling in and out of cupboards.

Things You Can Tell Just by Looking at Her (2000)

> Written and Directed by Rodrigo Garcia
> Starring Elpidia Carrillo, Glenn Close, Cameron Diaz, and Calista Flockhart

Featured dwarf: Danny Woodburn
"You gave a dwarf a ride home?"

This movie is meant to be a weepy drama, but is mostly just a waste of time, not to mention great dwarf talent. Now what sense does this make? You take awesome dwarf actor Danny Woodburn from TV's *Seinfeld*, put him in the movie just to more or less add a dwarf and don't give him anything to do. What a crock of shit. This movie is basically a bunch of estrogen-filled vignettes, none of which have payoffs worth watching. The one thing they did do right is wait up to the moment where the entire audience is about to fall asleep and then, with a curveball surprising for a chick flick/drama, they add a dwarf.

God bless them for their one moment of inspired genius. However, the genius stops there because, as mentioned before, they don't give the dwarf anything to do. Although they certainly make it seem like something is going to happen, trust me, it doesn't. In the segment with the dwarf, the mom from *Picket Fences* (tallie actress Kathy Baker) and her little teenage son (channeling Corey Haim in *The Lost Boys* (1987)) notice a dwarf has just moved in next door. They watch with curiosity as the little guy takes a box from the movers and hoists it above his head. It's a little box but he still has a difficult time carrying it. However, in the dwarf's defense, the box is half his size. From that point on, the mom's teenage kid seems to be as fascinated with dwarves as the authors of this book.

This was the only part of the movie I really liked because the kid's eyes kept lighting up when he used the word dwarf and he seemed to be as extremely fascinated with the mere use of the word dwarf as the fact that a dwarf had just moved in next door to him. The son keeps pestering the mother and using the word dwarf over and over until she becomes incredibly annoyed. The son quickly proclaims that he wants to invite the dwarf over for dinner and the mother protests the continued use of the word dwarf, yet somehow the son's curiosity piques the mother's interest as well.

Soon enough, in what ends up being perhaps the most awesome dwarfsploitation moment in the movie, the mother leaves her annoying son and goes to the store to pick up groceries. It's there that she sees her brand new neighbor dwarf pushing a shopping cart. She offers the dwarf a ride home after watching him have difficulty carry grocery bags home. From there on out, she and the dwarf spark up a relationship, which she fucks up by spying on him with the fascination of a tallie who has just discovered a hidden dwarf village, and of course, all this buildup leads to nothing and just ends. Lame.

"Did you see that? He's a dwarf!"
"You don't feel weird about meeting a dwarf, do you?"
"I certainly don't feel weird about introducing myself to a new neighbor, but please don't call him a dwarf."
"You'd better be careful, I'll tell you those little guys, they know how to work a lady."
Mother and son curiously watch their new dwarf neighbor as he moves in across the street.
Dwarf waddle.
Dwarf carries large box.
Mother curiously watches dwarf push large shopping cart through grocery store.
High angle - dwarf swipes card at cashier stand.
Dwarf walks carrying large bags of groceries back from store.
Mom gives dwarf a ride home.
Chivalrous dwarf opens door for female tallie.
Mom almost kills dwarf via shitty driving.
Dwarf has backstory about how he left home at 16, joined the circus and ran away.
Mother spies on sleeping, shirtless dwarf.
Mom watches dwarf water lawn at night.

This is Spinal Tap (1984)

Written by Christopher Guest, Michael McKean, Harry Shearer, Rob Reiner
Directed by Rob Reiner
Starring Christopher Guest, Bruno Kirby, Patrick Macnee, Michael McKean
Featured dwarves: Chris Romano, Daniel Rodgers
"Let's get the dwarf cannolis. The little ones."

Other than Billy Crystal dressed as a mime and making a comment about ordering dwarf cannolis, unfortunately, the only other dwarf related material in this movie is one concert gag: the one involving the miniature Stonehenge statue. Fortunately, it's hands down one of the funniest moments in the movie, although the entire film is hilarious and definitely one of Reiner's best. It set the stage for several mockumentaries and documentaries that blatantly ripped it off later on, including one of my favorite tallie movies: *Fear of a Black Hat* (1994) (although that film unfortunately didn't have dwarves).

The dwarf scene in *This Is Spinal Tap* (1984) revolves around a miscommunication from the band manager that results in a far smaller Stonehenge statue that was supposed to descend from the ceiling during one of the songs. Unable to get a larger statue in time, dwarves are brought in to dance around the miniature set piece in the hopes of making it look taller to the audience. This of course doesn't work and brings about a hysterically odd visual as the dwarves are dressed like elves and doing a happy jig as if they were in a commercial for a new Keebler cookie. I would protest the absence of more dwarves, but the movie's so good it deserves a pass.

3000 Miles to Graceland (2001)

> Written by Richard Recco, Demian Lichtenstein
> Directed by Demian Lichtenstein
> Starring Kurt Russell, Kevin Costner, Courteney Cox, Christian Slater, Kevin Pollak
> Featured dwarf: Jody Sadler

This movie features an outstanding cast but falls apart halfway through. It's a shame because it had potential. It's also a complete pass on the dwarfsploitation front. When the crew makes it to Vegas, some glamour shots of Sin City are spliced into the film, including a dwarf Elvis impersonator, who dances around for an incredibly short amount of time, then the fun's over.

> Dwarf Elvis impersonator.

Time Bandits (1981)

> Written by Michael Palin, Terry Gilliam
> Directed by Terry Gilliam

Starring Sean Connery, Shelley Duvall, John Cleese, and Katherine Helmond

Featured dwarves: David Rappaport, Kenny Baker, Malcolm Divon, Mike Edmonds, Jack Purvis, Tiny Rous

"That's what I like! Little things hitting each other."

A bunch of aspiring thief dwarves steal a map from the Supreme Being. They then use it to time travel and steal from famous people. The thing that's great about *Time Bandits* (1981) is that dwarves are present in nearly the entire movie, so you don't hit your dwarfless dead spots like so many of those dwarf poser movies. After recently viewing the movie again, I was as jealous of the kid actor for getting to be around dwarves for the entire film as was when I was as a kid and saw the film for the first time. So basically, my need for the company of dwarves hasn't changed. However, I must say the dwarves in this film didn't exactly prove to be good role models for the young boy who accompanies them on their adventures. They're constantly stealing, getting drunk, fighting each other and placing him in harm's way. They do, however introduce him to several historical figures, so they do provide some scholastic merit to counterbalance their overall blatant irresponsibility. These elements of less-than-adequate dwarf role models certainly provide for a bizarre kid's movie, and it's all topped off by an ending which has to be one of the grimmest in the history of both dwarf cinema and PG kid's movies. Yet, for some strange reason, it doesn't really feel that way due to the comic tone and great deal of fun the clearly dwarf-obsessed Terry Gilliam puts into the film. It's as much of a blast to watch as when I saw it for the first time and I was around that lucky bastard kid's age that gets to hang around all those cool dwarves for the entire movie.

Time Bandits (1981) is a must own for even the partially dwarf-curious.

Horse-mounted dwarves burst through closet into little boy's room.
Dwarves chased by large, floating cartoon head.
Dwarves jump through little time portal (aka time-traveling dwarves).
Dwarf reads from oversized map.
Rowing dwarf.
Dwarves get drunk and toast to a minor.
Dancing dwarves.

Dwarf-on-dwarf violence.
Dwarf fascinated honorary dwarf Napoleon.
Dwarves wear funny Napoleon hats.
Napoleon has the height of several famous short people memorized.
Dwarves get Napoleon all liquored up and steal from him.
Dwarves hang upside down in a booby trap.
Men spit over dwarves.
Robin Hood steals money from thief dwarves.
Evil man speaks through dwarf.
Dwarves crash banquet and perform magic for Sean Connery.
Dwarves steal Sean Connery's crown.
Dwarves fall on top of a couple and ruin their marriage proposal.
Dwarves in monkey suits drinking and smoking cigars.
Dwarves fall off the Titanic.
Dwarves caught in a net by ogre.
Dwarf tossed overboard by ogre.
Dwarves hide in cooking pot.
Dwarves knock ogre's wife overboard with pot.
Sailing dwarves.
Dwarves ride on giant's head.
Dwarves crash into invisible barrier.
Dwarf tosses skull through invisible barrier.
Dwarves run up really steep stairs.
Dwarves locked in cage.
Easily tricked dwarves.
Rat-eating dwarf.
Cage-climbing dwarf.
Rope-suspended dwarf.
Rope-swinging dwarf.
Pig-headed dwarf.
Flying dwarves.
Horseback-riding dwarves.
Dwarves abandon young boy.

Tiptoes (2003)

>Written by Bill Wiener
>Directed by Matthew Bright
>Starring Gary Oldman, Kate Beckinsale, Patricia Arquette, Matthew McConaughey
>Featured dwarves: Peter Dinklage, Ed Gale, Debbie Lee Carrington, Bridget Powers
>"You had a circle jerk with a bunch of little people? I would have loved to see that."

Tiptoes (2003) is a movie about a tallie man (Matthew McConaughey) who knocks up a tallie woman (Kate Beckinsale) and fears they will have a dwarf child because he himself comes from a family of dwarves, as if anyone would bitch about this in real life when they were about to get married to Kate Beckinsale, but that's beside the point. The important thing is that this movie features dwarf eye candy aplenty. Less than ten minutes in, we're treated to a dwarf convention. If anything else, you've gotta' give it props for that, plus it features dwarves as sex symbols (which I've always believed in). Patricia Arquette has the hots for Peter Dinklage, who plays an angry dwarf with a French accent. This of course leads to an extremely hot, *True Romance* (1993)-style love scene between the dwarf and Patricia Arquette which made me think of how much even more awesome *True Romance* (1993) would have been had the dwarf replaced Christian Slater's character.

The most bizarre and oddly fascinating part of *Tiptoes* (2003) involves Gary Oldman's character. He plays a dwarf. Maybe this wouldn't have been so strange if the rest of the cast weren't all dwarves! Essentially Gary Oldman is the only dwarf impostor in a cast filled with real dwarves, and he gets the lead. Not only is this seriously unrealistic due to the fact that Gary Oldman has tallie arms but it must have been the biggest insult to the world of dwarf casting since Peter Jackson made the *Lord of the Rings* movies and turned actors into dwarves in post-production.

And what's with Mathew McConaughey being ashamed to admit he has a dwarf family? He's friends with the dwarves at the convention, then refuses to acknowledge them around Kate Beckinsale. Not cool. So basically he's a closet dwarf appreciator. Again… not cool. However, this movie is worth checking out for its bizarro factor alone, and the sexiness of Bridget Powers (aka Bridget the Midget) as the smoking-hot platinum blonde love interest of dwarf impersonator Gary Oldman.

> Dwarf drives race car.
> Dwarf urinates on highway.
> Dwarf convention.
> Dwarf love scene with Patricia Arquette.
> Shirtless, drunk dwarf falls off bed and passes out.
> Tall security guard leeches off Bridget the Midget's money.
> Gun-toting shirtless dwarf.
> Dwarf with French accent.
> Kate Beckinsale is the only non dwarf at a dinner party.
> Interracial sex between Bridget the Midget and a tallie brother.
> Patricia Arquette gives dwarf dreadlocks.
> Kate Beckinsale kisses dwarf on the lips.
> Dwarf doctor cares for Beckinsale and McConauhey's dwarf baby.
> More dwarf and tallie sexual tension.

Total Recall (1990)

> Written by Ronald Shusett, Dan O'Bannon, Gary Goldman
> Directed by Paul Verhoeven
> Starring Arnold Schwarzenegger, Sharon Stone, Michael Ironside
> Featured dwarf: Debbie Lee Carrington
> "Let me know if you need any help with this one."

When Arnold goes on a simulated vacation to Mars, all kinds of crazy shit happens. Arnold doesn't know who he is, or whether everything's real or he's in some kind of matrix. What he does know for sure is that he sees a dwarf! The last pure, raw and real Arnold movie to date features a smoking hot dwarf in lingerie played by Debbie Lee Carrington.

When Arnold enters a smut den to meet his female contact, Debbie Carrington shows up as a prostitute named Thumbelina. She's dressed to the nines in sexy hooker garb and asks Arnold's contact Melina (Rachel Ticotin) if she needs any help, vaguely concealing the fact she's extremely horny for the great Arnold Schwarzenegger. He is merely amused by Thumbelina's advances and instead shifts his focus to his tallie female contact. Clearly the sexpot dwarf was attracted to Arnold, and she was a professional too so you could only imagine how great that would have been for Arnold! But then a bizarre thing happens… he foolishly turns down Thumbelina's offer for sex to get together with a tallie? We're all familiar with the term 'business before pleasure,' but an exception should always be made when it relates to super-hot dwarves. Now, the tallie Arnold got together with (Ticotin) was pretty attractive but she didn't have anything on Debbie Carrington in my book, that's for sure.

Skipping past all the non-dwarf parts in the movie, our favorite dwarf prostitute once again shows up when Michael Ironside and the rest of his evil corporate goons attack the smut palace, but does the sexy Thumbelina merely sit back and let the genocide continue? Hell no! In one of cinema's great moments of dwarf heroism, she grabs herself a fully automatic weapon, stands on the bar and blows the evil corporate tallies to Kingdom Come, and when that method is exhausted, she grabs a knife and keeps going after them. Thumbelina's heroism makes her even sexier. Why Arnold didn't dump Melina for the dwarf is beyond us.

> Dwarf prostitute horny for Arnold.
> Priceless dwarf prostitute reaction to three-boobed woman getting shot.
> Knife-wielding dwarf prostitute.
> Dwarf prostitute stands on bar and blows people away with a machine gun.
> Running-out-of-oxygen dwarf prostitute.
> Dwarf prostitute gazes in wonder at how Arnold has saved Mars.

The Toxic Avenger (1984)

> Story by Lloyd Kaufman
> Screenplay by Joe Ritter
> Directed by Michael Herz and Lloyd Kaufman (as Samuel Weil)
> Featured dwarf: Norma Pratt

The Toxic Avenger (1984) is a classic film from Troma studios that tells the tale of a nerdy mop boy, Melvin, who works at a fitness club where a couple of Fabios and their hot girlfriends hang out when they're not running people over for points. When they pull a prank on Melvin and he inadvertently lands in some toxic waste, he mutates into the muscular crime fighting machine that is "The Toxic Avenger." In a series of revenge scenes,

Toxie takes on the bad guys, crushing skulls left and right. As we all know, a good cult movie is not complete without a dwarf. Just over an hour in, we are introduced to Mrs. Haskell as she goes to get her son's pants cleaned (with some suspicious white stains covering the front). Toxie enters and chases her through the dry cleaners. When he catches her, he stuffs her in a dryer and we see her spinning around. When the clerk returns to the store we see her dead body lying on an ironing board. My only complaint about the scene is that it's too short (again, no pun intended). However, the movie is a brilliant cult classic that should be viewed by anyone who is a fan of cult cinema. Anyone looking just for dwarves might be disappointed.

> Cheesy line-delivering dwarf.
> Overly happy dwarf.
> Toxie pushes dwarf's head.
> Dwarf running away.
> Dwarf bouncing off Toxie.
> Toxie picks up dwarf.
> Dwarf stuffed in dryer.
> Dwarf rolling around in dryer.
> Dead dwarf.

Transformers 2: Revenge of the Fallen (2009)

> Written by Ehren Kruger, Roberto Orci, Alex Kurtzman
> Directed by Michael Bay
> Starring Shia Labeouf
> Featured dwarf: Deep Roy
> "Great, a munchkin. Tell him he's tall."

When the heroes of the film need to get across the border an hour and thirty four minutes into the movie, they face the ultimate adversary—Deep Roy. Among the heroes is a foot tall robot that throws out the only dwarf insult so that Michael Bay can say, "But it was said by a robot," like he did when the black community got upset with jive-talking robots… at least that's what I'm assuming. Anyway, the heroes get off easy because Deep Roy is a big fan of New York. This film is not worth anyone's time and is worth nothing more than a paycheck for some cool actors. Deep Roy's part is too small and insignificant to be worth your time.

Munchkin joke.
Height differential.

Troll (1986)

Written by Ed Naha
Directed by John Carl Buechler
Starring James Beck, Jenny Beck, Sonny Bono, Jesse Carfora
Featured dwarf: Phil Fondacaro

Troll (1986) features a dwarf (Phil Fondacaro) playing a troll with an incredibly stupid looking grin on his face that spreads from ear to ear. He lives in the basement of an apartment complex and hangs out near the washing machine. When a family moves in, the daughter goes into the basement to explore and the dwarf troll uses the powers of his magic ring to possess her body. This was clearly done to save budget on both dwarf and troll effects so unfortunately the dwarf scenes are limited to the kill scenes which involve the dwarf troll turning various people in the apartment complex into plant creatures, and the complex itself into a magical forest kingdom.

Fortunately, Phil Fondacaro plays a dual role outside the troll get-up as an English professor. Once again, Fondacaro defies conventional cinema dwarf stereotypes and plays a sensitive, intelligent and literate dwarf (in *Ghoulies 2* (1988), Fondacaro plays a Shakepeare-quoting thespian). Fondacaro's character is the only one the dwarf troll connects with and doesn't mercilessly attack (instead he grants his wish). There's an instant dwarf-on-dwarf bond between the two that is very special. The tallies in the apartment complex don't have it so easy though, as the dwarf troll takes as many down as he can, including a booze-swilling, swinging Sonny Bono who thinks he's far more hip than he really is.

Troll (1986) has earned a great deal of notoriety over the years for its infamous *Harry Potter* controversy. Michael Moriarty, who plays the young girl's father in the movie, is named Harry Potter Sr. and his son is named Harry Potter Jr. (Moriarty even wears a weird looking wizard-style hat in various parts of the movie). The world in the movie is one of a magical kingdom filled with various creatures and even a good witch who Potter Jr. begs to be an apprentice to. Hmm, I wonder if there's a connection here? Could it be that J.K. Rowling is a dwarf appreciator and found inspiration for her multi million dollar kid's book series once she saw *Troll* (1986)? I believe this is further proof of my hypothesis that dwarves inspire people in magical ways on a daily basis.

> Troll arm attacks little girl.
> Troll holds ball.
> Stupid looking, grinning troll dwarf.
> Dwarf troll uses ring to put himself into the body of a little girl.
> Dwarf troll attacks Sonny Bono.
> Dwarf troll looks at magazine while Bono turns into a plant in front of him.
> Dwarf troll stares at ghoulie looking trolls.
> Dwarf troll turns Bono's apartment into a ghoulie forest.
> Fondacaro dwarf wears suit.
> Dwarf troll sits in a chair and watches Julia Louis Dreyfuss dance as a plant woman for him.
> Dwarf troll dwarf POV
> Dwarf troll bonds with Fondacaro dwarf (who's an English professor) and thinks he's an elf.
> Dwarf troll has weirdest smile on his face.
> Fondacaro dwarf puppet.
> Dwarf troll is completely calm around Fondacaro dwarf.
> Dwarf troll fights princess.
> Dwarf troll slays main bad guy.
> Dwarf troll eager to attack cops.

Troll 2 (1990)

> Written by Claudio Fragasso, Rossella Drudi
> Directed by Claudio Fragasso
> Starring Michael Stephenson, George Hardy, Margo Prey, Connie Young, Robert Ormsby
> "Let me give you some advice, you dwarves. Get out of here or you're going to be in a lot of trouble."

Anyone who considers this to be the worst movie ever made hasn't seen some of the movies I've seen. I will agree with them, however, and place this movie in the category of one of the worst movies ever made. Over the years

Troll 2 (1990) has gained some serious cult status, so much so that regular sold out screenings are organized, attracting droves of people. Could this be because of its *Showgirls* (1995)-style, enjoyably bad movie dialogue and atrocious acting? Or is it because *Troll 2* (1990) has somehow tapped into the dwarf-obsessed subconscious? Perhaps the years to come will deliver the answer for mankind, or perhaps the mystery will continue to remain.

Troll 2 (1990) is about a family that goes to the town of Nilbog via an exchange program and fails to realize it's Goblin spelled backwards until nearly the end of the movie. The town is filled with human-looking goblins who claim to be vegetarians yet still desire to eat the meat of humans, but only after forcing them to eat their completely unappetizing green food, breaking them down into half plant, half human creatures, which is the favorite food of the trolls. But wouldn't this make them herbivores instead of vegetarians? Nevermind.

For some strange reason there are two sets of trolls. The first are forest troll dwarves which are basically dwarves with shitty masks who wear potato sacks and carry sticks. They're basically like an evil dwarf troll version of the Ewoks. The next are the human trolls which are trolls shape-shifted into their human form. The confusing part is that the dwarf trolls have the ability to morph into a human version which is understandable for catching humans but then some remain dwarf trolls and some remain humans. Clearly, the answer to this conundrum is because the producers didn't want to spend the extra budget to treat the audience to dwarf trolls all the time. Instead, they use dwarf trolls disguised as humans seventy-five percent of the time and actual dwarf trolls twenty-five percent of the time, if that.

Perhaps the biggest and crappiest reason for dwarfsploitation in this film is that the actors playing the dwarf trolls aren't even listed in the credits. So the producers wanted dwarves in the movie, yet refused to acknowledge them in the credits? WTF?! The dwarf trolls do talk in a few rare moments and prove to be just as skilled as all the shitty leads. Wait a minute... perhaps the actors playing the dwarf trolls realized this and decided to pull their names from the credits to save face? Regardless, it didn't work. They are now a part of what looks to be an immortal cult movie phenomenon.

> Running, stick-wielding, potato sack-wearing dwarf trolls.
> Man with crappy pointed hat and cheap Robin Hood looking outfit creeped out by multiple dwarf trolls in the forest.
> Grandpa scares grandson with tale of evil dwarf trolls.

Human-shape-shifting dwarf trolls.
Young boy has nightmare of turning into dwarf troll food.
Car-driving dwarf troll.
Dwarf trolls corner damsel in distress and horny teenage nerd.
Close up of dwarf troll's crappy looking mask.
Dwarf troll tosses stick at horny teenage nerd.
Dwarf trolls feast on human/plant food.
Dwarf trolls try to force feed ice cream to young boy.
Dwarf troll flicks its tongue at young boy.
Dwarf troll crawls on all fours after young boy.
Dwarf troll arm mutilation.
Dead preacher goblin turns into dead troll dwarf.
Breaking and entering troll dwarves.
Troll dwarf knocked down stairs in an obviously padded suit.
Back-jumping dwarf troll.
Father and daughter's boyfriend tag-team fight dwarf.
Young boy strangled by dwarf troll.
Dwarf troll punched in the face by ghost.
Dwarf trolls corner family.
Disappearing dwarf trolls.
Little boy thrown into dwarf troll mosh pit.
Dwarf trolls frightened by little boy eating a double decker baloney sandwich. Yes, it really is as ridiculous as it sounds.
Vomiting dwarf trolls.
Stunt dwarf troll falls off railing.

Twin Peaks: Fire Walk With Me (1992)

Written by David Lynch, Robert Engels
Directed by David Lynch
Starring Mädchen Amick, Dana Ashbrook, Phoebe Augustine, David Bowie, Eric DaRe
Featured dwarf: Michael J. Anderson

David Lynch is at his creepiest and most bizarre here as he goes much darker and less subtle than the TV series, and really turns up the freak factor. The film gets under your skin, to say the least. Michael J.

Anderson gives a brilliant performance as the dwarf in the red room. I have no idea what his scenes are all about, but then again, who knows whether Lynch did either. Nevertheless it's always fascinating when the film cuts back to those scenes with the dwarf. It is no doubt the role the filmmakers behind the bizarro TV series *Carnivale* saw when they decided to hire Anderson to play the leader of the freak show traveling circus act.

With *Twin Peaks: Fire Walk With Me* (1992), the film cuts back from its regularly scheduled weirdness to several scenes of a backwards-speaking, subtitled dwarf in a room with a red curtain. These scenes keep getting weirder as the film continues and so does the dwarf. Not only does he speak backward, he also stares at the camera as if he's about to suck the soul out of the viewer, makes weird noises, holds a ring right at the camera (which made me laugh because it make me think of a dwarf version of the Green Lantern), and sits next to a creepy guy that haunts Laura Palmer in the film and even does a disturbing ventriloquist routine on a tallie.

Twin Peaks: Fire Walk With Me (1992) is freaky stuff, and the dwarf is blatantly used to make the scenes more weird to unsettle the audience. There is no one like Lynch, but he is guilty of several stereotypical dwarf crimes here. However, he goes so far with it that the stereotypes seem to transcend into something that exists in some other bizarre dimension. Lynch, you are one weird guy. We appreciate your love of dwarves but can't you give an F.B.I agent role to Anderson in the next one and stop giving us nightmares by casting him as the creepy dwarf in the red room?

> Dwarf in room with red curtain.
> Backward speaking dwarf.
> Weird-noise-making dwarf.
> Dramatic zoom in on dwarf as he stares at screen and holds a ring in front of his face as if he were a dwarf version of the Green Lantern.
> Dwarf cut in to enhance frightening imagery.
> Dwarf sits next to creepy guy in room with red curtain.
> Bird's eye view of dwarf.
> Dwarf makes a creepy guy talk by putting his hand on his freaky shoulder.

UHF (1989)

Written by Al Yankovic and Jay Levey
Directed by Jay Levey
Starring 'Weird Al' Yankovic, Victoria Jackson, Kevin McCarthy, Michael Richards, Fran Drescher
Featured dwarf: Billy Barty

Barty was so good in *UHF* (1989) he deserved his own spinoff.

In *UHF* (1989), Weird Al Yankovic struggles to keep a fledgling TV station alive by employing a sideshow circus of various crazy characters to serve as talent and work behind the scenes, one of which is the great senior dwarf actor Billy Barty. He's expertly utilized at the beginning of the film as a cameraman for field reporter Fran Drescher. Dwarfsploitation quickly comes into play as Barty holds a camera that's about half the size of his body. Further dwarfsploitation also has angles from the dwarf's point of view when it cuts to the field report shots with Fran Drescher. Then Barty is tripped by one of the bad guys from the rival news station owned by *Invasion of the Body Snatcher's* (1978) Kevin McCarthy. It is there that we are shown the visual joke of dwarf eye squinting (as only Billy Barty can do so well) and grunting as he falls to the ground with the large camera in tow. Other visual gags in the movie include a morbidly obese black man who hoists the dwarf onto his shoulders to film a rousing speech given by Michael Richards (we all know him best as Kramer from *Seinfeld*). The little man/tall, fat man combo is truly a magnificent sight to behold.

The station also does their share to exploit Barty by getting him in front of the camera to advertise for the public to buy shares of the station so it can be community-owned. Although this film is high on dwarfsploitation whenever Barty is on screen, it doesn't stand out as much as it does in other films due to the fact Weird Al exploits everyone else in the movie as well, including himself.

UHF (1989) is one of those bizarre cult movies that keeps growing in status over the years. It is personally one of my all-time favorite movies. I can't describe why I find it so funny but every time I watch it, this movie never fails to crack me up. Weird Al's hiring of the dwarf was indeed the right thing to do to elevate it to such a high cult status. It's just a shame the dwarf never got his own little cameraman sequel. Imagine how awesome that would be: an entire show just about a dwarf cameraman. Hopefully one day Hollywood will wake up and make this dream become a reality.

> Dwarf cameraman shows up. Fran Drescher can't see him
>   when he first appears.
> Dwarf carries oversized news camera.
> Dwarf camera POV.
> Low Angle POV.
> Dwarf tripped by evil tallie.
> Dwarf bruises elbow.
> Dwarf propositions to get people to sell shares for the station

so they can all be owners.
Morbidly obese brother holds dwarf up in celebration.

Under the Rainbow (1981)

Written by Pat McCormick, Harry Hurwitz, Martin Smith, Pat Bradley, Fred Bauer
Directed by Steve Rash
Starring Chevy Chase, Carrie Fischer, Adam Arkin
Featured dwarf: Billy Barty

This movie's certainly got a lot going for it in the realm of dwarfsploitation. It covers all the dwarf cinema stereotypes: angry dwarves, horny dwarves, mischievous, drunken dwarves, shameless size gags, you name it. Since this film was made in the gloriously un-pc hey day of the 80s, it got away with a lot more dwarf insults than they'd ever get away with now, especially since there's currently a movement to ban the word 'midget' from everyone's vocabulary, which I kind of hope they do because then it's going to be a lot more fun to say. But back to the un-pc part. Check out the insults they gave dwarves in this movie:

"Careful, half pint."
"Don't look so shocked. Haven't you seen little people before?"
"You must be from Dusseldwarf."
"Can you tell me if a midget arrived here?"
"Look at all the children. It must be recess."
"This looks like the aerial view of an unemployment line."
"Don't worry, darling. When you grow up you'll get lots of beautiful girls."
"If you need rooms we'll just have to double up."
"I have a hundred and fifty little headaches ruining my hotel."
"You are bad little people. You deserve to be short."
"This is no time for pygmy perversion."
"Perfect. A midget posse. That's what was missing."

Amazing, isn't it? It's as if they were actually going out of their way to come up with every dwarf insult they could think of. So much so that I could imagine it must have been humiliating for a dwarf actor to be on set in this movie. But, then I think about those lucky dwarves who got to rip off Carrie Fisher's dress and chase her around in her underwear and I stop feeling sorry for those horny little bastards. This was, after all, around the time of *Return of the Jedi* (1983), and we all know how hot Carrie Fisher was in that movie. But aside from that bone the producers threw, it seemed they only put dwarves in the movie as an excuse to have a bunch of little people take over a hotel, get wasted, fondle the boobs of every female present, run under people's crotches, stair dive, swing from chandeliers like chimps and have a sword fight while wearing Oompa Loompa outfits. Classy, no. Impressive… you're damn straight.

Don't be going into this one expecting a good movie. But if you need your dwarf fix, and in multiple doses to boot, this movie's for you.

> Dwarf appears out of little tent.
> Dwarf drinks from an oversized coffee cup.
> Dwarf seig heil's Hitler.
> Dwarf in Hitler outfit complete with mustache.
> Dwarf hobo.
> Dwarves corralled into hotel.
> Dwarf walks under a drinking man's crotch.
> Dwarf operates Ventriloquist dummy.
> Dwarf grabs woman's breast.
> Woman pets dwarf.
> Man leans against dwarf in elevator and almost crushes him.
> Japanese man bows to dwarf.
> Hitler dwarf laughs from reading vital statistics column in paper.
> Dancing dwarves.
> Dwarf seig heil's Japanese man.
> Dwarves dance in train formation.
> Dancing, trumpet-playing dwarf.
> Drunken dwarves.
> Dwarf tips barmaid with cash down her shirt.
> Hitler dwarf wears munchkin outfit, complete with blond wig.
> Dwarf hits head on dresser drawer.
> Dwarf crawls out window.
> Drunken dwarves bang on pots and pans.
> Dwarf wears pot on head.
> Dwarf rips off Carrie Fisher's dress with a sword.
> Dwarves sword fight while dressed as munchkins.
> Hitler dwarf chases Carrie Fisher while she's in her underwear.

Dwarf hangs from chandelier.
Dwarf swings from rope.
Dwarf runs into wall.
Dwarf rappels down pillar.
Dwarves perform trapeze act on chandelier.
Dwarves trap Adam Arkin on chandelier.
Dwarf gives inspirational speech to drunken, disgruntled dwarves.
Drunk dwarf falls down stairs multiple times.
Dwarf on dwarf foot chase.
Dwarves trample tied-up man.
Dwarf crowd destroys movie set.
Hitler dwarf stops while being chased to ogle girls in dressing room.
Dwarf-on-dwarf chase featuring a bus and stagecoach.
Cowboy and Indian dwarves join chase via horseback.
Singing dwarves.

The Unknown (1927)

Written by: Tod Browning (story) and Waldemar Young (scenario)
Directed by: Tod Browning
Starring Lon Chaney
Featured dwarf: John George

Leave it to Tod Browning, best known for *Freaks* (1932) and *Dracula* (1931), to make one of the strangest films included in this book with this 49 minute silent film. The movie stars Lon Chaney as a murderer, posing as a limbless circus act, who has conveniently fallen in love with a woman who doesn't like to be touched. His competition, however, is a Don Juan Fabio who has two arms. The dwarf connection is Lon Chaney's sidekick, "Cojo" as played by John George, who not only serves as Chaney's Robin to his Batman but also serves as a conscience to an otherwise psychotic persona. Cojo mostly stands next to Chaney and makes the occasional facial reaction, but midway through starts pointing out the obvious—if he gets the girl, she's going to notice he has no arms. Chaney then goes to lose his arms but we also lose Cojo, who doesn't appear again once Chaney has returned home.

While the movie is definitely a very cool silent film, it does fail in the dwarf department. For starters, it would have been much better if John George were shorter to make him stand out more. It also would have been nice to see more of him rather than just "the guy next to Chaney." If it were to be remade, I'd vote for Warwick Davis to play Chaney's role.

Devil dwarf.
Cigar-chomping dwarf.
Angry dwarf.

A Very Unlucky Leprechaun (1998)

Written by Craig J. Nevius
Directed by Brian Kelly
Starring Tim Matheson
Featured dwarf: Warwick Davis

Warwick Davis is back as the leprechaun! Only, this time, it's a G-rated family comedy produced by the genius of Roger Corman. Instead of monster-like make up, this time around Davis has long red hair and a half beard and, unfortunately, doesn't go around killing people. Instead, we get the story of a young girl and her father who move from Chicago to Ireland to live in an old place that the father's dead brother left them. It just so happens that this old place happens to be inhabited by a leprechaun. As the girl begins talking to the leprechaun, chaos ensues because, well, he is very unlucky.

The movie is hard to watch and I'm not sure there is anything redeeming about it other than watching Warwick Davis at work, acting a bit goofier than normal. There are 'so bad they're brilliant' moments like Warwick chasing a starfish and a shooting star, a food fight, and the ultimate is a scene where Warwick has the little girl try to catch him.

Leprechaun hand close up.
Leprechaun crossing sign.
Speedy leprechaun.
Leprechaun giggling.
Leprechaun comes out of well.
Leprechaun feet close up.

Leprechaun legs close up.
Leprechaun flying.
Leprechaun flies out of window.
Leprechaun stumbling.
Leprechaun tiptoes.
Leprechaun stumbling.
Leprechaun in bag.
Leprechaun knocks over rocks.
Leprechaun hits head.
Leprechaun in fireplace.
Leprechaun on fridge.
Kid tries to catch leprechaun.
Leprechaun on high shelf.
Leprechaun chases starfish.
Leprechaun rolling on floor.
Leprechaun sobbing.
Leprechaun runs from dozer.
Leprechaun dancing.
Leprechaun hugging kid.
Leprechaun caught by old guy.
Leprechaun flying and waving.

Walk Hard: The Dewey Cox Story (2007)

Written by Judd Apatow, Jake Kasdan
Directed by Jake Kasdan
Starring John C. Reilly, Jenna Fischer, Tim Meadows, Kristen Wiig
"I've got to think about the other people."
"You mean, like your family?"
"No, I mean, like, people that's having injustices done to them. Like women and midgets and such."

In *Walk Hard: The Dewey Cox Story* (2007), a parody mainly of *Walk the Line* (2005), John C. Reilly plays a singer who goes through a variety of different musical careers in a life riddled with drama, alcohol, drugs and multiple wives. During a portion of the film where he tries to make a difference with his music and stand up for all those who have had injustices done to them ("like women and midgets and such," as he says in the film), the filmmakers give a nod to Bob Dylan, and have Reilly sing a ballad endorsing dwarves. However, in his song, he hypocritically refers to them as midgets. "I stand today for the midgets, half the size of a regular guy" and "I'm banging the drum, your big day will come, when they remake *The Wizard of Oz*" are some examples of the sizeist lyrics.

In the segment, the film switches to black and white and Reiley plays his pro-dwarf ballad while being supported by a bunch of dwarves wearing Black Panther style hats and holding signs that proudly proclaim "Short Power" and "Short Panther Party." The scene is hilarious but clearly dwarfsploitation thinly veiled as dwarf empowerment. I'm assuming the dwarf actors in the scene had a good sense of humor while this was being filmed although it didn't show on their faces when they held up the "Short Power" and "Short Panther Party" signs. Maybe they were just trying to act hard.

> Dwarves in black and white Bob Dylan-esque music video.
> Dwarf holds sign that says "Short Panther Party."
> Dwarf holds sign that says "Short Power."
> Black Panther looking dwarves.

Warrior of the Lost World (1983)

> Written and directed by David Worth
> Starring Robert Ginty and Fred Williamson

During a fight scene in the middle of nowhere, there are many oddball characters outlining the area they should be fighting in. On the bed of a truck stands a random dwarf. The dwarf jumps up and down, making weird noises. When the dwarf taunts the wrong tallie, he gets tossed. It's a random insertion of a dwarf that was unnecessary but used the dwarf, as usual, to spice up an otherwise bad movie. It is advised you avoid this movie unless you watch the *Mystery Science Theatre 3000* version.

> Dwarf makes weird noises
> Dwarf in stupid clothing
> Dwarf stands on higher object
> Dwarf taunts tallie

Dwarf tossing
Dwarf cheering

Watchmen (2009)

Written by David Hayter, Alex Tse
Directed by Zack Snyder
Starring Jackie Earle Haley, Patrick Wilson, Carla Gugino, and Malin Akerman
Featured dwarf: Danny Woodburn

I have a soft spot for this one because I'm such a fan of the source material. In *Watchmen* (2009), the film adaptation of the insanely popular graphic novel, one of the Watchmen, Rorschach (played with psychotic perfection by tallie Jackie Earle Haley) squares off against a sociopathic dwarf while he's being held in prison, played by outstanding dwarf actor Danny Woodburn.

Woodburn looks awesomely intimidating in this film, chomping a cigar with a bunch of large thugs standing behind him. During the section of the film where there's a riot in the prison, the dwarf approaches Rorschach's cell and the two trade taunts with one another. The dwarf doesn't give Rorschach much of a chance to speak as he quickly orders one of his tallie guards to saw Rorschach's hands off. Close but no cigar, though, as ultra bad-ass Rorschach dispatches of the tallie prison thug in record time and places a barrier between himself and the dwarf, who wants nothing more than his head on a platter. The dwarf, not having the time or desire to wait to take Rorschach out (this is a truly evil dwarf we're talking about here), orders his own tallie prison thug's hands cut off so he can get to Rorschach. This plan proves to be a miserable failure as well and the dwarf's other prison thug is quickly dispatched. The result leaves Rorschach and the dwarf squaring off with one another and, as there are no ape-like prison thugs to separate the two from one another, the dwarf suddenly doesn't look like such a bad-ass anymore. The cigar drops out of his mouth and he runs away from Rorschach like a little girl. Rorschach moves deliberately after him like *The Terminator* (1984) and corners him into a bathroom, where he flushes the little criminal in the toilet. Soon after, we see the dwarf's blood under the bathroom door. Unfortunately, there's not more dwarf in this film, but it was adapted from the graphic novel and, as as they were trying to stay as true to book as they could, the filmmakers get a pass on this one.

Watchmen (2009) is a very good example of using a dwarf for a short amount of time in a film and actually having it pay off. The filmmakers behind *Things You Can Tell Just By Looking At Her* (1999) could certainly learn a thing or two from this movie.

> Cigar-smoking dwarf.
> Prison-boss dwarf.
> Dwarf orders tallie's hands sawed off.
> Rorsharch taunts dwarf.
> Dwarf stands next to tallie.
> Dwarf gleefully waits for Rorschach to die.
> Cigar drops out of dwarf's mouth and he runs away from Rorschach.
> Dwarf runs into bathroom to excape Rorschach.
> Tallie stands over dwarf in bathroom.
> Tallie flushes dwarf down toilet (implied).
> Dwarf blood spills out of bathroom.

Waxwork (1988)

> Written and Directed by Anthony Hickox
> Starring Zach Galligan, Deborah Foreman, David Warner, Micah Grant, John Rhys-Davies
> Featured dwarf: Mihaly 'Michu' Meszaros

In *Waxwork* (1988) that crazy kid from *Gremlins* (1984) (and no, I'm not talking about Corey Feldman, I'm talking Zach Galligan!) switches from acting with puppets to acting with a dwarf. It's hard to tell which was the better move, because both puppets and dwarves are awesome. *Waxwork* (1988) is your basic take on a handful of spoiled teenagers who are thrown at the mercy of a living waxwork horrorshow. The museum's owner lures teens in with the diabolical plan of sacrificing them to the evil characters in the displays to make them come alive and bring about the end of humanity as we know it. He's aided by his tallie son and a butler dwarf in his quest for evil on earth.

When the clueless kiddies get to the door separated by the outside world from the one of waxwork inside, it swings open and standing behind it is the formerly mentioned dwarf butler. Other than creeping people out, the dwarf mostly serves as a visual sight gag for the variety of shots the director uses to display his lack of height. His character is endowed with some eccentricities though, such as marching around swinging his arms up and down like a Nazi. He's also partial to punching his boss's tallie son in the crotch, and he may look like a doll but he proves to be vicious in a fight as the end battle reveals, by cutting to his character pummeling a good tallie on the floor. This is a lesson the tallies never seem to learn from the *Chucky* movies as well.

>Dwarf butler isn't shown when the door first opens.
>Dwarf butler framed under tallies.
>Dwarf butler yells at tallie and punches him in leg for not waiting to open the door before entering.
>Bird's eye view of dwarf butler.
>"Gremlins" kid leans down to listen to dwarf butler.
>Nazi-acting dwarf butler.
>Dwarf says "bravo" and bows to tallie after he throws the *Gremlins* kid through the window.
>Dwarf butler's head framed between tallies.
>Dwarf butler scurries through fight.
>Dwarf butler beats on grounded tallie.
>Girl tosses dwarf butler into *Little Shop of Horror*-esque plant for a snack.
>Dwarf butler gets the cover as well.

Weirdsville (2007)

>Written by Willem Wennekers
>Directed by Allan Moyle
>Starring Scott Speedman, Wes Bentley, Taryn Manning, Matt Frewer
>Featured dwarf: Jordan Prentice

I guess it is hard for someone to make a movie with "weird" in the title and not include the use of dwarves. The DVD cover features three Fabio tallies posing with dwarves in knight outfits at the bottom. There's nothing to sell the movie as being weird other than dwarf knights. It's true exploitation of dwarves. The tagline is even "Where the days are long and the knights are short." After watching the film I was thinking something more along the lines of, "Where the movie is long and the dwarf screen time is too short."

From the director of *Pump Up the Volume* (1990) and *Empire Records* (1995) comes this tale of two losers who get mixed up with a lot of "strange" characters. They think their girlfriend has overdosed with drugs that they were supposed to sell to pay off a drug dealer. When they go to bury her, they get mixed up with some Satanists. Just when things couldn't get much worse, the drug dealer comes after them.

Just as the movie slows, the dwarf enters. The two slackers try to go to the mall when it's closed, but are quickly attacked and sprayed by a dwarf security guard. The dwarf is a knight re-enactor who apparently keeps medieval weaponry and clothing around the mall to use on such an occasion. He ends up getting excited when the slackers tell him of a cult that is after them and lets them go. Unfortunately, he ends up facing the cult on his own and gets drowned for information after being insulted and twirled around "like a little helicopter" by a tallie woman. Left for dead, the dwarf security guard comes up and calls his dwarf knight reenactor buddies. They show up in a car and the security guard piles in to go after the cult members. It's not long before they've found them and proceed to destroy the cult members' car and beat them senseless. Unfortunately we don't see the dwarf actors again until they randomly show up drunk, running into a building.

While the movie is decent, the dwarf screen time could have been so much more and made the movie great—they were far more entertaining than anything else in the film.

> Dwarf hits tallies in knees.
> Dwarf maces tallies.
> "Fuck the cops and their height requirements."
> Dwarf walks between two tallies.
> "Like the chief of police of Munchkinland,"
> "A Wizard of Oz joke. That's very original. I never hear those."
> Dwarf fights disrespectful tallies.
> Dwarf taken for little helicopter ride.
> Drowning dwarf.
> Dwarf knights.

Car with dwarf steps.
Dwarf growling.
Dwarves referred to as "midgets."
Drunken dwarves.

Werewolf of Washington (1973)

Written and directed by Milton Moses Ginsberg
Starring Dean Stockwell
Featured dwarf: Michael Dunn
"Are you real?"

When Dean Stockwell's character gets turned into a werewolf, it causes chaos at his job in the White House. As luck would have it, he runs into a dwarf doctor (Michael Dunn) who just happens to be doing experiments. At this point in the film I was bored and ready for something to happen. Upon their first meeting, the werewolf begins licking Dunn's face, making an unintentionally strange make-out scene. The potential is built with Dunn's appearance but it doesn't really go anywhere, although the werewolf is spared because Dunn's Doctor Kiss wants to research him (of course). Cult fans might enjoy this one, but most of you will be shaking your heads like me, wondering why the filmmakers squandered such wonderful possibilities.

Dwarf working on patient on table larger than him.
Dwarf licked by Wolfman.
Dwarf watches small screen in locker room.
Extreme close up of dwarf.

Where the Buffalo Roam (1980)

Written by John Kaye
Directed by Art Linson
Starring Bill Murray and Peter Boyle
Featured dwarves: Jerry Maren and Michael Lee Gogin

The writings of Hunter S. Thompson come to life in a lazy fashion, with Bill Murray as Thompson. When Thompson checks into a hotel, his weird antics draw the attention of two dwarf hotel employees. The two groups exchange several looks before moving on. As Thompson begins a football game in his hotel room, the dwarves are called upon to check in on the noise. Unfortunately, the scene cuts off at one of them falling into the room. We don't see the dwarves again until two black men are given the keys to the room and throw a party. In a downright classic scene, the dwarves are the center of the party, dancing away—Jerry Maren specifically looks great with his shades and trademark cigar.

Although not great, the movie is worth a look for the images of the party alone.

> Dwarf stares at crazy tallie.
> Dwarf looked down upon.
> Smoking dwarf.
> Dwarf accused of stealing wallet.
> Dwarf with keys around neck.
> Dwarves partying.

Who's Your Caddy (2007)

> Written by Don Michael Paul, Bradley Allenstein, Robert Henny
> Directed by Don Michael Paul
> Starring Big Boi, Jeffrey Jones, Terry Crews, and Mick Partridge
> Featured dwarves: Tony Cox, Dana Michael Woods
> "You can climb me like a tree."

This is a terrible, terrible movie. The filmmakers were clearly trying to top *Caddyshack* (1980), but failed miserably. Compared to *Who's Your Caddy* (2007), *Caddyshack 2* (1988) is actually funny. The only redeeming quality of this movie is the dwarves.

Jeffrey Jones plays a snobby fat cat who hires a couple of dwarves to get rid of a rapper that's been messing up things for him on his elitist golf course. His one brilliant moment of inspiration from his otherwise dull and lifeless imagination occurs when he hires dwarves to get rid of the rapper. He's surprised, of course, when the dwarves attempt to kill his mark instead of merely getting rid of him. This confused me. What was this ignorant tallie thinking? He didn't know the dwarves would rub out a tallie if they had the opportunity and got paid for it to boot? He clearly underestimated the hard-core nature of these dwarves. After all, a tallie would clearly be a fool to disrespect a dwarf, let alone a pair of dwarves. And why make a movie about a rapper and then use the edited version of *Straight Out of Compton?* (This doesn't have anything to do with dwarves, but it bothered me nonetheless.)

The dwarves in question, Tony Cox and Dana Michael Woods, are good though as they talk back to the tallies and punch them in the crotches. A female tallie in the rapper's crew is highly turned on by one of the dwarves and there is a pretty amusing scene where tallie Terry Crews tortures a tied up Tony Cox and fails to break him. The more pain Crews deals out to the dwarf, the more Cox insults and antagonizes him back. These small moments are just window dressing, however. The only really watchable part of the movie occurs as the dwarves walk away in slow motion from the explosion meant for their tallie mark. It was beautiful, to say the least. Seeing it made me cry in the hopes of an all dwarf version of *Die Hard* (1988). Then I cried harder when I realized that most likely will never happen; at least, not in the states.

If you are going to make the poor decision to watch this film, I highly recommend fast forwarding to the dwarves walking out of the explosion scene, then promptly throwing the movie in the trash.

> Tallie steps aside to reveal dwarf.
> Flashy suit wearing dwarves.
> Dwarf threatens tallie with gun.
> Dwarf hides under stage.
> Dwarves dressed in stealth gear in broad daylight.
> Dwarf looks through mini set of binoculars.
> Dwarves use mini walkie talkies.
> Dwarves leave bomb under stage meant to blow up tallies.
> Dwarf framed by stripper's legs on the stage.
> Dwarf looks up stripper's skirts while talking on the phone with tallie client.
> Dwarf feels no remorse for causing near destruction to tallie client mark.
> Tied up dwarf.

Slapped dwarf.
Interrogated dwarf.
Dwarf giggles at tallie like a mischievous little imp.
Dwarf gives in when interrogated by angry, tallie sister.
Dwarf shows up in flashy red suit and punches tallie in the crotch.
Dwarf turns on angry, tallie sister by punching tallie in the crotch.
"What do you mean little?"
"Small? What do you mean small? Are you trying to disrespect me?"
"You got a big ass mouth, bitch."
"The more time I spend hittin' you, the less time I spend hittin' that, tater tot!"
"Next time, bring it from the shoulder, you big pussy!"
"You can climb me like a tree."

Willow (1988)

Written by Bob Dolman
Directed by Ron Howard
Starring Val Kilmer, Joanne Whalley
Featured dwarves: Phil Fondacaro, Tony Cox, Warwick Davis
"Peck!"

Willow is continuously powerful proof that George Lucas is indeed dwarf-obsessed. From R2-D2 and the many other dwarves in suits in the *Star Wars* movies (let alone the Ewoks), to the Ewoks made-for-TV movies, to *Labyrinth* (1986), to *Howard the Duck* (1986), Lucas is definitely a man who loves his little people. Although he was only credited with the story and executive producer titles for *Willow* (1988), he did hire a former child actor (Ron Howard) to direct a village full of dwarves. Coincidence? I think not. Howard takes the reigns from Lucas and directs the charming Warwick Davis in the dwarf fantasy adventure of a lifetime. What impresses me the most is that both Lucas and Howard trusted a dwarf to have a lead role and be able to carry the movie. Seldom is this done, even on significantly smaller scales. Dwarves are often the sidekicks and butt of the joke, or the villain, but hardly ever the lead, let alone the lead hero. This isn't to say *Willow* (1988) doesn't contain its fair share of dwarfsploitative moments; it just does a better job of balancing those moments with positive dwarf qualities.

In *Willow* (1988), Warwick Davis is a family dwarf. He has a dwarf wife, two beautiful dwarf kids and is an aspiring wizard in a village of relatively happy dwarves. That is, until a tallie baby with a birthmark floats his way and he's selected to lead a dangerous mission to keep her safe and take her back to the Daikini (that's *Willow* talk for world of the tallies). Along the way, he's abandoned by his dwarf warrior friends (the great Phil Fondacaro and Tony Cox) and forced to enlist the help of a tempermental heightist, Madmartigan (Val Kilmer), who loves to constantly curse at Willow and call him a "peck" over and over again. At first, the tallie stranger and Willow argue constantly but before long they warm up to each other. After all, one can never stay angry with a good dwarf for very long.

Unlike the *Lord of the Rings* trilogy, the fights here are kept a little more realistic. Willow does take a few people down, but most of the time he's limited by his reach and the fact that he's a farmer by trade, not a warrior who hasn't mastered the craft of wizardry yet. On the other hand, like the *Lord of the Rings* trilogy, *Willow* (1988) is an inspiring movie that places the size of the individual on a much less lower level than their spirit. Good work, Opie!

>Dwarf children and baby.
>Dwarf operates a pig pulling plow.
>Impressive dwarf mullet.
>Mini dwarf house.
>Dwarf village.
>Dancing dwarves.
>Drinking dwarves.
>Fire-breathing dwarves.
>Dwarf magicians.
>Skullet dwarf.
>Drum banging dwarves.
>Dwarf wizard.
>Dwarves fight off evil hogs.
>Dwarves laugh at vomiting child.
>Dwarf abandoned by fellow dwarves.
>Temper mental dwarf.
>Dwarf battles bridge troll.

Crying dwarf.
Dwarf argues with talking goat.
Shetland pony riding dwarf.
Bird scats on skullet dwarf.

Willy Wonka and the Chocolate Factory (1971)

Written by Roald Dahl
Directed by Mel Stuart
Starring Gene Wilder
"They can't be real people…"

Before Tim Burton's remake with Johnny Depp, there was the Gene Wilder starrer that is VERY close to the remake. In this one, we get Oompa Loompas but they are in face paint and wearing colored wigs. At first it's distracting, but it feels to me that it fits in better with the color scheme even though it's obviously wigs and make up. The Oompa Loompas have to fight off Gene Wilder's wonderful performance but still manage to be the most memorable part of this classic family film. If you are not singing the Oompa Loompa songs by the end of the day then something is probably clinically wrong with you. An absolute must-see and recommended over the remake!

Dwarves referred to as "little men."
Dwarf responds to tallie's whistle.
Dwarves in make-up and wigs.
Dwarves singing and dancing.
Dwarf jumping.
Dwarf captain.
Dwarf in hat.
Dwarf ringing bell.
Dwarf referred to as "little guy."
Dwarves dance around blueberry girl.
Dwarf with egg.
Dwarf stroking egg.
Boxes crash on dwarves.
Dwarves in suits.
Dwarves carry large chocolate bar.
Dwarves carry off tallie.

Wizard of Oz (1939)

Written by Noel Langley, Florence Ryerson, Edgar Allan Woolf
Directed by Victor Fleming
Starring Judy Garland
Featured dwarves: The Singer Midgets

Many dwarf top-ten lists name this film, probably because it's a classic that most people have seen. The dwarf scene in Munchkinland is great, with a couple of large song and dance numbers with a very large amount of dwarves employed, but for me I would take *The Court Jester* (1955) over this one, which includes not only a large song and dance number but a huge battle scene). The greatest part of this one is the pure imagination and wonder that it adds to a classic fantasy film. The thought of that many little people together is astounding enough, but to see it come true with such vivid colors and great, catchy music is just an amazing experience. Personally, it's the only part of the movie I can remember the next day.

The Lollipop Guild are especially gifted at mocking tallies.

Back to run more tallies through the ringer.

Everyone knows the story but in case you don't, here's the important part…When Dorothy's house lands on the Wicked Witch of the East, she becomes the heroine of Munchkinland. Munchkinland is filled with little people referred to as Munchkins (coining the phrase into popular culture, causing many little people in cinema to then be referred to as Munchkin). This movie is a classic that is a definite must see, although I feel you'll be like me and disappointed that they didn't get more screen time.

Dwarves with flowers on their heads.
Dwarves popping up from bushes.
Dwarves referred to as Munchkins.
Dwarves giggling.
Dwarves referred to as little people.
Scared dwarves.
Dwarf comes out of manhole.
Dwarves in costume dancing.
Dwarves in fat suits.
Dwarves with funny hair.
Dwarves with funny voices.
Dwarves wake out of eggshells.
Dwarf with large lollipop.
Dwarves jumping up and down.
Dwarves scared of witch.
Dwarves bow.
Dwarves wave.

The Wonderful World of the Brother's Grimm (1962)

Written by David P. Harmon, Charles Beaumont, William Roberts
Directed by Henry Levin
Starring Lawrence Harvey, Claire Bloom, Karl Boehm, Walter Slezak, Oscar Homolka
Featured dwarf: Billy Barty
"Nasty little man!"

In this film about the inspiration for the tales created by the Brother's Grimm, the dwarves are few and far between. However the filmmakers do score some pretty good points for using the dwarves in unique and creative ways. In the first dwarf appearance, a woodsman shows up in front of a king with bright red hair that looks so creepy he'd give the Burger King mascot nightmares, and we all know how creepy that guy is. To make things even creepier for the woodsman, the king has a dwarf jester sidekick with a jester hand puppet. Now here's a twist I liked quite a bit, kind of a dwarf-within-a-dwarf thing. The freaky jester dwarf laughs every time the king does, and indicates for him to do the same. He also gets excited, hops around, does somersaults, and frantically crawls around the woodsman on all fours like some kind of a happy, rabid dog.

In the second dwarf entrance, Wilhelm Grimm is very ill as a giant comes to him, showing his face through his window. He sends some friends to give Wilhelm inspiration to live and commit the tales to paper, and as we all know, the best form of inspiration is a dwarf! Sure enough, a dwarf with a red hat appears, shakes his finger at Rumplestiltskin for not showing compassion toward the dying Wilhelm, calls him a nasty little man, and then jumps down from the windowsill and into the dying tallie's room. What happens next is truly beautiful as multiple dwarves appear through the windowsill, jump down into Willhelm's room and surround him by his bed.

If only more dwarves were scattered throughout the movie instead of just appearing in a couple of very small doses, I would have been a much more satisfied viewer, but it was an interesting movie nonetheless.

>   Dwarf jester.
>   Dwarf jester with hand puppet.
>   Dwarf jester acts as toadie for creepie king that looks like the Burger King mascot.
>   Dwarf jester laughs every time the king does.
>   Hopping dwarf jester.
>   Somersaulting dwarf jester.
>   Dwarf jester walks around woodsman like a dog.
>   Dwarf dances with tallie.
>   Tallie hoists dwarf in the air while dancing.
>   Dwarf in windowsill.
>   Dwarf jumps down from windowsill.
>   Dwarf stands on the nightstand next to Wilhelm's head to console him.
>   Multiple dwarves jump through windowsill.
>   Dwarf body posed in the back of Wilhelm Grimm.
>   Dwarves harass Wilhelm Grimm to write about their exploits.

One dwarf stands tall, ready to take on all.

Afterword
by Brad Paulson

It all started with *Slaughter Party* (2005). That's when fellow micro-cinema filmmaker Chris Watson told me the idea for his follow up to *Zombiegeddon* (2003). The plot revealed to me revolved around a crazed dwarf chasing scantily clad women around the desert with a knife. Instantly I thought back to those pitch seminars I'd paid so many of my hard earned dollars to attend. At one of the seminars we had a speaker who told us the most effective pitches were one sentence or less, a.k.a 'high concept.' Watson's description of *Slaughter Party* (2005) instantly struck me as the perfect Hollywood pitch. That is, if Hollywood were more open minded. As an audience member, just hearing the words, "Mad dwarf chases girls in bikinis around the desert with knife," I'm instantly sold. If I were a studio head, I would have bought it on the spot. But what do studio heads buy? You know, the same trash they always buy: giant robots chase after annoying teenagers or crappy 3-D remakes of good movies, etc. But alas, Hollywood's mostly safe, generic taste is beside the point. The point is, the mere mention of *Slaughter Party's* plot and the fact I got so excited when I heard the killer was a dwarf, unleashed my true love for dwarves. Instantly I began to rekindle my obsession with little people. Needless to say, when Chris Watson asked me to co-author this book with him I was thrilled.

Thinking back, I don't know when it was I first became obsessed with dwarves. Was it when I was a child and rode my bike across town four times to see *Howard the Duck* (1986) in the theatre? Was it the fact I went to go see *Willow* (1988) because it featured an entire village of dwarves and was fascinated by the fact there were dwarves inside of those "Ewok" outfits? Was it gun-toting dwarf Debbie Lee Carrington in *Total Recall* (1990), exposing all that sexy dwarf cleavage when blowing people away? It's hard to say. There have been so many great dwarf cinematic memories. Perhaps it was the time I bought two dwarf girls a drink in a bar, became aroused after giving one a massage and attempted to jump in the closed window of a cab to try and get her to go home with me? Was it when I got my first dwarf drinking buddy and it was one of the happiest times in my life? It's hard to tell, really. I have a different reaction to dwarves than most people do. I simply appreciate. I see them as very unique, fascinating human beings and the fact there's not that many around make them even more special to me.

I'm also a firm believer in the theory that dwarves highly enhance the viewing quality of movies, not unlike the popular theory that a lesbian scene improves a film regardless of the genre. Take a great film like *High Plains Drifter* (1973), for example. Without the dwarf, it could have still been a great Western but add the talents of excellent dwarf actor Billy Curtis and it becomes something truly legendary. There's not a whole lot (movie-wise, at least) more cool than Clint Eastwood strolling through town fighting bad guys with a dwarf by his side for the entire journey. The only thing that could top that in my book is if the dwarf were the anti-hero gunslinger with Clint Eastwood as the Sheriff sidekick, always cheering him on, talking him up and kneeling down to light his cigar. Eastwood was certainly onto something brilliant with casting the dwarf, but could have elevated opportunities for dwarf actors to unseen heights had he made that decision.

Writing this book with Chris Watson has been a wonderful journey and my love and obsession for dwarves has blossomed. Both of us have gained much more insight into the way the cinema represents dwarves: mostly as stereotypes (hungry, horny, impish, etc). Most of the time, they're the butt of jokes or used just to make a movie weird. Sci-fi dwarves are often covered from head to toe in alien outfits, the list goes on. Worst of all though, dwarves almost always play second fiddle. It seems like Hollywood just never has enough faith in their talents to cast them in lead roles. In fact, dwarf actors have been so ignored, Watson and I weren't even able to find a book about them (until now that is). Talk about a travesty! Things have changed over the years, though, as we see the roles for dwarves starting to get larger and the public's love for them growing as well. All one needs to do to recognize that is take a look at *The Station*

Agent (2003), starring Peter Dinklage, often referred to in this book as the finest working dwarf actor today.

I hope that after reading this you've gained some insight and or at least appreciation for the gifts dwarves have given the world of cinema over the years, and hopefully, this book is only the beginning...

Special Thanks

Brad Paulson: Special thanks to Chris Watson for making this project possible and for sharing a mutual fascination and admiration for all things dwarf. I've had a great time on everything I've worked on with Watson. To BJ Paulson for being the best big brother anyone could ask for and for constantly appreciating and spreading the good word about my projects. To Joe Bob Briggs, Joe Estevez and Joe R. Lansdale. It's great to meet your heroes and find out they're not only excellent human beings but supporters of guys like Chris Watson and myself. To Paul Gebeau for lending me access to his dwarf stocked film library. And most importantly to all the dwarf actors out there who have transcended size, become larger than life on the silver screen and captured our hearts. This book is for you. We hope one day you finally get the appreciation you so rightly deserve.

Chris Watson: This book is undoubtedly dedicated to all the little people. We hope this book serves as a celebration and defense of little people everywhere. *Dwarfsploitation* wouldn't be possible without the assistance of Brad Paulson—a fellow dwarf appreciator. Jose Prendes and Eric Spudic deserve big thanks for letting me borrow numerous little people movies. Tony Longworth, as always, came through with the cover. Thanks to Lloyd Kaufman for taking the time to write the introduction and not go overboard in advertising. To the numerous people who would call, text, or barrage me with every little person sighting—I salute you.

About the Authors

Brad Paulson was born in Glasgow, Montana and attended Montana State University where he received his bachelor's degree in film/video. He's reviewed movies for his hometown paper, *The Missoulian*, KECI-TV (an NBC affiliate) and hosted the public access show, *The Big Picture*. He's written and/or directed several independent films and is a co-partner of the website www.deadharvey.com. He has been fascinated with dwarves ever since that magical moment he saw *Howard the Duck* in the theatre. He dreams of one day being a professional dwarf historian. *Dwarfsploitation* is his second book with Chris Watson, the other being *Wiping Off the Sheen*, an interview book about independent film icon Joe Estevez. Paulson currently lives in Los Angeles where he feels for a town of its enormous size, there's not nearly enough dwarves around.

Chris Watson is an award-winning filmmaker of several internationally distributed films. Watson previously co-wrote the books *Reflections on Blaxploitation, Dwarfsploitation, Wiping Off the Sheen* and *Dirty Talk*. Watson has also written for *Inside Kung-Fu Magazine, Paracinema Magazine, B-Independent, Rogue Cinema, Strictly Splatter, East Side Boxing* and numerous other magazines and websites.

www.ingramcontent.com/pod-product-compliance
Lightning Source LLC
Chambersburg PA
CBHW050336230426
43663CB00010B/1876